UNDER

LASH

A HISTORY OF CORPORAL PUNISHMENT IN THE BRITISH ARMED FORCES

By SCOTT CLAVER

Including
A Digest of the Report of
The Royal Commission, 1835-36
and
The First Reprint of
"Certain Immoral Practices in
His Majesty's Navy"
(1821)

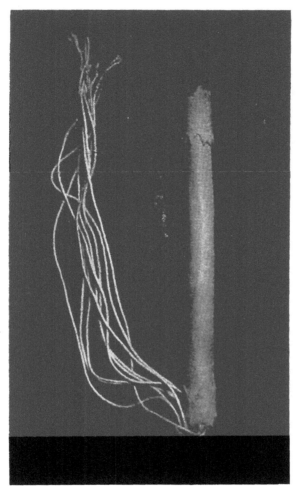

CAT-O'-NINE-TAILS FORMERLY IN USE IN THE INDIAN NAVY
By permission of the Royal United Service Museum, Whitehall, London, where it is on view.

CONTENTS

CONTENTS

LIST OF PLATES

PREFACE

I have found that there are three subjects over which tempers become strained. The first is religion; the second, politics; and the third, corporal punishment. There are countless books on both religion and politics, but the subject of corporal punishment has not been documented very extensively—at least, not for the last century. The more recent books on this subject—and there are only a handful—have been, for the most part, pseudo-scientific essays primarily intended for a basically uncritical market; directed mainly at a reading public less interested in history than in gratifying personal curiosity.

If the Bible is the holiest, and some political books are the liveliest, then this must surely be the bloodiest book ever written. On several occasions I have paused to consider whether such a volume might not be looked upon as "sensational", rather than factual or historical; but the urge to put "on record" something never before attempted has overcome the urge to stop. Friends who knew I was preparing this volume have said to me, with awe in their voices, "I was reading in the paper the other day about a soldier who received *three* hundred lashes —have you put that in your book"? When you commence reading here about hundreds of sentences of *one thousand* lashes, of men tied to guns and flogged senseless, of men shot from a gun, and of men made to sit on wet gunpowder swabs and sharp ridges of wood, I wonder whether you will have the stomach to finish reading this work.

But, I believe, with due modesty, that this book will fulfil a long required need. To the student it will act as the only modern textbook on the subject of corporal punishment, its growth, changes and evolution in the British military forces.

It is designed to make available to those interested in
this vital subject (such as judges, lawyers, barristers,
magistrates, social workers, doctors, psychiatrists, penal
workers, members of Parliament, *etcetera*)—hitherto
unpublished and inaccessible records. To the student of
the Army and Navy is presented an accurate portrait of
life and punishments never before dealt with, except
superficially.

*   *   *   *

In the following pages, discipline may have *seemed*
severe; but if patriotism is to mean anything at all, then
discipline is utterly necessary. Too often, people think
of a soldier as a free man. But the facts are the opposite;
he is, in fact, a self-dedicated slave to a laudable,
respected and admired sense of patriotism; a tiny cog in
a huge machine designed to protect the interests of his
family, himself, his friends and countrymen; failure to
recognise this truth is anarchy—a violation of the
essential discipline which is the vital oil to the larger
machine, thereby risking its destruction, his own
destruction, and the inevitable destruction of all.

It was for the person who by nature was more
interested in his own skin than in those of the majority,
that the punishment of flogging—the corporal punishment most frequently used and most heatedly debated—
was so ironically apt and, because of its aptness, proved
such an effective punishment. More important, it
proved an effective *deterrent* to the committal of crimes
by the potentially selfish youth, who witnessed its infliction at Drum Head Courts Martial in the barracks
square.

*   *   *   *

Some of the following chapters may seem out of
place in a work of this kind. The digest version of *The
Soldier's Wife* is included because of its obvious authen-
ticity as regards recruiting, conditions in the barracks,

the realistic flogging scenes, the branding and shooting to death of deserters, and the agitation to do away with corporal punishment which commenced as a murmur about 1810 and grew to a roar by 1844. *Certain Immoral Practices in His Majesty's Navy* is included because of exposure of conditions in H.M. Ships at the period; and details of punishments in the Merchant Navy are included as a comparison to those of the Royal Navy.

*   *   *   *

While anxious to avoid "taking sides", by compiling this work—which is by no means a plea for the reintroduction of the birch, whip, or cat-o'-nine-tails—I have *perhaps* been swayed to a small sympathy with those who advocate the return of flogging. This particular punishment seems the best retribution for those violent crimes committed by individuals whose past character and behaviour show them to be men unlikely to be impressed for the better by any other punishments. These are the thugs who laugh derisively at admonishment, humanitarianism, the "psychological approach". We all know these types. "A good hiding" is, it seems, the only chastisement they understand: an opinion voiced by many experienced authorities, mature brains in the best positions to judge. And it was that very type —for this "tough-guy" is not peculiar to the twentieth century, whatever some may say about "products of modern civilisation"—who have been an ageless blot on civilisation since the earliest times of recorded history, though they bore different group-names in each period. Moreover, it was these especially selfish young men who most frequently found themselves bound to the halberts.

Far too many of those flogged, as we shall show, were undeserving of such severe discipline—a disciplinary punishment akin to torture, and, in many cases, a protracted death sentence. But the majority of the thousands who had corporal punishment of that nature inflicted upon them were a type of human closely related to our modern gangster, rapist, gun-man, and those other well-known social misfits of seemingly "tender years" with minds old in vice, deception and deceit : the sort who are now causing prison congestion all over the country and serving long terms because no alternative punishment is any longer available to our judges.

Nobody would suggest to-day that men should be flogged with hundreds of lashes, but some might feel that a couple of dozen strokes with either a "cat" or possibly a leather whip, under strict medical supervision, might help these thugs to think twice before using the "cosh" a second time. Many might think that if these whippings were given in full view of other men of violence in a prison yard and, to increase the humiliation, were inflicted on the "breech", it would act, as pointed out and reiterated by members of the Royal Commission over one hundred years ago, as a deterrent *by example*. It is not argued "that punishment should 'fit' the crime", but I am, in passing, favourable to *any* suggested punishment which, though apparently "ruthless", might put a halt to waves of violence.

This is the place to point out that any compulsory imprisoning, or shutting up of the body, is in fact a *corporal* punishment; an important aspect of penal conditions which is ignored to-day. From questions put to a representative number of men in the forces to-day, a great many would sooner have a short, sharp lesson with a minimum of confinement, than a long, demoralising, stagnating, undermining and physically frustrating sojourn in the cells—possibly with hardened criminals who will use their conversational hour to "educate" the novice in crime; and this echoes the sentiments frequently expressed by privates when examined by the Royal Commissioners in 1835 . . .

SCOTT CLAVER.

Several persons who have read the manuscript of this book have expressed disbelief in the startling facts. The author wishes to reiterate, therefore, that *every incident reported in this history is factual and is drawn from contemporary records.*

BOOK I

CHAPTER ONE

MILITARY PUNISHMENTS (History Sketched) 1189 to 1812

I

In the Army and Navy, the end and final aim of Regulations is the complete discipline of the men under arms, the immediate, unhesitating, unquestioning reaction to orders—in one word : OBEDIENCE.

To achieve this discipline, this unswerving obedience, Naval and Military punishment had to be proportionately severe. It had to be adaptable to both the home barracks in days of peace and the battlefield in times of war. Fear of punishment, the example of suffering for crime as a deterrent to potential offenders, had to come even before justice in a military body that depended on its very existence and for the success of all its enterprises upon the strictest discipline. And it is upon this unpalatable truth that military punishments were designed and enforced. There was justice, of course, but only as much as could be afforded, a secondary matter to that of deterring by example and of punishing offences to maintain unquestioning discipline.

Major-General Sir Charles Napier wrote in 1837 : "Military laws have for their object to force an unhesitating and instant compliance with whatever the military chief chooses to issue, and to sustain a constant and unnatural state of irksome existence in obedience to rules which interfere every instant with our wishes and time : all this inconvenience being endured for a small pay, for which the soldier gives up a home and domestic comfort . . . Our military law changes daily, as circumstances demand; every order issued from the King, or from a Lance Corporal, is part of our law. OBEY ! that is our law''.

Tytler thus describes the military code of this country : "A British soldier, enjoying in common with his fellow subjects, every benefit of the laws of his country, is bound by the military code, solely to the observance of the peculiar duties of his profession—a code which is simple in itself, reasonable in its enactments, easy in all its obligations, level to the meanest understanding, and more effectually promulgated and better known than any of the ordinary statute laws of the realm''.

Sir Charles Napier, a later writer on military law, and a much better authority on the usages of the Army than Mr. Tytler, gives a somewhat different account of the British military code : "Dreadful," says he, "is the calling of a soldier, and dreadful must be the means by which that calling is fulfilled during war. A state of war is the natural state of an army, and military institutions must have war for their object, or they are without sense''.

"As a soldier, OBEDIENCE is 'the Law and the Prophets'. His religion, law, and morals, are in the 'orderly-book'. If that says 'spare', he spares : if that says 'destroy', he destroys ! The conscience of a good soldier is in the keeping of his General, who has the whole responsibility before God and man for what the soldier does in obedience to his orders. Perfect obedience is a yoke which every soldier of the British Army voluntarily places upon his own neck when he enlists.''

"Those alone," says Count Alfred de Vigny—a retired officer of the French Army, "who have been soldiers, know what servitude is. To the soldier alone is obedience, passive and active, the law of his life—the law of every day and of every moment; obedience not stopping at sacrifice, nor even at crime. In him alone is the abnegation of his self-will, of his liberty of independent action, absolute and unreserved; the grand distinction of humanity, the responsibility of a moral agent, being made over once for all to superior authority." In fact, nothing short of this severity has been found necessary, in order that one individual might be master of one hundred thousand armed men. Passive obedience from grade to grade, is a condition essential to the existence and efficiency of an army. "When the clock-maker has made a clock, it goes without asking why. Soldier, you must be like the clock; march, turn, halt, and, above all, not a word."

It is essential that the reader should continually bear in mind that the object of military law is not to punish moral delinquencies, in other words, to make men virtuous and good, but to produce prompt and entire obedience; hence, a military offence may not be a crime in its moral sense.

Military crimes were usually arranged under the following classes : —

1. Mutiny.

2. Desertion.

3. Violence to a superior; Insubordination.

4. Disobedience and neglect of duty.

5. Quitting or sleeping on post.

6. Drunk on duty, under arms.

7. Habitual drunkenness.

8. Disgraceful conduct.

9. Absent without leave.

10. Making away with necessaries.

11. Miscellaneous crimes (see Article of War, 70).

Crimes of civil or social life were commonly classed under two heads, namely : 1st, offences against the person; 2nd, offences against property. The difference of the character of the requirements of social and military law, is therefore obvious.

B

Military law (obedience) has in all ages been enforced by more rigorous penalties than the punishments of civilian law.

II

The first regulation on record which refers to punishment in the Army is the *Charter*, as it is called, of Richard I, which was addressed to all his men going by sea and land to Jerusalem, and purports to have been made in the first year of that monarch's reign, for the emergency described. The ordinance being short, it is here inserted verbatim : —

CHINON. 1st RICHARD, 1189

"Richard, by the grace of God, King of England, Duke of Normandy, etc., To all his men going by sea to Jerusalem, greeting : Know ye, by the common counsel of all good men, we have made the underwritten ordinances.

He who kills a man on shipboard shall be bound to the dead man and thrown into the sea [*this punishment was still being used for the same offence six hundred years later*]; if the man is killed on shore the slayer shall be bound to the dead body and buried with it. Any one convicted by lawful witnesses of having drawn his knife to stick another, or who shall have drawn blood of him, to lose his hand; if he shall have only struck with the palm of his hand, without drawing blood, he shall be thrice ducked in the sea. Any one who shall reproach, abuse, or curse his companion shall, for every time he is convicted thereof, give him so many ounces of silver. Any one convicted of theft shall be shorn like a champion, boiling pitch shall be poured on his head, and down of feathers shaken over it, that he may be known, and he shall be set on shore at the first land at which the ship touches."

Many of these punishments lasted for over five hundred years.

King Richard's articles of war were obviously framed after the original idea of punishment, which was to inflict pain on a person as a satisfaction or atonement for some offence which he had committed. The law of retaliation, *lex talionis*, was recognised by the Mosaic law, the punishments awarded by which are : 1. *Death* by the sword, or by stoning, followed in some instances by gibbeting the corpse of a criminal for a few hours (Deut. xxi. 23). 2. *Exile* from the congregation. 3. *Corporal punishments*, the maximum number of stripes being fixed at forty,* while the amount of the sentence, which could not legally exceed that number, was left to be determined by the circumstances of the case and the discretion of the judges. 4. *Fines.* 5. *Offerings* to make atonement for sin.

For the five hundred years following the first Richard's Charter, not only the capital but the secondary punishments were of a most ferocious and sanguinary description, such as dismemberment, maiming, or fracturing of the limbs, boring of the tongue with a red-hot iron, and burning or branding the cheeks and cutting off the left ear.

Grose (*Military Antiquities*) informs us that in many instances where a corps, or a considerable body of men, were guilty of a crime for which the established punishment was death, to prevent too great weakening of the army the delinquents were decimated, every tenth man being executed; sometimes corps were decimated by ranks and files. In cases where only a few were condemned to suffer for the sake of example, the whole were ordered to cast dice on the drum-head, sometimes under the gallows, and the requisite number of persons who drew the low numbers were doomed to death. In India, 1790, in consequence of marauding, the majority of a corps were prisoners to the minority. In this case a few delinquents were selected by ballot from the whole number, and flogged at the halberts.

* An injunction in the Holy Word, that was ignored by the Military.

The ordinances of war, during the sixteenth and part of the seventeenth century, contained a minute enumeration of military crimes, and a clear denunciation, so far as they admitted of precision, of their correspondent punishments. Death, fines, and forfeitures appear to have been very common punishments. The income of the Earl-Marshal depended in a great measure upon the fines which were imposed in this way. Under such a system of temptation, where officers had a beneficial interest in the delinquencies of soldiers, neither honesty nor humanity could be expected to prevail.

The punishments mentioned in the *Lawes and Ordinances Militarie* of Robert Earl of Leicester, Captain-General of Her Majesty's Army and Forces in the Low Countries, etc., etc., 1579, are as follows : —

"Death with torments. Death. Loss either of life or limb. Banished the Army. Fines. Loss of place and wages. Imprisonment."

The *Lawes and Ordinances of Warre*, etc., were promulgated by His Excellency the Earl of Northumberland, who commanded the Royal Army in 1640. An article in these is as follows : "No man shall resist, draw, lift, or offer to draw, his weapon against an officer correcting him *orderly* for his offence, upon pain of death". Resistance to a Commanding Officer, or contumacy in a soldier, such as taking hold of an officer's rod, or cane, wherewith he was beaten, was by the Romans deemed a capital offence.

In 1642, the Earl of Essex, who commanded the Parliamentary Army, published a code of *Lawes and Ordinances of Warre*, etc., which seems to have been the foundation of the present Articles of War. This code enumerates certain crimes which are to be punished with death, while the punishment of all other offences is left to the discretion of a council of war. There were from forty to fifty delinquencies mentioned in this code for which death might be awarded. The Secondary Punishments, specially enumerated, were, "Boring the tongue with a red-hot iron; loss of pay; confinement in prison with only bread and water; riding the wooden horse (see illustration p. 12); and degradation to serve as pioneers and scavengers".

The offence of blasphemy, namely impugning the doctrine of the Trinity, was treated with a much heavier penalty, the blasphemer being liable to have his tongue bored through with a red-hot iron, even at so late a period as the reign of King James II. *Vide* : Fourth Article of War, James II.

We are informed that "a soldier of Okey's Regiment was on the 26th July, 1750, sentenced by a court martial *to be bored through the tongue with a red-hot iron*, and to run the *gantelop* through four companies, for uttering blasphemous words, he being at the time in a ranting humour with drinking too much".

The punishment of the "gantelop" will be better understood by the following sentence, which was passed on two soldiers for deer-stealing; the punishment took place in September, 1649 : "That they be stripped naked from the waist upward, and a lane to be made by half of the Lord General's regiment of foot, and half of Colonel Pride's regiment with every soldier a cudgel in his hand, and they to run through them in this posture, every soldier having a stroke at their naked backs and breasts, arms, or where it shall light; and after they have run the gantelop in this manner, they are to be cashiered the regiment". A hundred years later, we find the cudgels replaced by whips, lashes, rope's ends and canes.

It may be mentioned that commissioned officers were as liable to be sentenced by a court martial to the corporal punishment of having the tongue bored with a red-hot iron for blasphemy as were privates. This punishment remained on the military statute-book until the reign of Queen Anne, 1710.

III

Markham, who published his *Epistles of Warre* about the year 1622, gives us the following account of the duties of a Provost-Marshal, from which the nature of the military punishments then inflicted may be inferred. "The Provost-Marshall hath the charge of all manner of *tortures, as gyves, shackels, bolts, chains, bilbowes, manacles, whips,* and the like, and may, by his officers, use them either in case of judgment or commandment from a marshall court or otherwise upon unruliness at his own discretion; he is, by his officers, to see all places of execution prepared and furnished with engines fitting to the judgment whether it be *gallows, gybbets, scaffolds, pillories, stocks,* or *strappadoes,* or any other engine which is set up for terror and affright to such as behold it."

Sir James Turner furnishes us with a fairly full account of the military punishments of the seventeenth century, in his *Pallas Armata,* a work which was published in 1683. In one chapter he treats of military laws and articles, of courts of war, of the Judge Martial, and of the Provost-Master General : in another chapter he describes "our modern military punishments and rewards".

"The fairest and justest way of punishment," says Sir James, "is by courts of war, if the case do not require a present animadversion. As to capital punishments, the most honourable death," says Sir James, "for a delinquent soldier, is beheading, the next to that is shooting—if he be a horseman, with pistols—if a foot soldier, with muskets."

The *Secondary* military punishments, according to the same authority, are "the strappado", hanging up by the thumbs, "so that the delinquent's toes can only touch the ground, laying muskets on their shoulders, more or fewer, for a longer or shorter time, according to the quality of the fault; to be kept in prison so many

THE STRAPPADO

[*Face page* 8

days or weeks, with irons on them", and sometimes to be fed only with bread and water while in prison. "There is also *riding the wooden horse*, on which sometimes he hath his hands tied behind his back, and sometimes muskets, or other weights, tied to his feet. As likewise to be turned out of the Army by the *hangman*, to have their ears cut off by the *hangman*, and to be whipped by the *hangman*. I have known some who thought that soldiers who are whipped at *Gatloupe* should be turned out of the Army, which is a gross mistake, for they are appointed to be whipped by their comrades, that they may be kept in the Army; *for after an officer or a soldier is put into a hangman's hands, he should serve no more in any army*." Gustavus Adolphus, King of Sweden, first began it (the Gantlope) in imitation of the customs of the Roman centurions to whip their soldiers.

When the punishment of the *gatloupe, gantelope*, or *gantlope*, was inflicted, the Provost-Marshal furnished the rods, and gave the delinquent the first stroke; but if there was neither Provost nor Deputy Provost present, then a drummer gave the rods.

The punishment of the strappado, *etrapade* (French), was as follows : "The delinquent is hoisted up by means of a rope fastened to the arms behind his back, and then suddenly dropped down with a jerk, by which process his shoulder joints were generally dislocated. He was sometimes hoisted up, and again let fall two or three times". (See illustration, p. 8.)

Sir James next discusses "some nice questions" regarding the mode of beating soldiers; for example, "a corporal", he says, "must only beat with a musket rest; and if he broke one of them in beating a soldier, who should pay for it? the corporal or the soldier, is a hard question". Sir James does not attempt to resolve this difficulty.

It does not appear that drummers were specially employed to execute the sentences of courts martial

before the beginning of the eighteenth century. Sir
James Turner says, "When regimental hangmen are
wanting, capital crimes must be punished by harque-
busiers, and scourging must be converted into the
gatloupe".

The cat-o'-nine-tails appears to be an invention of
a later date than the reign of William III.

The duty of carrying the sentence of a court martial
into effect belonged, during the reign of William III,
to the Provost-Marshal, who made out a contingent
bill to defray expenses for execution, including his fees.
The contingent expenses of a Dutchman who was
Provost-Master General in Ireland under William III,
amounted, in one campaign, to £307 10s. 0d.—a
manuscript copy of this contingent bill is preserved in
the British Museum.

And here is the "expense account", tendered by the
Provost-Marshal, after the execution of two men :—

	£	s.	d.
For 33 days' diet, at 6d. each day ...	1	13	0
For extraordinary treats after the sentence of death of the patients, as otherwise, each 6s.		12	0
Paid unto 3 servants that have sat up with, and served the patients after the sentence of death, according to custome, half-a-crown a day, for two days and a night		15	0
For the reading of the sentences ...		2	6
Unto the executioner, for hanging and taking downe, as otherwise, 10 shillings apiece is together	1	0	0
For the ladder, ropes, and bolts ...		3	0
For the locking, and unlocking of each, 2s. 6d.		5	0
For assisting in the execution, according to custom, for me		10	0

For the Liftenent   4   0
  Paid for burying, unto the servant,
  2s. 6d. each   5   0
(Grose, *Military Antiquities*.)

IV

It seems probable that the military punishment of flogging was derived through the gauntelet from the Roman *Fustuarium*, or the *bastinado, stick-beating*, which was much practised in the Roman Army.

When a soldier was to suffer the bastinado the Tribune first struck him gently with a staff, on which signal the soldiers of the legion fell upon him with sticks and saplings.

Bruce, who published his work *The Institutions of Military Law* in 1717, has a long chapter on military crimes, with the punishments awarded. The punishments he enumerates were *death*, which might be awarded for a great number of delinquencies, the secondary punishments being *stigmatizing* (branding) *in the forehead, cutting off the ears, forfeiture of three months' pay, degradation to the quality of a pioneer-scavenger*, and *riding the wooden horse*. Flogging is not mentioned.

Among the punishments to which sutlers and camp-followers were liable we may mention the *Whirligig*. This was a circular wooden cage, which, according to Grose : "turned on a pivot, and when set in motion wheeled round with such velocity that the delinquent became extremely sick, and commonly emptied his or her body through every aperture".

A military essay was published in 1761, by Lieut.-Colonel Dalrymple, from which we learn that by that period whipping was employed as a military punishment. As a means of preventing crime in the Army, Colonel Dalrymple recommended that the regiments should be raised and recruited in particular counties. "It is very difficult," says that author, "from the kind of men we get, to avoid frequent and severe punishments, especially in time of war, when, from the scarcity of men, we are not to whip out of a regiment perhaps a good but vicious soldier; *yet we do that more than perhaps is absolutely necessary.*" Colonel Dalrymple is the first author that we have met with who mentions the word "flogging", and who bears testimony to the *inefficiency* of this mode of punishment.

Whipping or flogging was, according to Samuel (*Account of the British Army,* 1816), a refinement on the former modes of chastisement, increasing the rigour of punishment by prolonging the duration of it.

When the pursuit of a military life became preferred as a profession, a pecuniary expiation of crimes could not be countenanced in the military code; and hence, from altered circumstances, flogging was substituted in its stead. "A species of punishment," says Samuel, "which, if not exceptionable in itself, is, from the frequency of its use, and the strange extent of its application, not less discreditable, as it is supposed by many well-directed minds, to the spirit of the military law than the general character of our armies."

British soldiers had for many ages been liable to "manual correction" by officers; and the result, a motion before Parliament on the 7th February, 1750, may be considered tantamount to approval by the House of Commons. It was not until after the commencement of the nineteenth century that effectual measures were taken to prevent soldiers being beaten by officers; but manual correction, or, in fact, correction with the cane, did not fall into disuse in the East India Company's Army for a number of years after it had been practically abolished in the British Army.

It may be inferred, from a work which was published in 1761, entitled *Cautions and Advices to Officers of the Army, by an Old Officer,* that soldiers were at that time very liable to receive "manual correction" from officers, without any previous legal investigation.

"Give yourself no trouble" (said a soldier who had been convicted of intemperance, to the members of a court martial, who were deliberating upon the amount of his punishment) "in regard to the number of lashes; just put down the usual 200."

One of the lesser known, but none-the-less important, liberties, was that a soldier who thought that he had been aggrieved in the Army might, even after his being discharged, appeal to the civil jurisdiction of the country, and by that means obtain a legal investigation of the alleged grievance.

As long ago as July, 1763, at the assizes of Winchester, before a special jury, a case was tried, wherein George Dawson, lately a soldier in the 85th Regiment, was plaintiff, and three Lieutenants and three Drummers were defendants. The action was brought for trespass and assault, and false imprisonment of the soldier. In the course of the evidence it appeared that one of the defendants, a lieutenant, had caned and imprisoned the plaintiff without just cause, and that the plaintiff received 300 lashes with a cat-o'-nine-tails, at the halberts, under colour of the sentence of a court martial, of the proceedings of which no evidence was given by the defendants; and, after a long hearing, the jury found a verdict for the plaintiff, with £300 damages —against one Lieutenant £200, and £50 each against the other two.

In 1693, three soldiers of Prince Hesse's Regiment were brought to St. George's Fields, being condemned by a court martial for deserting their colours, where they threw dice upon a drum for their lives and one of them was shot to death (*Lutterell*).

In 1704 at Gibraltar, the Journal of Rev. Thomas Pocock, the Chaplain of the Renelagh, reads : "Great disorders were committed by the boats' crews that came ashore and marines . . . one marine was hanged after he had threw dice with a Dutchman, who hove 10 and the Englishman 9".

Barclay, in his *Icon Animarum*, talks of an English-man on the Spanish side in Flanders who was taken prisoner with many and various others. They were given dice with which to throw for their lives. He won. Later, the Englishman noted a Spaniard about to throw for his own life; the Spaniard was shivering and quaking with fright. The Englishman offered to throw for him for twelve pence. He won again. The Spaniard fainted.

And here is a description of a military execution in 1795. It is based on an account in the Annual Register of that year. If the imagination is used just a little, a macabre and awful picture presents itself . . . the valley with hills around . . . the three thousand cavalry in the wonderous uniforms of the period, the horses in their glinting trappings . . . the twelve executioners . . . the officers, plumed, stern, erect and autocratic . . . the clergyman . . . the two "miserables" kneeling on their coffins . . . the whole fantastic spectacle thrown into leaping light and shadow by thousands of flaming torches . . . awaiting the dawn. Here is the account : —

"Brighton, 14th June, 1795. The Oxfordshire Regi-ment marched on Friday night last at 11 o'clock, from Seaford, in order to attend the execution of the two men who were condemned by a general court martial for riotous and disorderly conduct. The hour of four after midnight was the time appointed to assemble. On the march the regiment halted, and twelve of the men who had taken part in the riot were called out. The Com-manding Officer ordered them to fix their flints, and to prepare to execute sentence. This was done to demonstrate to the men that state of obedience in which the officers were determined to hold them, and by this measure they felt more pointedly the folly of their former conduct, when those persons, whom they had made their leaders, were now to suffer death at their hands. The regiment was then conducted to a spacious valley and divided into two wings, which were stationed

THE PICKET

[*Face page* 16

on each side of the place of execution. On the rising ground above the valley, three thousand cavalry were posted; they were followed by all the Horse Artillery. The guns were pointed and matches lighted. From the disposition of the ground, and from the arrangement of the troops, a more magnificent and a more awful spectacle were never exhibited in this country. After the corporal punishments had been inflicted on the two offenders of less note, Cooke and Parish (flogging by torchlight), the two unfortunate men condemned to die were brought forward with a very strong escort. They walked along the vale in slow and solemn procession, accompanied by the clergyman, who had devoted his time so conscientiously to them from the moment the sentence had been made known, that they were fully prepared to meet their fate. They approached the fatal spot with resignation, and expressed much concern and penitence for the crime. They then kneeled down upon their coffins with cool and deliberate firmness; when the one who was to drop the signal said to his comrade : 'Are you ready', upon the reply being made, he dropped a prayer book; and the party did their duty at about six yards distance. One of them not appearing to be dead entirely was instantly shot through the head; the same ceremony was performed to the other. After this the whole line was ordered to march round the dead bodies." (See *The Soldier's Wife*.)

V

The following brief but comprehensive account of the punishments in the British Army, is given in a work published about the year 1762, entitled *Essay on the Art of War*, etc. "*To be hanged, shot, sent to the galleys, chained to a wheelbarrow, or run the gantelope, are the military punishments of crimes now in use. The wooden mare, the picket, imprisonment, chains, bread and water, are the punishments of faults.*"

The history of the punishment of flogging is thus given by Grose : —

"The gantelope," says he, "was in cases of theft, or some offence that affected the character or interest of the corps, practised in two ways. In one, called running the gantelope, the regiment was formed six deep, and the ranks opened and faced inwards, each man being furnished with a switch. The offender, naked to the waist, was led through the ranks, preceded by a Sergeant, the point of whose reversed halbert was presented to his breast to prevent him running too fast; as he thus passed through the ranks every soldier gave him a stroke. But this method being found inconvenient, and in many cases objectionable, the offender was tied to four halberts, in the ordinary way, three being placed in a triangle, and the fourth across two of them, to keep him on the outside. In this situation the regiment filed off from the right, and marched by. When they came near the halberts, a cat was given to the first man; who, having given a stroke to the culprit, threw down the cat and passed on. This was repeated by the whole regiment, each man giving him a lash. This, likewise, being found objectionable, as degrading soldiers to executioners, has been likewise in a great measure left off, and the infliction of the punishment put into the hands of the Drummers, under the inspection of the Drum-Major and Adjutant : the first to see the halberts are properly fixed, the cats in order, that each Drummer does his duty, and is properly relieved after having given twenty-five lashes. The Surgeon is to take care that the prisoner does not receive more lashes than he is able to bear without *endangering his life*, or injuring his constitution; and the Adjutant to cause the sentence of the court martial to be properly inflicted, and to oblige the Drum-Major to make his Drummers do their duty."

"Whipping," says Grose, "is almost the only corporal punishment now in use [1786]. This was formerly inflicted with switches; but for these *thirty years* at least, except running the gantelope, with what is called a cat-of-nine-tails; being a whip with nine lashes, each lash knotted with nine knots. This punishment is inflicted either by the soldiers or Drummers of the regiment, according to the sentence of the court martial."

The punishment of the gantelope, from which the more modern punishment of flogging in the Army originated, had not been completely abandoned when Dr. Hamilton published his work, *The Duties of a Regimental Surgeon Considered*, in 1787. "Different regiments," says he, "use different methods of punishing; in some to run the gantlet is customary. Here, instead of cats, rods of willow are made use of. The whole regiment is drawn up in a line two deep, face to face—every man is furnished with a willow. The prisoner runs *naked* the whole length of the line, and every man strikes as he passes. No regard can be paid in this way to the part they strike, hence the ribs as well as the shoulders are wounded." While the delinquent runs the drums beat at each end of the ranks; sometimes he runs three, five, or seven times along the line, according to the nature of the offence. The Major of a regiment superintends the punishment, and takes care that every soldier does his duty. In 1805, when Major James published the Second Edition of his *Dictionary*, this punishment had become unknown in the British Army. "The punishment of the gantlet, as I have seen it executed on board a man-of-war, is conducted in the following manner : The whole ship's crew is disposed in two rows, standing face to face, on both sides of the deck, so as to form a lane whereby to go forward on one side and aft on the other, each person being furnished with a small twisted cord or rope called a *knittel*, having two or three knots upon it. The delinquent is then stripped naked above the waist and brought to the gangway, where he receives one dozen from a boatswain's mate. Next follows what may be called a procession,

c

which takes place between the two rows of men in the following order : First, a Drummer, who beats the Rogue's March. Second, the Master-at-Arms, having a drawn cutlass under his arm, with the point directed behind him towards the delinquent. Third, the culprit. Fourth, the Surgeon's Mate. The delinquent passes forward between the two rows of men on one side, and aft on the other, a certain number of times, rarely exceeding three, during which every person lays on him with their knittels. All the officers are present at the punishment, and when the Captain sees fit he directs the flogging to cease.

"The ordinary effects of the gantlet are, excessive tumefaction of the shoulders and ribs; the parts do not usually ulcerate, but the sufferer is commonly some time on the sick list, being unfit for duty." (Marshall.)

VI

To the foregoing punishments, the following may be added, the great number of which were in use when Grose wrote, in 1786, and some of them were employed until the early nineteenth century.

Removal to the Navy.—"A soldier, who behaved ill, and who, in consequence of frequent delinquencies, was deemed incorrigible, was occasionally turned over to a press-gang. This transfer did not, however, occur without some sort of concurrence on the part of the soldier, who was left to choose between the execution and continuance of a severe military punishment, or to enter on board one of His Majesty's ships."

Cold Burning—Bottling.—"This punishment is thus inflicted. The offender is set against the wall with the arm which is to be *burned,* tied as high above his head as possible. The executioner then ascends a stool, and having a bottle of cold water, pours it slowly down the sleeve of the delinquent, patting him, and leading the water gently down his body till it runs out at his feet;

this is repeated to the other arm if he is sentenced to be burned in both. Bottling was, at one time, much in use in the Cavalry branch of the Service."

"*Cobbing* is a punishment inflicted upon a soldier by his comrades for petty offences committed among themselves, sometimes with the sanction of the Commissioned Officers of a Company, or of a Commanding Officer of a corps. It consisted in bastonading an offender on the posterior with a cobbing-stick or a cross-belt. Cobbing was chiefly practised in the Infantry."

"*Booting* is a punishment which was principally used in the Cavalry. It consisted in flogging a man with a belt on the soles of the feet. Previous to the infliction of Cobbing, or Booting, the delinquent is fairly tried by a Court consisting of a president, the oldest soldier; members : next two oldest soldiers, youngest soldier, next youngest soldier."

"*Venereal Fine.*—Until about the end of the [18th] century, a soldier who incurred the misfortune to have it alleged by a medical officer that he had the venereal disease was, in many regiments, mulcted of five shillings, which sum went into the pocket of the surgeon. Hence, medical officers had a beneficial interest in the moral delinquencies of soldiers !" In the Navy the fine was fifteen shillings.

Blistering.—Boiling oil or water was used to blister the backs of habitual drunkards, usually by their own comrades, and while drunk. It appears to have been, according to Sir Charles Napier, a most successful alternative to flogging.

The principal punishments inflicted upon soldiers subsequently to the year 1790, by military law, and military usage, were death, and flogging with the cat-o'-nine-tails. The minor punishments inflicted by a Commanding Officer were imprisonment in a guard-house or black-hole—in which case, bread and water was the usual diet.

Pecuniary fines had long ceased to be awarded as a punishment for military crimes; but when martial law was proclaimed in Ireland, in 1798, this mode of punishment appears to have been temporarily restored. In this year (1798) the following proclamation was issued :—

TO THE INHABITANTS OF BELFAST

"This is to give notice, that if any person is taken up by the patrols after ten o'clock he will be fined five shillings for the benefit of the poor. If the delinquent is not able to pay five shillings, he will be brought to the drum-head court martial, and will *receive one hundred lashes.*

JAMES DENHAM, Colonel Commandant.

By this notice, Colonel Denham seems to have considered five shillings equivalent to one hundred lashes, and any man who could not raise five shillings might be flogged as a matter of course.

In practice, flogging was almost the only punishment employed, as at this time confinement had not been much approved as a mode of chastisement. We learn from Dr. Hamilton that private Anthony Gregory, of the 10th Foot, was punished with a hundred severe lashes, "well laid-on", "for suffering the queue of his hair to drop off when on duty", which, perhaps, he had that morning rather carelessly tied on; "and as late as 1811, an African recruit, who did not know a word of our language, was brought to a drum-head court martial and flogged, in consequence of some of his appointments being less clean than they ought to have been. Unsteadiness in the ranks caused, perhaps, by a man brushing a fly from his face, and the disgraceful offence of stealing from a comrade, met with a similar chastisement, differing, perhaps, a little in the amount of infliction, but the same in ignominy".

In the *Conversations of Paley,* by the Rev. Mr. Best, there is a case recorded which may be here noticed.

About the end of the eighteenth century several regiments of boys were raised, for the purpose of being sent to India. One of these regiments was quartered at Lincoln. "The cat-o'-nine-tails, though administered," says Mr. Best, "as was supposed, with due regard to the tender age of these young soldiers, was not idle. One boy died a day or two after a punishment. The officers wished to impute it to some other cause."

The subject of corporal punishment was brought prominently forward by Sir Robert Wilson, in a letter which he addressed to the Right Hon. William Pitt, in 1804. The report was entitled *An Inquiry into the Present State of the Military Force of the British Empire, with a View to its Re-organisation.* In this inquiry the author asserts that the principal checks to recruiting are comprised in the system of enlisting for life, and *the frequency of corporal punishments.* "There is no mode of punishment," says Sir Robert, "so disgraceful as flogging, and none more inconsistent with the military character, which should be esteemed as the essence of honour, and the pride of manhood; but when what should be used in very extreme cases as the *ultimum supplicum,* producing the moral death of the criminal, becomes the common penalty for offences in which there is no moral turpitude, or but a petty violation of martial law, the evil requires serious attention."

The famous author Southey (*Espriella's Letters*), describes the principal military punishments of this country in 1807 : "The martial laws of England are the most barbarous which at this day exist in Europe. The offender is sometimes sentenced to receive a thousand lashes—a surgeon stands by to feel his pulse during the execution, and determine how long the flogging can be continued without killing him. When human nature can stand no more he is remanded to prison (hospital). His wound, for from the shoulders to the loins it leaves him one wound, is dressed, and as soon as it is sufficiently healed to be laid open in the same manner he is brought out to undergo the remainder of his sentence. And this is repeatedly and openly practised in a country where they read in their churches, and in their houses *that Bible*, in their own language, which saith 'Forty stripes may the judge inflict upon the offender, and not exceed' ".

Mr. Windham's Army Bill passed in 1806, substituted service for a limited term of years, for that indefinite and hopeless bondage to which soldiers had hitherto been doomed. This Bill had for a long time been called for by humane and enlightened men in civil life, but it met with but little support from military officers. But in 1808, a Bill by Lord Castlereagh passed the House, permitting recruits to enlist for life, negating the Bill of 1806. By the consequent offer of a higher bounty to recruits who enlisted for life, the liberal provisions of Mr. Windham's measure was rendered abortive, and enlistment for life again became the rule of the Army.

When the Bill for establishing the local Militia was introduced, it met with great opposition from Sir Francis Burdett, partly because the men were to be placed under military law. The Marquis of Buckingham viewed it in the same light, and when the Bill was brought into the Upper House he proposed, but without success, as an amendment to the clause, which subjected the local Militia to the Mutiny Act, "that no sentence of a court martial for inflicting corporal punishment should be carried into effect until submitted to His Majesty or to the Commander-in-Chief".

During the month of June, 1808, Sir Francis Burdett renewed the subject of martial law, by moving "That there be laid before the House early in the next session of Parliament, regimental returns of all corporal punishments sentenced and inflicted during the last ten years in every regiment of regulars, Militia, garrisons, and Artillery, specifying the causes, the sentences, and number of lashes given at one or more periods". This motion gave rise to a long and interesting discussion. Four members only, however, voted in favour of it.

Public opinion had, however, by this time become, *in some measure*, alive to the abuses of corporal punishment in the Army; "and when the public mind becomes intelligent and benevolent, the reign of Justice and humanity will certainly follow". "Public opinion," says Lord Lauderdale, "cannot be held too sacred by public men. The voice of enlightened public opinion is irresistible." These observations of his Lordship were amply fulfilled in regard to the practice of flogging in the Army.

Flogging was, we believe, carried to a greater extent in the Army at this time than at any future period. "When at Jersey, in the year 1808, it was my painful duty," says Lieut. Shipp, "to witness the infliction of corporal punishment almost every week. One of the battalions of the 60th, which was chiefly composed of foreigners, including a number of Frenchmen, was then stationed at Jersey. Many of the men deserted, and most of them were taken in the attempt. Being tried for desertion, they were sentenced to receive a thousand lashes each." According to our authority, "this punishment was rigidly inflicted, with the additional torture which must have resulted from the number of *five* being slowly counted between each lash; consequently the space of three hours and twenty minutes was occupied in inflicting the total punishment, as though a thousand lashes were not of themselves a sufficiently awful sentence without so cruel and unnecessary a prolongation of misery. Many of these poor creatures fainted several times, but having been restored to their senses by medicinal application, the moment they could move their heads the castigation was recommenced in all its rigour. Numbers of them were taken down and carried from the square in a state of utter insensibility. The spectacle, altogether, instead of operating as an example to others, created disgust and abhorrence in the breast of every soldier who was worthy of the name of man".

In the month of June, 1809, an alleged mutiny broke out amongst the local Militia at Ely, which was suppressed by the arrival of four squadrons of the German Light Cavalry, under the command of General Auckland. Five of the ringleaders were tried by a court martial, and sentenced to receive five hundred lashes each, part of which punishment they received, and a part was remitted. "A stoppage for their knapsacks was the ground of complaint that excited this mutinous spirit."

Mr. Cobbett, in his *Political Register* of the 1st July, 1809, argued strongly against the impolicy and injustice of flogging the alleged mutineers at Ely, and his arguments eventually excited the attention of the Government; for on the 15th June, 1810, he was tried for seditious libel, nearly twelve months after his remarks had been published. He was found guilty. "A few days after, on the 9th July, he was sentenced to be imprisoned in Newgate for two years, to pay a fine of £1,000 to the King, and at the expiration of the two years to give bail, himself to the amount of £3,000, with two sureties to the amount of £1,000 each, for his keeping the peace for seven years."

In his defence Mr. Cobbett stated, "that the disturbance at Ely was not to be called a mutiny—that it was a mere squabble between the men and the officers for a trifle of money—that the men were persons who had just thrown off their smock-frocks to put on the garb of a soldier, and still continued so much labourers as to be ignorant of their duty as soldiers, and had become so much soldiers as to have lost the inclination to labour". Which remark, though nearly a century-and-a-half old, is still apt to-day.

Messrs. Hunt, the proprietors of a weekly newspaper, *The Examiner*, were tried at Westminster for a seditious libel, 22nd February, 1811, having published some remarks in regard to the punishment of flogging, extracted from the *Stamford News*, a paper edited by Mr. Drakard. They were acquitted.

At the assizes at Lincoln, on the 13th March, 1811, Mr. Drakard, of the *Stamford News*, was tried for a seditious libel, which he had published in his papers, in regard to the flogging of soldiers. He was found guilty, and adjudged to pay a fine of £200 to the King, and be imprisoned in His Majesty's jail at Lincoln for the space of eighteen months, and find security for good behaviour for three years, himself in £400 and two sureties in £200 each.

When the Mutiny Act was brought before Parliament, in 1811, a new clause was introduced, which empowered courts martial to imprison instead of to inflict the penalty of flogging. It may be mentioned here that a court martial had always the power of sentencing men to be imprisoned, or, indeed, to any other mode of punishment, but confinement was not the *established usage*, the "old system", commonly employed for punishing military delinquents. We are informed by Major James, in the Second Edition of his *Dictionary* (1805), that solitary confinement had then been tried by some Commanding Officers. This punishment became gradually more frequently adopted in the Army.

"The first instances I find on our books," says Sir John Woodford, Grenadier Guards, "of commutation of corporal punishment are in 1807, when part of the regiment was in Sicily. A close kind of military confinement, when the soldier was off duty, was substituted, combined with punishment-drill . . . The first instance of such a sentence in the 1st Regiment of Guards at home occurred at Knightsbridge Barracks, on the 28th December, 1814; consequently it would appear that corporal punishment first fell into partial disuse on foreign stations." (*Evidence on Military Punishments; Question 3,846.*)

The mean number of lashes inflicted monthly in a regiment then serving in India, in 1812, was for some time 17,000; and we have no reason to think the practice of flogging in this corps differed materially from other regiments on the same service, and liable to the same temptations.

Strange to say, it is probable that the amelioration of the punishment of soldiers was materially promoted by the West Indies slave owners. In defending the cruelties inflicted upon the negroes, and the inhuman treatment they endured, the slave proprietors frequently referred to the severe punishments in the Army.

CHAPTER TWO

MILITARY PUNISHMENTS (History Sketched) 1812 to 1840

With Especial Reference to Flogging in the Army

Although the Duke of York, in 1812, issued a confidential letter as a circular to all Commanding Officers, advising the use of the cat-o'-nine-tails only when unavoidable, and limiting the number of lashes to three hundred, officers had still a frightful opportunity of abusing the power with which they were invested. They could sentence a man to receive three hundred lashes for a *small offence*, such as being absent at *tattoo*, although, perhaps, he might be in an adjoining barrack-room, or for the constructive crime of "unsoldierlike" conduct. Many old officers, however, individuals who had been educated in the school of vindictive routine, believed, and did not hesitate to say, that "to limit the number of lashes to 300 would destroy the discipline of the Army". We are all prone to consider those means by which we have long been accustomed to adopt in furtherance of an object, as not only completely justifiable, but indispensably necessary. One officer swore that he could not, and would not, comply with the order, "for," says he, "my conscience would not allow me to award a sentence of 300 lashes when I felt convinced that the man *deserved* 600". At a later date, a Governor of the United East India Company, writing to an officer who had been appointed Judge of Civil Affairs in India, said : "Sir, I expect my will and orders shall be your will, and not the laws of England, which are a heap of nonsense, compiled by a number of country gentlemen, who hardly know how to govern their own families, much less regulate *our* affairs".

At one time the efficiency of an officer to command

seemed to be estimated by his disposition to inflict corporal punishment.

"I understand you have got a new commanding officer," said an officer of one regiment to that of another, "How do you like him?"

"We like him pretty well," answered the other, "only he does not flog enough."

In the spring of 1812, shortly after the issuing of the Duke of York's circular, an Act was passed by the American Congress expressly putting an end to flogging in the American Army.

By the regulations and orders of the Army (1822), soldiers were permitted, upon application, to commute for service abroad, without limitation, the punishment awarded by a court martial; but before permission was granted a man was obliged to sign the following declaration : —

"I do hereby declare, that I am willing to serve, without limitation, in any regiment abroad, to which I may be attached, if the punishment, *or remainder of the punishment* (as the case may be), awarded me for ——————————, is remitted."

The question respecting corporal punishment had, by 1815, been so fully discussed from time to time, in the House of Commons, and the opinion of the few officers who had in their publications disapproved of frequent flogging, so often quoted—namely, Sir Robert Wilson, Brigadier-General Stuart, and General Mooney—that hopes began to be entertained that flogging would not long be practised in the British service, except for thieving, or some notoriously disgraceful act.

"Perhaps the relative frequency of punishments in different regiments depends more upon the disposition of Commanding Officers than on insubordination of the men," writes one author. "Let the returns of each regiment in the Service be called for, for a series of years, and it will be found in some corps not a man has

been flogged, and in others a considerable number. A
similar result may be observed in the same regiment
under different Commanding Officers. As the men are
pretty much alike in all corps, the difference in regard
to the number of punishments must be chiefly owing to
the dispositions of the Commanders." But it was 1840
when he wrote, though agitation against flogging was
already thirty years old, and the recommendations of
the Royal Commission had become historic.

Many men who underwent corporal infliction were
good soldiers, not a few of them later having been made
non-commissioned officers, and some having been promoted to the rank of commissioned officers. The promotion of soldiers who have been corporally punished
during the early nineteenth century need not surprise,
when we take into consideration the numbers who had
undergone that infliction, amounting, it was alleged, in
some regiments, to one-third or one-half of the
strength, and also the trivial natures of the offences for
which men were at one time flogged. No one
acquainted with the usages of the Army at this date
could deny that the punishments awarded to delinquents
were sometimes enormous—far, very far beyond what
the average man was able to endure. Even in 1807,
this cruel absurdity attracted the attention of His
Majesty, George III. A general order, of the 30th
January, 1807, promulgating the sentence of a court
martial on a private of the 54th Regiment, who had been
sentenced to *fifteen hundred lashes* for mutinous conduct, contained the following observations : "It appearing to His Majesty, that a punishment to the extent of
one thousand lashes, is a sufficient example for any
breach of military discipline, short of capital offence;
and as even that number cannot be safely inflicted at any
one period, His Majesty has been graciously pleased to
express his opinion, that no sentence for corporal
punishment should exceed *one thousand lashes*".

But in May, of the same year, a man belonging to

the 67th Regiment, was tried by a court martial in Bengal, and sentenced to receive *fifteen hundred lashes,* which sentence was approved and confirmed by competent authority. (The only excuse could have been the slowness of transport conveying Royal Orders in those days !)

This is the largest amount of flogging to which we can find a man sentenced, *and that sentence approved and confirmed.*

At this date it was the custom of the Service to complete a sentence at a period subsequent to the first infliction. The award of the court sometimes expressly stated that the delinquent was to be punished at such a *time* or *times* and *in such portion or portions,* as the Commanding Officer might think fit to appoint, but the express permission to carry the sentence of a court martial into effect by instalments does not appear to have been considered indispensably necessary; second punishments were a usage of the Army, and, indeed, it may be observed that a court, in awarding such a punishment as one thousand lashes, must, one should think, have contemplated the probability of a second infliction, if not the certainty of it, unless a part of the sentence was remitted.

"We tolerate," says Sir Samuel Romilly, "this species of punishment, this refinement of cruelty; we permit a fellow creature to be driven to the very verge of existence, a Surgeon standing by to feel the pulse of the sufferer, and to pronounce at that moment exhausted nature can bear no additional infliction. Then, when his soul is about to forsake his body and leap into eternity, then, indeed, the poor wretch is taken down from the halberts, and removed into an hospital, where he is left, his body more at ease, but his mind still upon the rack, reflecting that the faster his wounds heal the nearer he is to a renewal of his sufferings, and that his life is thus cherished by his tormentors only that it may be again subjected to their torments."

In the evidence given on military punishments before the Royal Commission, 1836, it appears (Question 822) that a court martial held at Dinapore on the 12th September, 1825, sentenced a man to receive *nineteen hundred lashes,* which sentence was remitted by the Commander-in-Chief to *twelve hundred lashes,* completely disregarding His Majesty's direction of January, 1807. Ships, we know, were slow in those days, and there was no wireless, aeroplane or telephone, but, surely, the King of England could get his orders delivered in less than eighteen years !

"There are sentences of court martial," said Sir Charles Grey, in his place in the House of Commons, 14th March, 1834, "which, if inflicted would amount to loss of life; and I think when the punishment is to the extent which we sometimes hear of, it is *degrading rather to them who inflict it* than to the sufferer, and especially degrading to the noblest art which human talent can attain—I mean the art of healing—when the attendance of a medical man is rendered necessary, *not to assuage pain and relieve suffering,* but to ascertain the extreme limit of human endurance."

Henry Marshall, Deputy-Inspector-General of Army Hospitals, writes : —

"In 1811 or 1812, I recollect seeing thirty-two punished men at one time in a regimental hospital on a foreign station. The ratio of men admitted into hospital, in consequence of punishment, in Jamaica, during the year 1817, the first year of which we have any correct record, was one in five of the strength; but if we deduct the non-commissioned officers, who were not likely to incur the punishment of flogging, it would be nearly one in four privates. It may be observed that this may not be the full amount of corporal punishments, inasmuch as men were not admitted into hospital unless the infliction had been so severe as to unfit them for duty."

The same writer tells us : —

"It is a notorious fact that when flogging was at its height, it was counted no great disgrace, indeed it was sometimes made a boast of, and instances have occurred where to have suffered from the lash, was reckoned a qualification necessary for becoming a good comrade. A soldier who had been frequently punished, was ordered to strip to receive another flagellation. He refused at first to take off his clothes; but when coercive measures were resorted to, he submitted, and received his quantum of punishment, without complaining; and when taken down, he said to the Colonel, 'Colonel, honey ! if you will give me six drams of liquor, I will take six hundred lashes more'. This man prided himself exceedingly on the number of lashes he had received, and used to expose the marks on his back to his comrades."

And : "Major ———, while he commanded the African corps—a corps which has been always notorious for corporal punishment, was one Sunday reading the morning service of the Church to the men, who were formed into a square. The Major, who was from north of the Tweed, spoke and read the English language with the broad accent of the natives of one of the counties in the north of Scotland; upon reading the Creed, and pronouncing the words, 'Suffered under Pontius Pilate', in his own queer way, a wag in the ranks, well-known for his uncontrollable propensity to joking and fun, exclaimed 'Wha's Ponshews Peelate, I wonder?' The Major paused, and laying aside the Prayer Book, said, 'Ah, John, is that you at your jokes again? Just come out here, my man'. The soldier stepped forward—a drum-head court martial was held—the triangles rigged out, and another flogging having been completed, the Major resumed the Prayer Book, and finished the service of the day''.

By 1812, flogging had been for a considerable time almost the only punishment used in the Army, and having been frequently inflicted, it came at length to be

RUNNING THE GAUNTLET IN THE ARMY
c. 1780

[Face page 34

considered an indispensable and efficacious specific—a moral *panacea* eminently calculated to prevent insubordination and other military offences—a measure without which all other means of preserving discipline were unavailing.

The frequency and severity of corporal infliction in the Army eventually excited, as has been observed, the attention of the public, press, and a handful of members of Parliament. Measures of restriction were officially promulgated, and reports from General Officers called for, by which means it soon became known that any excess or heedlessness in the infliction of punishment would not pass unnoticed at the Horse Guards. A new system in the course of time had sprung up in the Army, and it became the general practice of Commanding Officers to check the offences of soldiers in a great degree, by the infliction of what were called minor punishments, viz. punishments inflicted upon their own authority, such as extra drills, heavy marching drills, additional parades, extra guards, confinements to barracks, gagging, wearing the jacket inside out, drinking salt-water, bread and water diet, stopping a man's ration of grog, or diluting it with an unusual portion of water, trotting round in a circle, standing fully equipped in heavy marching order with the face to the wall, parading at the guard-room fully equipped every hour during the day, the stocks, the log, the dry-room, and the black-hole. The last four modes of punishment require a little explanation.

The Stocks.—Military authorities were much divided in regard to the use of the stocks as a reforming and deterring punishment. Some officers recommended it, while others considered it too ignominious as a military punishment. Lord Hill thought the punishment of the log (and the stocks, was liable to the same objection) as too degrading. "I think," said his Lordship, "the log is a punishment more for a beast than a man, and I should think it was not desirable to restore

D

it." (*Evidence on Military Punishments*, Question 5,744.)

The Log.—This punishment consisted of a log, or a large round shot or shell, which was connected to a delinquent's leg by means of a chain. The delinquent was obliged to drag or carry the log about with him on all occasions, except when he mounted guard. *In one regiment, which was quartered in Richmond Barracks, Dublin, in 1821, from twenty to twenty-five men were frequently seen marching together round the barrack-square, and dragging logs behind them.*

The Dry-Room.—The dry-room, or penitentiary, was, originally, an East Indian punishment; and it obtained its name from the circumstance of the men being kept in a state of confinement, and deprived of their spirit rations—hence, the term dry-room. The delinquents were much at drill, and sometimes their diet was reduced to bread and water. From forty to fifty men belonging to a regiment were sometimes in the dry-room at one time. The ignominy of a punishment diminishes in proportion to the numbers who undergo the penalty together. To confine thirty or forty offenders in one apartment was a sure means of corrupting the moral atmosphere and rendering the bad worse.

The Black-Hole.—(A cell with scarcely any light.) The name of this kind of punishment is sufficiently characteristic of the place in which soldiers were frequently imprisoned.

The very informative Deputy-Inspector-General, tells us : —

"Until lately (1840) it was the practice in some regiments to confine a man to the black-hole for forty-eight hours, and after an interval of twenty-four hours to repeat the confinement for forty-eight hours, and so on."

"The black-hole," says an old soldier, "was no doubt invented by some gloomy and good-natured soul, who loved a sedentary life, for the punishment of the minor offences incident to a soldier's life and which when frequent, are in their opinion and wise judgment, subversive of military discipline and highly disgraceful to the profession. I will instance," says he, "some of these offences which call for incarceration in solitude; sneezing in the ranks—scratching your head—letting the butt of your firelock fall on your Captain's toes—singeing his whiskers by filling your pan too full—wiping your nose on a chilly morning—treading upon the Captain's heels—looking cross. These, with a hundred others equally shocking, happen daily, and all are considered as deserving of seven days' solitary confinement in the black-hole." (*The Military Bijou*, by Lieutenant Shipp.)

Now that the reader has become familiar with the sentences and punishments usual to the eighteenth and nineteenth centuries, we will define the procedure adopted for corporal punishment.

FLOGGING—PROCEDURE

Quoting Henry Marshall, the Deputy-Inspector-General of Army Hospitals, a man who was an authority on the subject : —

"The usual mode of inflicting punishment is on the back of the delinquent : but at one time, it was very common to flog also upon the breech. Sometimes the punishment was inflicted on the breech for the purpose of rendering it more painful, sometimes to render it more disgraceful than on the back, and occasionally with the view of saving the back, when the skin was inflamed or otherwise unsound, from repeated punishments. Sometimes a man was flogged on the calves of the legs perhaps in consequence of both the back and breech being unsound from former inflictions, and consequently very liable to tedious ulceration. In one regiment it was customary for a time to give twenty-five lashes alternately on the back and breech. The Commanding Officer of another corps used to order a man to receive twenty-five lashes on one shoulder, and then twenty-five on the other; a similar plan being adopted with the breech, twenty-five lashes being inflicted by a left-handed Drummer upon the left buttock, and twenty-five by a right-handed Drummer on the right side. This amount of punishment was frequently inflicted on a march, the delinquent being obliged to carry his knapsack after the punishment.''

Although laid down very precisely in Articles issued, the procedure of a drum-head court martial varied considerably from regiment to regiment and from time to time. But so that the reader may construct a fairly accurate mental picture typical of such an execution we include some descriptions from contemporary records and Articles : —

THE DRUM-HEAD COURT MARTIAL

This is used when immediate punishment is necessary and derives its name from the fact that the man's sentence was often written on the drum at the head of a marching column.

If corporal punishment was ordered the sufferer was tied by the wrists, ankles and often round the legs below the breech to a tree, ladder or three sergeants' halberts tied together so as to form a triangle. (See illustration, p. 66.)

Lashes were limited to a maximum of three hundred by the Army Order of 1812. Procedure should be as follows: The court decided on its punishment. Should the man be found guilty (see list of offences punishable corporally below), *he is marched in, stood to attention and addressed by the President of the Court thus:*

"You (name of man), *having been found guilty of* (name crime), *are ordered a corporal punishment of* (name number of lashes) *lashes across the bare*

back with a cat-o'-nine-tails." "Strip sir." (The prisoner then removes his shirt.) *The order is then given : "You will take your punishment."* (The prisoner approaches the ladder or triangle, and is tied as in second paragraph.) *The President then says (to the executioner) : "Do your duty". The man not giving the cat stands on one side and numbers and writes down each stroke as he calls it aloud. The President may stop the punishment any time he thinks fit and continue the remaining strokes at a later time.*

If the crime is an aggravated one, strokes with the cat may be given on the bare buttocks and the strokes in this case must not exceed one hundred. Exactly the same procedure as the above is followed except for the substitution of "bare buttocks". The man's trousers or shorts in this case are let down AFTER he is tied up. The strokes must be given with a space equal to three steps in slow time between each.

Crimes punishable by above : Abusive language, indecency, excessive drinking, being late and general slovenly marching.

*   *   *   *

The following defines procedure even more graphically : —

"Corporal Punishment is inflicted on the bare shoulders of the offender by the drummers of infantry, or trumpeters and shoeing-smiths of cavalry, each of whom in succession give twenty-five lashes until the punishment is completed, or interrupted by order of the Commanding Officer. The Drum-, or Trumpet-Major numbers each lash, allowing between each a pause equal to three paces in slow time. A Commanding Officer is not justified in prolonging the infliction beyond the usual time.

"The Commanding Officer is responsible that the punishment is inflicted according to the custom of the service. In General Order, No. 511, His Majesty declared, with reference to an irregularity which occurred in a regiment (where cats were steeped in brine, previous to the infliction of the punishment, though not with the knowledge of the Commanding Officer) : —

"That whatever may be the opinion, or sentence of a General Court Martial, His Majesty will continue to require that Officers be held responsible for what passes in regiments under their command. It matters not whether such irregularities proceed from design, inattention, or ignorance, on the part of the Commanding Officer. Whatever may be the cause, it is equally clear that the officer who may either authorise, or allow such acts, or during whose command such acts may take place, is in no way fit to be entrusted with the charge of a body of troops; and it is therefore the imperative duty of the General Commanding in Chief, whenever such a case is brought forward, to make a special report of it, for the serious consideration of His Majesty."

"By Article 102 of Rules and Articles of War, the following Criminal Offences are listed as being punishable with whipping, by order of General Court Martial : Larcency by clerks or servants; stealing, or severing with intent to steal ore, etc., from a mine; stealing, or destroying plants in a garden; stealing, or cutting trees; hunting, or stealing deer in enclosed places; stealing, or dredging for oysters; larcency by lodgers; embezzlement by clerks, or servants; setting fire to crops; damaging ships with intent, etc.; destroying sea banks, locks, and piles; threatening letter demanding money; or threatening to accuse a man of sodomy, or unnatural crime, or threatening to kill, or burn, etc."

Most of the above held alternative sentences such as transportation for a number of years : some alternated the whipping with fines, imprisonment, or both.

At this time (1841), the death sentence was passed for such crimes as : "Riotously *beginning* to demolish a house" (no case is listed as to what happened to any unfortunate who successfully completed the job !); "ravishing women, carnally abusing children, sodomy committed either with mankind or animals, stabbing with intent to murder, setting fire to ships with intent to destroy, burning ships with intent to murder, burglary attended with violence, exhibiting false signs, burning houses and people being therein, piracy with violence", etc.

"The infliction of the cat on the breech is more painful than on the back, probably in consequence of the greater sensibility of the extreme parts of the body."

"It is alleged that flogging on the breech occasionally caused an erection, sometimes to such a degree as to attract the attention of the men in the ranks, and to excite their suppressed laughter."

"When the soldier has received the punishment awarded to him, or when the Commanding Officer remits part of the sentence, he is released from the triangles, and his shirt being loosely thrown over his shoulders, he is marched off to hospital.

"Here his back is dressed by being covered with cloths wetted with a dilute solution of the sugar of lead. The dressings are kept in their place by means of a cloth, technically known by the name of a 'saddle', and sometimes by that of a 'wrestling jacket'." (Marshall.)

CORPORAL PUNISHMENT. (*Flogging*).—In awarding the sentence of corporal punishment, the court martial commonly stated, that the infliction should be "*on the bare back, with a cat-o'-nine-tails, in the usual manner*"; but the last four words were sometimes omitted, it was alleged, for the purpose of conveying to the officer ordering the execution of the sentence, a power to inflict the punishment on the back or breech at his discretion. The mode of inflicting corporal punishment is detailed on p. 37.

"Untoward circumstances may be occasioned by tying a man too tight as well as by allowing him more freedom than is necessary. For want of due attention to this circumstance, the hands, above the ligatures, from the stoppage of circulation, have turned black, and remained numb for several days, which partly arises from a man's hanging, as it were, by the hands. When the ligatures are too loose he is liable to move from side to side, by which means the *cats* are apt to fall on unsuitable parts of the body; if too low the instrument is applied to the ribs, and if too high the tails of the cat may twist round the neck, injure the face and endanger the eyes." Sergeant Teesdale (*A Letter to the People of England, 1835*) informs us : "that a remarkably fine young soldier, belonging to the ———— Regiment, who was undergoing corporal punishment on board a transport, having been insufficiently secured, disentangled himself from the ropes, jumped overboard and was drowned. Two of his comrades, who were good swimmers, leaped over the ship's side with a view to save him, but without success".

Our previous authority, Marshall, goes on : —

"A culprit having been secured, the requisite number of Drummers, who have been previously *told off* by the Drum-Major, to inflict the punishment, commence their operations, by each taking off his cap, coat, or jacket. The Commanding Officer then says, 'Go on', and, 'Drum-Major, see that the Drummers do their duty'. The Drum-Major gives the time to the Drummers, audibly calling, 'one', 'two', 'three', etc., in slow time.

"When the first Drummer has inflicted twenty-five lashes, the Drum-Major calls out, in a loud voice, '*Stop, twenty-five*', and then orders a second Drummer to supply the place of the first. When another twenty-five lashes have been inflicted, the Drum-Major again calls out '*Stop, fifty*' : and so on till the punishment is completed. It is the duty of the Adjutant, who stands near to the triangles, to record the number of lashes inflicted. Water is always at hand for the purpose of a delinquent's drinking, or to restore him from fainting by sprinkling a little on his face.

"The first stroke of the cat occasions an instantaneous discolouration of the skin from effused blood, the back appearing as if it was thickly sprinkled with strong coffee even before the second stroke is inflicted. Sometimes the blood flows copiously by the time the first fifty or one hundred lashes are inflicted; at other times little or no blood appears when two hundred lashes have been inflicted. During the infliction of the first hundred and fifty or two hundred lashes, a man commonly appears to suffer much, considerably more, indeed, than during the subsequent part of a punishment, however large it may be. The effused blood in the skin, or, perhaps, some disorganisation of the nerves of sensation, seems to occasion a blunting of its sensibility, and thereby lessening the acuteness of the pain arising from the application of the cat. Left-handed Drummers, whose cats are applied to a portion of sound skin and Drummers who have not been sufficiently drilled to flogging, spread the lashes unnecessarily, and excite an unusual degree of pain. Delinquents frequently call out to the Drummer to strike higher, then lower, and sometimes alternately. A story is told of a Drummer, who, while he was flogging a man, had been frequently found fault with by the floggee, and who, forgetting the usual etiquette of a military parade, said, in an audible voice, 'Flog high, or flog low, there is no pleasing you, Barney McKanna'."

An ex-Drum-boy, who had attained the rank of a commissioned officer, gave the result of his own manual experience in the following terms : —

"From the very first day I entered the service as Drum-boy, and for eight years after, I can venture to assert, that, at the lowest calculation, it was my disgusting duty to flog men *at least three times a week.* From

this painful task there was no possibility of shrinking,
without the certainty of a rattan over my own shoulders
by the Drum-Major, or of my being sent to the black-
hole.   When the infliction is ordered to commence,
each Drum-boy, in rotation, is ordered to strip, for the
purpose of administering twenty-five lashes (slowly
counted by the Drum-Major) with freedom and vigour.
After a poor fellow had received about one hundred
lashes, the blood would pour down his back in streams,
and fly about in all directions with every additional
blow of the cat, so that by the time he had received
three hundred, I have found my clothes all over blood
from the knees to the crown of the head.   Horrified at
my disgusting appearance, I have, immediately after
parade, run into the barrack-room, to escape from the
observations of the soldiers, and to rid my clothes and
person of my comrade's blood."

The Drum-Major was presumed to see that the ends
of the cords of the cats were not entangled during the
infliction, so as to produce a more serious blow than
intended, but that they were disentangled from time to
time; should the cords become heavy with coagulated
blood, they were sometimes washed with water.   Nine
of every ten of the Drummers were right-handed, and
consequently stood on the left of the delinquent, the
right shoulder suffering much more severely than the
left.   Left-handed Drummers appeared, as has already
been observed, to inflict more pain than right-handed
punishers, in consequence of the cat being applied to a
sound and sensible part of the skin of the back.   The
Drum-Major stood behind the inflicting Drummer with
a cane in his hand, and his eyes fixed on the sufferer's
back, ready to lay it hard and heavy on the shoulders or
thighs of the punisher, should he think he was laying on
lightly or *unfair*.   "I have seen a Drum-Major 'lay on'
a Drummer with merciless severity," writes one author.
It would appear, that the Drum-Major was formerly
admonished to do his duty in a similar way to that by

which he occasionally excites the Drummers, namely, by the infliction of the cane. "The Adjutant," says Dr. Hamilton, "charges the Drum-Major, and often enforces it *with a stroke of his rattan*, to make the Drummers *do their duty*; he, in return, strikes the punisher, who, if he is able, is compelled to add force to his next stroke on the delinquent." The practice of rattaning a Drum-Major upon punishment parades, did not fall into complete disuse for several years after the commencement of the nineteenth century. "I have been assured by an officer now living, and not an old man, that he has seen a Drum-Major chastised on parade, with a cane, by an Adjutant, for alleged leniency in the performance of his duty," remarks Henry Marshall.

In some cavalry regiments it was customary to count ten between each stroke of the cat; in many corps the cats were not washed, the blood being allowed to dry upon them, for the purpose of rendering the punishment more severe (Hamilton). A previous preparation of cats was by steeping them in brine, and washing them in salt and water during the punishment.

The instrument of punishment, namely, the cat-o'-nine-tails, seems to have varied. Dr. Hamilton describes the cats used, when he wrote, as consisting, generally, of six cords. When Governor Wall was tried for flogging Sergeant Armstrong to death, the Lord Chief Baron Macdonald carefully described what he called the legitimate instrument of punishment : "The cat-of-nine-tails," said he, "is an instrument of punishment composed of small cords—the cords are *nine* in number; and they are generally whipped at the end with threads that are turned up and twisted round with a bit of thread, in order to prevent their unfolding; the handle of this instrument is wood". No notice is here taken of knots being on the cords, but this is, probably, an omission.

We may here observe that Armstrong was tied to a gun-carriage, and flogged by Africans, each man inflicting twenty-five lashes in turn. The instrument, employed in this case, was a rope one inch in diameter, and he received eight hundred lashes. (Howell's *State Trials*, Vol. XXVIII, p. 57.)

An officer, who had risen from the humble station of a Drum-boy, and who has already been quoted, gives the following account of the cat-o'-nine-tails : —

"I am ignorant," says he, "what sort of cats were used when flogging was first introduced into the Army, but they are now, I believe, very different in different regiments, and, indeed, there is sometimes, a variety kept in the same corps. Those which I have seen, *and used*, were made of a thick strong kind of whip-cord, and on each lash, nine in number, and generally about two feet long, were tied *three* large knots, so that a poor wretch, who was doomed to receive one thousand lashes, had twenty-seven thousand knots cutting into his back, and men have declared to me, that the sensation experienced at each lash, was as though the talons of a hawk were tearing the flesh off their bones."

According to Captain Simmons, "the cat-of-nine-tails consists of a drum-stick, or handle of wood of equal length, having fixed to it nine ends of whip-cord about sixteen inches long, each knotted with three knots, one being near the end". (*Remarks on Courts Martial*, 1830, p. 276.) So far as we know, there was no pattern cat deposited in any of the public offices nor any specific instructions issued by authority for the construction of this instrument of punishment.

The *delinquents* usually paid 1s., or in some regiments 6d., for the use of the cats; and this charge was regularly entered in a soldier's monthly account, thus : —

"Drum-Major's charge, 6d."

Should a soldier complain of the charge, which he sometimes did, as is recorded, the Drum-Major offered to present him with the cat *or cats*, which had been employed in punishing him; and this proposal generally put an end to the business.

"In cases where there are a considerable number of men to be punished, or when time is very limited, two triangles are sometimes put up in one square, by which means two men undergo punishment at the same time. I have seen two triangles actively employed in the square of a regiment, and I have heard of three being in use at the same time. Occasionally, also, punishment takes place at night, by means of torch-light, or rather by the light of a lantern. All the men who are to be punished are usually brought into the square at one time, and consequently some of the prisoners have to endure the anguish of seeing their comrades undergo a similar punishment to that which is awaiting themselves. The agony of the prisoners may be imagined. Two men belonging to —— Regiment were brought out for punishment, one a young lad, the other comparatively an old soldier. The lad, who was tied up first, screamed dreadfully, by which means the old soldier was completely unmanned; and while the staff of the regiment were superintending the punishment, he insidiously extracted a razor from his pocket, with which he made an attempt to cut his throat. He was, however, secured before he effected his purpose, and he finally recovered.

"Some men evince great fortitude during punishment, and will endure seven or eight hundred lashes without complaining. I recollect attending at the punishment of seven men, each of whom received six hundred lashes without one of them saying a word. Where there are a number of men punished at one time, the fortitude of individuals is strongly exercised by way of rivalship; and those who behave best, or evince the greatest powers of endurance, become the heroes of the day : they enjoy a kind of triumph."

"Many implore for a remission of their punishment, and frequently exclaim, 'Oh, Colonel, forgive me !— Oh, Doctor, take me down, and I'll never come here

again ! Five-and-twenty are as good as five hundred';
and I must say that I usually entertained a similar
opinion with the delinquent."

"In general, offenders conduct themselves with as
much submission and propriety while they are undergoing punishment, as could be expected. Sometimes
their expressions are calculated to excite a smile.

" 'Oh, Colonel, take me down,' said a man of the
———— Regiment; 'take me down, I say, for God's sake !'
After being silent for a short time, he again addressed
the Colonel as follows : 'I see, Colonel, that you do not
intend to order me down. I always thought you were
a gentleman until now'. The Colonel was a kind man,
and took no notice of the implied stain upon his
character.

"Occasionally, a man will set the whole regiment
laughing, in some instances apparently from intention,
and in others from simplicity. One man, after
imploring the intercession of a long catalogue of the
saints in the Roman Catholic calendar, exclaimed,
'Oh, son of David, take me down'. A smile was
excited in some of the spectators by the *equivoque*, the
Commanding Officer's name being Davidson. The
Colonel observed that there was no resisting such an
appeal, and ordered the punishment to cease." On
another occasion : —

"During the time a private belonging to the Artillery
was receiving corporal punishment, he begged earnestly
to be forgiven, and frequently called upon Major D.,
the Commanding Officer, to take him down. The Major
replied, by saying that he would not remit one lash of
the sentence which the court martial had awarded. 'It
is with reluctance,' said the Major, 'that I bring a man
to a court martial; and even at this moment I feel as
much pain as you do.' 'Oh, then,' said the man,
'just come and take my place'; apparently implying
that it was inexpedient for both to be suffering punishment.

"Some men appear to amuse themselves by a kind of soliloquy while they are receiving punishment. 'I think,' said an old soldier, belonging to the —— Regiment, who was in this situation, 'that when I receive the present sentence, I shall have got about twelve thousand lashes, which are quite enough, and I do not intend to come here any more.' This man was soon after discharged."

The following story, from Dr. Bell's work on diseases among soldiers in the West Indies, 1838, is instructive in many respects :—

"A private soldier in the 5th Regiment, had been repeatedly sentenced by courts martial to be punished for theft; but the punishment of flogging had always been changed for that of confinement, as on the instant he was brought to the halberts he was attacked with convulsions; and the medical gentleman who attended, thinking it not proper that in these circumstances the punishment should be inflicted, the man was released."

He was again convicted of stealing, and again he was sentenced to be flogged. At this time Dr. Bell attended his punishment.

"These convulsive fits," says Dr. Bell, "were either feigned or real; but in either case it was deemed proper that the punishment should go on. If they were feigned, the pain of flogging would soon put an end to every exertion of artifice; and, if they were real, it appeared probable that severe pain, to which he had not been accustomed, and the operation of terror on his mind, at the time the fit was approaching, might prevent the attack, and, by breaking the habit, might prove a useful remedy. I never had seen him in any of these fits, but I was informed that he was frequently attacked by them when guilty of any irregularity, and consequently was sent to hospital instead of the guard-house. On the morning of his punishment I informed him, in presence of the Sergeant of the hospital, and that of another person, that the Commanding Officer was determined to inflict every lash, although death should be the consequence, and that I would on no account interfere in having him taken down. He was told, that if he *dared* to fall into fits, the Sergeant and my servant had orders to burn him to the bone with red-hot irons, which they kept ready heated for the purpose in the mess-kitchen, at the door of which he was punished. While the drummers were tying him to the halberts I placed myself opposite to him, and his eyes were steadily fixed on mine. His countenance was marked with the strongest symptoms of terror, which was not lessened by turning his head towards the door of the kitchen, where he saw a person prepared, as he thought, for the purpose of which he had been informed. He firmly believed that what had been threatened would be executed. The punishment went on—the pain it occasioned was almost forgot in his apprehension of that which he more dreaded. He received three hundred lashes; and while I remained in the regiment I never heard of his being attacked with any convulsive disorder, nor of his being tried by a court martial for his old crime."

Dr. Bell leaves the nature of the case still doubtful, and concluded with the following expression: "Whether the fits were real or feigned, impressing the mind with terror produced the effect that was desired".

Dr. Hamilton very graphically described the cruel consequences of *second* punishments.

"Let us suppose," says he, "that a man is taken down at the end of two hundred and fifty or three hundred lashes, and that his sentence was one thousand, all of which he must receive, whether at two, three, or more times, before he is released from confinement. Let us suppose he is conveyed either to the guard-house or hospital, is daily dressed until the wounds are healed, and a new cuticle formed, which may be in a month or five weeks. He is now become able to wear his clothes, yet perhaps scarcely able to suffer the weight and friction of his cross-belts, or the pressure of his haversack—the

Date.		Year.	N. of Company.	NAMES.		Quality.	For what Offence.
Day and Month.							
28th July		1820	14	William	Hart	Pte	Disobedience of orders
" " July, August			43	Richard	Edwards	..	Making away with part of his Necessaries
12th			42	John	Miller	Gun	Irregular behaviour in making use of threatening language to Serjeant on duty Lyning of the 1st inst. the Serjeant being in the execution of his Duty
26th			71	Michael	Walsh	Ptr	for Drunkenness and irregular Conduct
4th September			64	James	Refain	,	for Drunkenness and irregular behaviour
4th			43	Thomas	Hetchings	,	for being absent without leave and making away with part of their Necessaries
"			43	William	Bennett	,	
9th October			3	James	Orran	,	Absenting himself nights without leave & making away with part of his Necessaries
21st			11	John	Chew	,	for Irregular Conduct, also repeatedly absent without leave
21st			66	Mark	Budd	,	for Irregular Conduct
2d November			91	Michael	Walsh	,	for Irregular Conduct and being absent from General Muster without leave
18th			39	Thomas	Rogers	,	for absenting himself from the Quarters without leave and making away with part of his Necessaries

PAGES FROM A COURT MARTIAL BOOK

How Tried, by General or Regimental.	Sentence.	Punishment.	REMARKS.
Regimental	150 Lashes	Forgiven	*[illegible]*
	180 "	100 Lashes	And put under Stoppages
	200 "	125 "	and by weeks Solitary confinement on Bread & Water in the Common Gaol of this County
	100 Lashes	100 Lashes	
			Six weeks Solitary Confinement on bread and water in the Common Gaol of the County & to be put under Stoppages not exceeding one half of his Pay until the expiration of the Money taken & made good to *[illegible] McDermot (the remaining to Ed. Maye]*
	200 Lashes	150 Lashes	Put under Stoppages & Confined to barracks six weeks from the time of his quitting the Hosp.
	200 "	100 "	Put under Stoppages & Confined to barracks *[illegible]* months from the time of his quitting the Hosp.
			Six weeks Solitary Confinement in the Common Gaol of this County. and at the expiration of the said term of six weeks to be placed under Stoppages not exceeding the half of his Pay until his Necessaries be made good.
	200 Lashes	200 Lashes	
	" "	" "	
	300 "	200 "	Forgiven 100 Lashes by the Commanding Officer
	150 "	150 "	
	? "	" "	
	150 "	150 "	And put under Stoppages.

parts are as yet red and tender; notwithstanding, he is ordered a second time to the halberts, and at the end of two hundred or three hundred more is a second time taken down, cured as before, a third time brought there, and so on till the whole judgment be inflicted . . ."

" . . . the first few lashes tore open the newly cicatrised skin, so much that his back became instantly covered with blood, which flowed downwards under his clothes."

Dr. Hamilton gives another account of a case of second punishment, similar to the one mentioned above : —

"Hall," says he, "was sentenced to receive five hundred lashes for house-breaking; he got four hundred of them before he was taken down; and in the space of six weeks was judged able to sustain the remainder of his punishment, as his back was entirely skinned over. The first twenty-five lashes of the second punishment tore the young flesh more than the former four hundred, the blood pouring at the same time in streams. By the time he got seventy-five his back was ten times more cut by the 'cats' than with the former four hundred—so that it was thought prudent to remit the remaining twenty-five, and take him down. Hall declared that his first punishment was trifling to what he suffered by the second. Other examples might be added," says Dr. Hamilton, "but to multiply cases of this kind is disagreeable."

"Some men suffer much more than others from the same amount of punishment, more especially persons of a sanguine temperament, with red or fair hair, and a tall, slender frame of body."

"Edwards, in the end of 1781, was sentenced to receive fifty lashes. He had got drunk, and otherwise misbehaved. In the Army, this number is accounted next to nothing. So much, however, did this small punishment affect him, that, notwithstanding every degree of attention to his case, it was upwards of three months before he could bear his cross-belt, or even move

E

his arms to work. Perhaps fifty more would have placed his life in most imminent danger. He was of a thin, tall, genteel shape—his hair black, but soft, woolly, and thin on his head, with a skin remarkably white and smooth." (Hamilton, Vol. II, p. 40.)

"Henley, for desertion, received two hundred lashes only; ' acute inflammation followed, and the back sloughed. When the wounds were cleaned and the sloughed integuments removed, the back-bone and part of the shoulder bone were laid bare. I never had seen so much of the muscular parts destroyed in any case of punishment before . . . It was upwards of seven months before he was so far recovered as to do his duty." (Hamilton, Vol. II, p. 44.)

"In 1806, I recollect having two similar cases of sloughing from punishment to dress; they having occurred in the regiment to which I belonged. One man died, the whole of the muscles of the back having sloughed, and the other was never fit for duty, and required to be invalided." (Marshall.)

Hamilton mentions the case of a man who died at the halberts : —

"Lately, in England, not far from the metropolis," says the authority he quotes, "a soldier received four hundred lashes; he scorned to flinch for some time, till by a repetition of stripes he groaned and died. Fever and sloughing of the back are the consequences of flogging which are most to be dreaded."

Dr. Marshall remarks : —

"In such a punishment as flogging, accident will be sure to assist the intrinsic rigour of the system, oversight will conspire with design, and congenial circumstances will develop strict discipline into cruelty."

Bombardier Alexander incidentally mentions an interesting case in his *Memoirs* : —

"In 1803, at Chatham, a private of the 9th Regiment, having been found asleep on his post, was tried by a court martial, and sentenced to be flogged. The soldier was a fine-looking lad, and bore an excellent character in his regiment. The officers were much interested in his behalf, and it was said they endeavoured to prevail upon the General in command, to give his case a favourable consideration, but without success. All the troops were assembled to witness the punishment; *and during the infliction I saw the Drum-Major strike a drummer to the ground for not using his strength sufficiently.* The man's back became black as the darkest mahogany, and greatly swelled. He was taken down at the recommendation of the medical officer, after he had received two hundred and twenty-nine lashes, and sent to the hospital, where he died in eight days, his back having mortified. I have witnessed seven hundred lashes inflicted but I have never seen a man's back so black and swelled."

"One culprit," writes Dr. Hamilton, "had so great a discharge from his back, accompanied with a smell so great, that though a more than ordinary robust man, it made him extremely faint and uneasy; he complained more of this than of the pain he suffered, yet he was carefully dressed and washed twice a day, and for some time shirted once every day."

"Dale was punished for stealing, and smelled so offensively, though the greatest attention was paid to dressing and washing his back, as well as to changing his linen; and so great an effect did it produce on his health, that he fell into a fever, and narrowly escaped with his life. He was removed to a ward by himself, the smell being extremely offensive to the other patients. From the putrid smell of his sores, it was no easy task to dress him; and such was the precarious state of his health, that I durst trust it to no one but myself." (Hamilton, Vol. II, p. 60.)

"In cases where great ulceration and sloughing occurs, the cicatrix is long, and, in some cases, permanently so sensible and tender, as not to permit a man to wear his cross-belts, or at any rate to carry his knapsack. I have seen a soldier permanently disabled for duty by this means, and rendered unfit for the service. It is alleged, by persons who have witnessed much flogging, that the back becomes callous by frequent corporal punishment, a circumstance which is probably occasioned by the repeated effusion of lymph." (Marshall.)

"Although that few or none die, which," says Dr. Hamilton, "I believe to be the fact, immediately from punishments moderately inflicted, I know, from experience in the Service, that constitutions are impaired by them. We sometimes find the body melt away into a spectre of skin and bone, from the large suppurations that have followed; nor were they ever afterwards, as long as I knew them, able to bear the same hardships as before; and they must from thence also be more incident, but to other complaints to which fatigue or hardships of duty may expose them." (Hamilton, Vol. II, p. 56.)

"Sergeant Armstrong," says Dr. Marshall, "who was flogged to death by the orders of Governor Wall, passed blood constantly after his punishment, both by urine and stool; and the Surgeon stated also, that he had asthma from the extraordinary absorption of the blood."

And here is Simmons' description of a flogging in 1863. It is historic and we give it in its full text, for it is, so far as we are able to trace, the last description given in a semi-official book on how a sentence of corporal punishment should be carried out.

"The brigade, garrison, regiment, or detachment, being under arms, is formed in some retired spot, often in the ditch of an outwork of a fortified place or fort, to receive the prisoner, who is brought to the centre by an escort.

"The Commanding Officer, or the Brigade Major, the Town Major, or Adjutant, as the case may be, proceeds aloud to read the charge, sometimes the proceedings, but invariably the sentence of the court and the approval; the prisoner being uncovered, and advanced a pace or two in front of the escort.

"The culprit is then directed to strip to the waist, and under ordinary circumstances, is tied to a machine termed a triangle, which consists of three legs or poles, connected by a bolt at the top, and separated by about four feet at bottom; to two of its legs a bar is fixed, at a convenient distance, that the prisoner's chest may rest against it, his ankles being tied to the legs. Halberds were sometimes rigged out for the purpose, when has originated the common saying, 'bring a man to the halberds', as synonymous with bringing him to corporal punishment.

"At other times the prisoner is lashed to a gun-wheel, and receives on his bare shoulders twenty-five lashes, from the drummers of infantry, or the trumpeters or shoeing-smiths of cavalry, in succession, until the punishment is completed, or interrupted by order of the Commanding Officer. The Drum- or Trumpet-Major counts each lash, or rather directs it, the lash not being inflicted until it is numbered. Between each, a pause equal to three paces in slow time takes place, which is marked by the time taken to circle the cat round the head, or formerly, in some cases, by taps of the drum. A Commanding Officer is not justified in prolonging the infliction beyond the usual time; and charges have been grounded on the non-observance of such caution. No punishment is to be inflicted save in the presence of the surgeon or of the assistant surgeon in case of any other indispensable duty preventing the attendance of the surgeon. Should any symptoms arise which indicate the propriety of suspending the infliction, it is the duty of the medical officer to report to the senior officer on the parade, who directs accordingly.

"The cat-o'-nine-tails consists of a drum stick, or handle of wood of similar length, having fixed to it nine ends of common whip-cord; a larger description of cord, or the substitution of a rope, could not be justified; each end is about sixteen inches long, and knotted with three knots, one being near the end; the Drum-Major sees that the ends are not entangled during the infliction, so as to produce a more serious blow than was intended, but that they are disengaged from time to time, and, if necessary, washed in water. A previous preparation of cats, by steeping them in brine and washing them in salt water during the punishment, has been made the subject of a charge against a Commanding Officer; and although the officer referred to (Lieutenant-Colonel Bayly, of the 98th Regiment) was acquitted of all knowledge of, or participation in, the cruel and unprecedented practices of steeping the cats in brine, and washing them in salt water, during the infliction of the punishments, yet His Majesty, ever alive to the reputation of the Army, and desirous of tempering with mercy the unavoidable severity of military punishment, was pleased to command that *the admonition* to which he had been sentenced by the court, should be communicated to that officer, accompanied by the expression of His Majesty's regret and displeasure, that punishments deemed necessary in their nature to the maintenance of discipline, and legally authorised, should have been inflicted in any corps in so cruel and unprecedented a manner as the evidence on the face of the proceedings clearly establishes to have been the case in this instance, and that so unquestionable a proof should have been afforded of neglect of duty on the part of an officer in command of any regiment or detachment of His Majesty's troops, as is too clearly chargeable upon Lieutenant-Colonel Bayly, and as is justly so held by the court, when an occurrence so prejudiced to military discipline, and tending so manifestly to bring the Army into disrepute, could have been preconcerted without his knowledge, and afterwards take place, without his notice, in the depot under his immediate command."

Simmons points out that the use of left-hand and

right-hand Drummers used at an infliction was never
sanctioned legally, and that it is therefore not to take
place as it is not "according to the usual manner".
The Regulations of 1837 forbade the completion of an
award of a flogging if the culprit was unable to bear the
whole flogging at the first infliction.

The confirming authority had the power to commute
or mitigate corporal punishment to imprisonment.
Twenty years later, when prisoners were to undergo a
mitigated sentence of corporal punishment within the
prison, the commitment had to contain a special order
for such punishment with a certified extract of the sentence of the court. (*Rules and Regulations for Military
Prisons, War Office, 1851.*)

Corporal punishment in a military prison was always
administered according to the practice of the service.
After 1851, the infliction of such mitigated punishment,
in no case exceeding twenty-five lashes, had to be
attended by a visitor, the governor, and the medical
officer, whose instructions thereon, for preventing
injury to health, were to be obeyed. But warders, *and
prisoners*, were not required to be present, unless
deemed specially expedient. On the other hand,
Queen's Regulations at this date allowed fifty lashes to
be given to soldiers of the second class and, except on
actual service in the field, for particularised offences.

"The proper end of human punishment," says
Paley, "is not the satisfaction of justice, but the prevention of crimes. By the satisfaction of justice, I mean
the retribution of so much pain for so much guilt."

BOOK II

CHAPTER ONE

TYPICAL AND ECCENTRIC EXAMPLES OF FLOGGING IN THE ARMY

I

For two hundred and fifty years the most popular and habitual chastisement was by flogging.

From the mid-seventeenth century to the middle of the nineteenth century, flogging was the most prevalent form of punishment in both the Services. Indeed, it might be said without fear of serious contradiction that during those two hundred years, law and order was kept throughout the realm largely by fear of the gallows-tree, and in the armed forces by fear of the lash.

The mind, if unaccustomed to statistics, reels when faced with the figures documenting the thousands of stalwart young men who for offences serious—but, also, too, often trivial—suffered on their backs, buttocks, thighs and calves, millions of searing cuts with whips, lashes, rope's ends and rattans. Faced with the accumulated facts one is inclined to speculate, when thinking of England's greatness, upon how much we all owe to-day, not only to the pioneers, the explorers, the emigrants, the politicians, the Admirals and the Field-Marshals, but also to the anonymous soldiers and sailors —not only for their endurance, but also for their heroism and stoic obedience; it is a sobering thought to reflect that possibly as much blood from drum-head floggings has stained the barrack-squares and decks of ships as was ever spilt upon the battlefields of Europe and Empire . . .

In his *Recollections of a Highland Subaltern,* writing of 1857, Colonel Gordon-Alexander says, "As an illustration of the nonsense since talked in Parliament, at the time of the abolition of corporal punishment in the Army in 1881, I may here relate what occurred at a punishment parade at Portsmouth a short time before we embarked for China. A man of my Company had been tried by regimental court martial, and very properly sentenced to receive fifty lashes for assaulting a non-commissioned officer. He was a particularly brave, clean and smart soldier, but was of an insubordinate disposition, and when he took too much drink developed a murderously violent temper. He had been arrested, by the orders of the sergeant of the guard, when coming into the barrack gate, for being drunk; but before he could be overpowered he succeeded in crowning the sergeant with a large tub of slops, and was very violent. After receiving his fifty lashes, which were most effectively administered by the Drummers, he not uttering a sound, and whilst putting his shirt on, previous to being marched to the hospital as usual after a flogging, to be detained there under the doctor's care until his back was healed, he turned round to Colonel Leith Hay, who was in command of the parade, and defiantly shouted to him, so that all the men might hear : —

" 'Dae ye ca' THAT a flogging? Hoots ! I've got many a warse licking frae ma mither !'

"It was bravado, of course, and he had to be punished for it; but there was not the slightest feeling of 'degradation' which, according to the sentimentalists, led by the late Sir George Morgan, overwhelms not only the man who is flogged but all his comrades, as being liable to the same punishment".

The Colonel goes on to contend that the abolition of corporal punishment was a mistake which would have to be reconsidered at a later date. He claims that fifty lashes does not have any ill effects and that seldom more than twenty-five were ordered for a first offence. He says that as recently as 1897, a French private soldier was sentenced to death for the technical offence of throwing a button at his superior officer; and a month before that another private soldier in the French Army had been shot at Toulon for striking a corporal.

"As for flogging having deterred good men from entering the ranks; in the name of common sense," asks the Colonel, "how could it deter any except those who thought themselves capable of committing the serious military crimes for which alone they could be sentenced to be flogged?"* Surely such recruits were not desirable, contends General Sir John Alexander Ewart, K.C.B., of an offending soldier who had become hardened to "the shame of showing his back to the halberds". On one of his *weekly* trips to be flogged this much-scarred warrior addressed the officers thus : —

"Gentlemen, I am sorry to give you this frequent trouble on my account; but if you will be pleased to order me one hundred and fifty lashes every Monday morning I will regularly come and receive them. This will be better for all of us, it will save you the trouble of meeting so often, and me the confinement between whippings."

However, his suggestion, rational as it seemed, was ignored, and the man was again sentenced to be whipped. The Commanding Officer was determined to try an experiment, and, if it failed, he privately resolved to discharge the soldier from the regiment as worthless. Accordingly, when the man had—with great calmness and resignation—suffered his hands to be tied up, the Commanding Officer ordered the soldier's breeches to be let down and the lash to be applied to his naked buttocks. (This he thought himself entitled to do as the court martial had ordered a certain number of lashes without specifying on what part of the anatomy they should be given.)

The soldier, hearing the orders, begged and

---

* According to the law, that is, but many liberties were taken with the law in those days.

beseeched with the greatest emotion that he might be
punished as a man and not as an un-bearded youth, even
that he might be shot rather than whipped in such a
manner before all the regiment. However, the Commanding Officer was adamant and the soldier received
the cutting lashes as directed, being humiliated before
all his comrades-at-arms. The "Old Officer", who
recounts this episode, tells us that "the effect of this
degrading punishment was beyond all expectation and
worked a total reformation", upon the oft-offending
soldier, who rapidly became one of the best men in the
regiment and was shortly made a Sergeant as a reward
for his good behaviour in the months that followed.

II

Although it may be thought that soldiers were sentenced out-of-hand to very many strokes of the lash,
this was not always the case. Some of the court martial
findings were queried and some were argued in the
courts of justice. The case of Sergeant Samuel Grant
shows that care was shown as regards almost every sentence passed, and all which exceeded four or five
hundred lashes.

Grant's case was argued in the court of Common
Pleas in 1792, and has become known as Grant v. Sir
Charles Gould. This important case arose on a motion
for a prohibition to prevent the execution of a sentence
passed against the plaintiff Grant, by a general court
martial, held at Chatham Barracks. The court were of
the opinion that he, the said Samuel Grant, "was guilty
of having promoted, and having been instrumental
towards the enlisting of Francis Heritage and Francis
Stephenson into the service of the East India Company,
knowing them at the same time to belong to the said
regiment of foot guards; and, deeming this crime to be
of exactly the same nature with that which is set forth
in this charge, and to differ only in this, that it is rather

inferior, but in a very slight degree, in point of aggrava-
tion, they did adjudge him to be reduced from the ranks
and pay of a Sergeant, and to serve as a private soldier
in the ranks; and the said court did adjudge him to
receive one thousand lashes on the bare back with a
cat-o'-nine-tails by the Drummers of such corps or corp,
at such time or times, and in such proportion as His
Majesty should think fit to appoint".

In the summing-up, Lord Loughborough, delivering
the opinion of the court, observed that "in this case
which arises on a motion for a prohibition, the novelty
of the application was a sufficient reason why the court
should grant a rule to shew cause, and give it that consideration which the importance of it seemed justly to
demand. It has been very fully argued on both sides,
and with great ingenuity and ability. Everything has
been said, in support of the motion, by my brother
Marshall, that any talents, ability or ingenuity could
suggest. But, upon the result of the whole, the court
are clearly of opinion that the prohibition ought not to
issue". The summing-up continued with each argument
that had been used, being examined, rejected, or
retained by Lord Chief Justice Loughborough.

And when eventually Samuel Grant took off his
shirt and bared his back for punishment, he did so in
the knowledge that justice—British justice—had fully
argued his case and had, in its opinion, come to the
right conclusion.

Among many others, one of the longest and most
argued cases on record concerned a Sergeant, Joseph
Ginger, who, at the Cape of Good Hope, May 1802,
was tried by a regimental court martial for disobedience
of orders, being out of barracks after hours, and for
unsoldierlike behaviour to Lieutenant Dawson. He
was found guilty and sentenced to be reduced to the
ranks, to serve as a private soldier. He was also ordered
to receive five hundred lashes on his bare back. The
irregularity of this sentence was aggravated by Sergeant

Ginger having, for the *same* offence, previous to the said trial, been degraded by the Colonel of the regiment from the rank of Sergeant-Major to that of Sergeant. A general court martial was accordingly assembled to try the appellant, Sergeant Ginger, and the court passed the following resolution : "It having been clearly proved that the appellant was Sergeant-Major of the 34th Regiment, and regularly mustered as such, and tried by the regimental court martial from which he has appealed as a Sergeant. It therefore appears to the court, that the proceedings of the regimental court martial were invalid, in as much as the appellant was not by any sufficient authority reduced from the rank and pay of a Sergeant-Major to that of a Sergeant. The general court martial, therefore, rest their proceedings until this opinion be submitted to the Commander-in-Chief, and receive his orders as to any further investigation".

The result, after further investigation had taken place, was that the Commander-in-Chief confirmed the opinion of the general court martial, with respect to the irregularity of the regimental court martial, directed the proceedings to be cancelled accordingly, and ordered Sergeant Ginger to be released, and return to his duty as Sergeant-Major of His Majesty's 34th Regiment.

Sergeant-Major Ginger escaped, therefore, with nothing worse than a shock and a deal of worry. There is no record of his ever having again been in trouble.

III

But there is no doubt that while many were against flogging as a punishment almost equal numbers were in favour of the whip. Indeed many soldiers developed a pride in the punishment, boasting and bragging of their capacity to endure more lashes than the next man, keeping a score and tally of the cuts received, displaying their scarred backs at the least provocation.

Dr. Hamilton, in *The Duties of a Regimental Surgeon*, tells of a soldier who, in the middle of a flogging, turned round and said : —

"Well, I get my three thousand a year, which is more than many of you can say !"

In *Sketches of a Soldier's Life* is a record of a regiment known as the "Bloody Regiment" because of the number of floggings undergone by the soldiers in it. Every soldier made it a boast of manhood that he had received *thousands* of lashes on his back, on the calves of his legs, and on the fleshy backs of the thighs. He who could name and prove the greatest number of lashes was the barrack-room hero "and considered himself an honourable soldier".

Sergeant Teesdale, writing in 1835, gives us a very graphic picture of the frequency of flogging in the Army in the early 1800's and also the type of offences for which this severe punishment was at that time thought justified and suitable.

"During our stay in Bremen," writes the Sergeant, "we had a parade to attend each morning and evening. The officers commanding companies received orders from Major B——— to inspect their men closely and to turn out to the front such as they found dirty; a square was then formed for punishment and the men who had been found fault with were marched in, tried by a drumhead court martial, and flogged to a man without reference to character. Not a lash was remitted and I have known from ten and fifteen to twenty-five fellows flogged one after another at a parade under this frivilous pretext. This practice was continued at every parade until it was put a stop to . . ." (probably by Sir Edward Paget).

"At one of the above flogging parades," continues our informative Sergeant, "when we had been nearly two hours witnessing the horrible scene of bloodshed, and when the hands and feet of every soldier in the regiment were benumbed from cold, and from remaining such a length of time in one position, a soldier of excellent and unblemished character coughed in the ranks. He moved his head to one side to discharge the phlegm. Major B——— swore that he had been unsteady in the ranks, put him through a mock drumhead court martial, placed him before the halberts, stripped him, tied him up, and had him given fifty lashes; the soldier weeping bitterly the whole time and imploring mercy."

As to stoicism and perhaps the most restrained understatement ever delivered under acute physical and emotional stress, we have to thank Dr. G. Smith for recording this remark by a Private P——— of the 12th Dragoons : —

This young man was ordered one thousand lashes. These he bore without a word of complaint. As soon as he was taken down from the halberts he turned, still steady on his feet, his face ashen grey, his back and legs a scarlet pulp of bruised, cut and bloody flesh, and said to the officers : —

"Gentlemen, you have seen me take my punishment like a soldier. I hope you will give me my discharge, and if you won't I will vex you all." (He was as good as his word and seldom was out of the guard-house for the next two years. Finally he was discharged and was employed as a valet.)

It seems that on one occasion a Scottish soldier complained repeatedly under the lash and was finally moved to say : "O, Colonel, take me down, for ye ken I'm just a puir ·auld drunken bodie like yoursel' ". There was no resisting such humour under such conditions and the man was forthwith unpinioned.

There was serving in the 94th Scots Brigade in 1812, a Captain L———, and about him we are told : "Having neither the education nor the breeding of a gentleman, he felt jealous in the company of the officers. He generally passed his time in gossiping with his barber, or his cook, or, indeed, any of the men, with

an affectation of entering into their affairs. By this
eavesdropping, he became acquainted with little circumstances which another Commanding Officer would
have disdained to listen to, and of which he always made
a bad use. The full extent of his malevolence was not
known, however, until he got command of the regiment,
when he introduced flogging for every trivial offence.
In fact, the triangles were generally the accompaniment
of every evening parade. In addition to this, he
invented more disgraceful and torturing methods of
inflicting and receiving the punishment. The
Drummers, for instance, were always stripped to the
waist, as in an inquisition torture cellar. They were
told, on occasions, to take a step back, or a short run,
before bringing down the cat; this to give extra weight
to the stroke. As for the prisoner, he never knew how
he would be ordered to take his punishment until his
time of pain was about to start—for Captain L———
was no believer in convention, and the tying-up of a
man for whipping meant not the usual stripes on the
back, but where and how the Captain ordered. His
favourite seems to have been the tying-up in the normal
manner and then giving the order for the lowering of
the culprit's breeches. The breeches would be lowered
to just above the knee, where the prisoner had been
bound to the cross bar of the triangle. The Captain
would then give the order for the number of lashes to
be given alternately on the back and across the breech,
or on the breech alone. His other method was to have
the prisoner bound across a barrel, with, of course,
breeches pulled down. He also ordered defaulters to
wear a yellow and black cloth patch sewn on the sleeve
of the regimental jacket, and a hole cut in it for each
time they had been flogged".

At a later date, a regiment was near Wrexham and
two Sergeants took it into their heads to go and see
their sweethearts. When they came thoroughly to their
senses they were far on their journey, and thinking their

FLOGGING IN THE ARMY, TIED TO THE HALBERTS

[*Face page* 66

punishment, at a later date, would be the same, they continued into the town.

A party was sent after them and marched them back, prisoners, to their regiment. Reduction to the ranks was the punishment expected, but they were tried by a regimental general court martial. They were each sentenced to be reduced to the ranks, to receive five hundred lashes and to be branded on the side with the letter "D", and afterwards to be sent to a banished regiment. "One of them was an intelligent young man who had been well brought up; the other a fine lad scarcely twenty years of age. The first died of a broken heart, and did not live to go abroad."

Major-General Sir Charles J. Napier, in his book published in 1837, took strong objection to flogging on the grounds that it was torture, pure and simple, and substantiated his claim by pointing out that the infliction of any sentence ordered varied according to the expertness, temperament, skill, and strength of the Drummers executing it. Napier tells of men covered with blood from the poll of their necks to their buttocks after twenty lashes, whereas he has seen others receive three hundred vicious cuts without much blood running below the wounds made by the lash. "Some men," he says, "can take forty or fifty lashes without blood flowing, but the man's back appears covered with welts and black bruises."

"In these cases," says Napier, "I have noticed that the sufferer usually bears his torments with strong courage, but the danger to life seems greater—for I have often noticed that the surgeon soon stops the punishments . . ."

"I have heard men," says Napier, "whilst receiving the lash, set the whole regiment laughing; others blaspheme; others bear their agonies with a fortitude which elicits the admiration of the spectators."

Moreover, Napier thought that no stronger argument for the abolition of the cat could be quoted than

F

that of the indelible marks it left, "and are with a man throughout his career. Whatever the victim says, he cannot prove that he was guiltless, or, possibly, that he was flogged for a prank when he was young".

Sir Charles continues : —

"I have now to trace the progress of punishment during the same period, and I must again revert to the day when I was a subaltern. I then frequently saw six hundred lashes ordered by a regimental court martial; and generally every lash inflicted. I have heard of twelve hundred having been inflicted, but never witnessed such an execution.

"Even a general court martial cannot do this now (1837). Its sentence cannot exceed two hundred lashes. I, then, often saw the unhappy victim of such barbarous work, brought out from the hospital three and four times to receive the remainder of his punishment, too severe to be borne, without danger of death, at one flogging; and, sometimes, I have witnessed this prolonged torture applied for the avowed purpose of adding to its severity.

"On these occasions it was terrible to see the new tender skin of the scarcely healed back or buttocks, again laid bare to receive the lash. I declare, that accustomed as I was to such scenes I could not, on these occasions, bear to look at the first blows, the feeling of horror which ran through the ranks was evident, and all soldiers know the frequent faintings that take place amongst recruits when they first see a soldier flogged. The bringing a man from hospital to receive a second and third infliction, cannot now take place.

"There were Commanding Officers who distributed the lashes from the poll of the neck to the heel, thus, flaying the shoulders, posteriors, thighs, and calves of the legs, multiplying the torment enormously, but I believe it was done (and legally too) according to the wording of the sentence which ordered, or permitted, such cruelty. It could not be done now. Here we have proof upon proof how much punishment is now ameliorated, both in quantity and mode of infliction, and this has been produced by public feeling."

Napier goes on to claim that too much punishment makes the victims into heroes; that the Government itself at that very time was "crimping recruits", a term expressive of every sort of fraud and infamous conduct. He finishes his essay, "I have seen many hundreds of men flogged, and have always observed that when the skin is thoroughly cut up, or flayed off, the great pain subsides. Men are frequently convulsed and screaming, during the time they receive from one lash to three hundred lashes, and then they will bear the remainder, even to a thousand lashes, without a groan. They will often lie as if without life, and the Drummers appear to be flogging a lump of dead, raw flesh".

Napier's report on flogging is a balanced and dispassionate recital of conditions in the Army of his day, and all he suggests after recounting spine-chilling examples of flagellistic tortures by the hundred, is that since the discipline of the Army has improved so considerably during his lifetime, excessive flogging tends to defeat its own purpose : that two hundred lashes prove more effectual than a thousand because less revolting to the spectators, that excessive flogging tends to make a soldier unreliable and to endanger his health and, too often, to give the victim the sympathy of his comrades —a mutinous mass reaction to be avoided. where possible. But he does not suggest TOTAL abolition !

And as a contrasting example of how humanitarian reactions were received by authority, especially when they emanated from the ranks, let us quote an incident that occurred after the defeat at Roleia : —

The Commanding Officer, who mostly ruled by fear, established a permanent court, and this court had no other work except to try soldiers. Flogging became frequent and instantaneous, and as the halberts were going up on one occasion, the culprit ordered to strip, the Sergeant stepped forward and said, "May it please your Honour, the soldier is guilty, but he is a good and brave man, and I will answer with my own body for any future crimes if you will show him mercy on this occasion".

"You mutinous rascal!" exclaimed the Commanding Officer; with which remark, the Sergeant was there and then demoted, tried, sentenced, stripped of his shirt and tied to the halberts. "As the lash rose and fell, and the blood spurted, and the man writhed in agony, he ground his teeth and swore vengeance . . ."

The most memorable sentence we have come across is one given after the notorious Black Watch mutiny of the eighteenth century. The death sentence and transportation were the sentences mostly imposed, so from some points of view Private Campbell was a lucky man . . .

His was the only sentence of flogging passed at the courts martial that tried the mutineers. The sentence made it clear that Campbell must receive every lash of the sentence ordered and that there was to be no question of the surgeon ordering him down from the halberts as unfit for punishment halfway through the execution. To make sure that justice was done—and could be done—the soldier was medically examined before sentence to see what punishment he could stand without danger to life or permanent injury, and it was decided that being an especially well-proportioned youth of fine physique he would be able to endure one thousand lashes, to be delivered two hundred at a time. The sentence made no mention—purposely—of where he was to receive the lashes, thus leaving the buttock-area within punishment range. Private Campbell appealed against this sentence but his appeal was dismissed and the sentence of a thousand lashes was fully executed, the soldier being brought out five times in as many days for flogging before the assembled regiment; the last day suffering the ignominy of standing at the halberts with his breeches round his ankles, receiving two hundred lashes on his naked buttocks.

IV

In 1836, Captain W. Hough of the 48th Regiment Bengal N.I. published a book on the proposed Military Police and the Mutiny Acts and Articles of War. He gives interesting figures as to the number of men flogged in the Native Armies of Bengal (amongst others). He states that in the five years, 1829-1833, the average number of men in the regiment was 59,264 men. The average number of lashes was 8,062 inflicted, and that one man in 1,481 was flogged. He adds, "I think that seeing one man flogged in a year or two would not deter men of good character from entering the army . . . no, I fear it is the slow promotion which deters them". He argues with Sir Henry Fane, Commander-in-Chief, that a slow corporal punishment such as solitary confinement, may undermine the constitution more than a sharper and quicker correction.

The suggestion in 1836 was that natives in the Army in India should no longer be subjected to the cat and the rattan, but that only Christian natives were still to be so subjected . . . The natives were given the cat on their naked backs in the usual manner. The rattan, a cane of some five feet, was given them on the buttocks, a damp muslin cloth, similar to a very large handkerchief, being bound tightly to the thighs. Records show that the muslin was soon torn and the bamboo rattan had a habit of splitting and cutting beneath the skin.

At the time of the Peninsular War, the amount of lashes that could be given ranged from twenty-five to one thousand two hundred strokes, but the latter was seldom ordered; being a sentence which could kill, or maim for life. On the other hand, the man had a chance to live, whereas the crimes for which one thousand lashes could be given were often capital ones in many foreign armies at this period, including that of the

French. Professor Oman, in his book, *Wellington's Army*, can find only fifty cases of one thousand lashes. "It was at this time," says Oman, "that two other punishments were invented . . . those of penal servitude in New South Wales, or banishment to a regiment in a colony." Violence meant the addition of a flogging. "Everyday affairs" were the seven hundred, five hundred, three hundred lashes for theft, selling Army goods, plundering. etc.

V

To example that the Irish have little changed their trouble-starting and sense of humour, we quote the following two stories : —

The order against plundering had just been made, and Sir Arthur Wellesley, in a cross-country ride, saw a man of the Connaught Rangers with his great coat wrapped round his head, a beehive balanced on it, and a swarm of furious bees buzzing round. The Commander-in-Chief called out, "Hullo, Sir, where did you get that beehive?" Pat, unable to see anything, answered in a fine Irish brogue, "Just over the hill there, and be-Jasus, if ye don't hurry they'll all be gone".

Wellesley told this tale at a dinner in the week, thus, with a joke, giving away the soldier's delectable pastime : and the men of the 53rd caught stealing honey, not only received the nickname the "honeysuckers" but were flogged without mercy.

The second tale concerns the enterprising Private Chas. Reilly, sent to bring back pipes of wine for the troops, in a cart pulled by two fat, white bullocks. He returned, after some delay, with the cart pulled by two skinny black ones. His imaginative explanation : "Och ! plaise your Honour, and wasn't the white beasts lazy, and didn't I bate them until they were black?" did not convince the court, and poor Reilly's back received five hundred strokes of the cat.

We quote a personal account by a victim of flogging :

William Lawrence, of the 1/40th, a private in 1809, writes : —

"I absented myself without leave from guard for twenty-four hours, and when I returned I found I was in a fine state, for I was immediately put in the guard-room. It was my first offence, but that did not save me much, and I was sentenced to four hundred lashes.

"I found the regiment assembled all ready to witness my punishment; the place chosen for it was the square of a convent. As soon as I had been brought up by the guard, the sentence of the court martial was read over to me by the Colonel, and I was told to strip which I did firmly, and without using the help that was offered to me, as I had by that time got hardened to my lot. I was then lashed to the halberds, and the Colonel gave the order for the Drummers to commence, each one having to give me twenty-five lashes in turn. I bore it very well until I had received one hundred and seventy-five, when I got so enraged with the pain that I began pushing the halberds, which did not stand at all firm (being planted on stone), right across the square, amid the laughter of the regiment. The Colonel, thinking, I suppose, that I had had sufficient, ordered 'the sulky rascal down', in those very words. Perhaps a more true word could not have been spoken, for, indeed, I was sulky. I did not give vent to a sound the whole time, though the blood ran down my trousers from top to bottom. I was unbound, and a Corporal hove my shirt and jacket over my shoulders, and conveyed me to hospital, presenting as miserable a picture as I could. Perhaps it was as good a thing to me as could have happened, as it prevented me from committing greater crimes, which might have at last brought me to my ruin. But I think a good deal of that punishment might have been abandoned, with more credit to those who then ruled the Army."

Lawrence received one hundred and seventy-five of the four hundred lashes ordered and he did not receive the remaining two hundred and twenty-five. He was in hospital nineteen days. There were many men who took three or four hundred lashes as well as Lawrence took his one hundred and seventy-five, and took them without a sound.

In the year 1812, "corporal punishment was going on all the year round", writes a veteran officer of the 34th. "Men were flogged for the smallest offences, and for the graver ones often flogged to death—the lashes were often awarded by court martial. I have seen men suffer five hundred and even seven hundred before being 'taken down', the blood running down into their shoes, and their backs flayed like raw, red, chopped sausage meat. Some of them bore this awful punishment, without flinching, for two or three hundred lashes, chewing a musket ball or a bit of leather to stifle or prevent their cries of agony. After two hundred lashes they did not seem to feel the same torture. Sometimes the head dropped over to one side, but the lashing still went on, the surgeon in attendance examining the patient from time to time to see what more he could bear. I DID see, with horror, one prisoner receive seven hundred before being taken down. This was the sentence for a court martial, carried into effect before the whole brigade for an example."

CHAPTER TWO

FURTHER EXAMPLES, TYPÍCAL AND ECCENTRIC, OF FLOGGING IN THE BRITISH ARMY

I

Over all other military figures of his day (1812), Lord Wellington was way and above his contemporaries; his attitude, therefore, toward corporal punishment is especially noteworthy, reflecting as it does the Commanding Officer, tactician, autocratic and military man's attitude of the day.

Wellington was the disciplinarian *par excellence*, but had he been even a "jot" less strict and demanding than he was it is very unlikely that he and the armies under his command could have achieved the outstanding successes they did.

Wellington was the greatest champion of the whip. "They are the scum of the earth," he said of his soldiers, to the Royal Commission. "English soldiers are fellows who have enlisted for drink . . . they have ALL enlisted for drink !" And again : "I have no idea of any great effect being produced on British soldiers by anything but the fear of immediate corporal punishment". Under Wellington's immediate command floggings of a thousand and twelve hundred lashes were frequent, and the ever-present threat of a summary firing-squad kept within the ranks incalculable numbers of cruelly whipped potential deserters.

However, each in its own way, the following three episodes seem to give some substance to Wellington's sweeping assertion : —

The monotony of a voyage on a transport to Denmark in 1813, says Sergeant Morris, of the 73rd Regiment of Foot, was one morning broken by the swish of the lash. The officer had, by some means, obtained some fresh vegetables. What remained were put on deck with a sentry to guard them. But one soldier made off with a couple of carrots. He was detected and sentenced to receive one hundred and fifty lashes. On the morning of the punishment there was a stiff breeze and the motion of the ship prevented the Drummers from always hitting one spot, so that the lashes fell on the neck, shoulders and back, giving the impression that the man had been dreadfully punished, whereas he did not suffer so much as if he had always been struck on the same place. However, it was considered quite unnecessary, and rather too severe for the offence; had they stopped his grog for a few days, it would have been quite sufficient, being at that time a severe punishment indeed.

Later, celebrating after a victory, there were not men sober enough to bury the dead, and the third morning afterwards a punishment parade was called. The regiment was taken to a secluded spot some way from their village, and there, the court martial proceedings which had been held the day before were read out, and eight men were tied to the triangle in succession and received two hundred lashes each; one hundred each short of their sentence. The Colonel threatened that in future he would give the full sentence to any man found too drunk for duty.

And at Courtray, on the River Leys, the following interesting events took place in the 73rd. Genuine Hollands spirit was sold at this time in the chandlers' shops, and the price was only 8d. per quart. The consequence was that there was much drunkenness and crime, and flogging parades were frequent. These took place on the esplanade, a piece of ground overlooked by some private houses. The inhabitants were not amused by the spectacle of young men being tied-up and whipped, and a remonstrance was presented which resulted in other punishments being substituted, such as solitary confinement for serious crimes, and extra guards and punishment drills for the more common crimes. Sometimes the man would have to mount guard with a log of wood tied to his leg by a chain. Solitary confinement was especially dreaded by the men. Here is an example of one of the floggings referred to above. It is interesting because it shows the result of a lashing taken under the influence of spirits.

Two prisoners were brought out, the crime having been the same—drunkenness and insubordination, under very aggravated circumstances. The first prisoner was a young man belonging to the Grenadiers; his sentence was eight hundred lashes, out of which he received five hundred. The other prisoner was a Drummer, young, small and weakly; he had been punished before, and his back was scarcely healed from the last infliction. The first few strokes of the cat laid the back bare to the bone. Someone, from mistaken motives of kindness, had given the poor wretch a copious draught of Hollands, the effect of which was not apparent until he was tied up; then it maddened him. Instead of wincing from the stripes, he abused the Commanding Officer, and sang a variety of scraps of songs. The Major who commanded that morning, was exasperated at the apparent levity of the prisoner, and abused the Drum-Major for not making the Drummers do their duty more effectively; and for every stroke the Drummer gave the prisoner, he received one from the Drum-Major across his own shoulders! At length, the Major suspended the punishment, selected one of the Drummers, and formed a drum-head court martial. The Drum-Major swore the Drummer could punish more effectually if he chose. He was found guilty of refusing to do his duty and there and then was tied up and received one hundred and fifty lashes across his own back. The other punishment proceeded with, but the effects of the spirits having worn off, the prisoner fainted and was carried to the hospital.

Here are some especially interesting excerpts from records of military punishments executed, arranged chronologically : —

In 1802, John Hilton of the Royal Horse Guards was accused by Captain M——— of the Bedfordshire Regiment of Militia of having refused to go to quarters when ordered by the Captain to do so. It was proved that the Captain "had engaged in a disgraceful personal conflict with the soldier", and he was displaced from his captaincy. The Royal Horse Guard was ordered one thousand lashes, but in view of the Captain's behaviour, the punishment was mitigated to as many lashes as the soldier could bear at one time, which was two hundred.

On 1st May, 1807, three men of the 67th Regiment were confined by Lieutenant-Colonel Gordon, for having caused, excited, and joined in a mutiny in the 67th Regiment, for having grounded arms when being lawfully ordered to shoulder arms, and for obstinately remaining stationary when ordered to "right about". A similar charge in the French Army of this period would have unreservedly resulted in a death sentence, or a life sentence with ball and chain . . . The three men concerned were ordered : Wm. Shea, one thousand five hundred lashes; Jos. Bagnall, one thousand two hundred lashes; Wm. Kennedy, eight hundred lashes. Kennedy was pardoned because of good character.

On 13th July, 1809, Private Edwd. Salter, 7th (or Queen's) L.G., for having fixed to the barrack wall a paper accusing the Commanding Officer of scandalous and infamous behaviour, such conduct having the effect of exciting mutiny and discontent, and such charges being utterly untrue, was ordered to be tied up and to receive five hundred lashes on his back.

In Madras, on 26th November, 1810, Private Timothy Driskill, 38th Regiment, was found guilty of striking the Adjutant of the regiment, whilst he, Driskill, was prisoner. Whilst not approving of the sentiment that spared Driskill's life for such an offence, Adjutant-General T. H. S. Conway gave his consent to the private receiving one thousand three hundred lashes with a cat.

In 1811 and again in 1816, two Sergeants came too close to the swish of the cat. For attempting to cut Corporal John Andrew with a sword, and for refusing to put it away, Sergeant W. Rogers of the 80th Regiment was ordered one thousand lashes and to be reduced to the rank and pay of a private. In 1816, Sergeant Wm. Whiting of the 8th Regiment, N.I., was at Bombay ordered to receive one thousand lashes and to be reduced to the pay and rank of a private. He had struck his Sergeant-Major with a stick.

For threatening Lieutenant Picking on parade, in 1813, Private Edward Riley, 34th Regiment, was ordered one thousand lashes.

In June, 1815, William Smith, Matross, of the Horse Artillery, charged with making away with ammunition and discharging a pistol at the Sergeant of the 1st Troop of Horse Artillery, was "let off" his six hundred lashes on account of the excellent character given him by all officers who knew him. The Commander-in-Chief, Lieutenant-Colonel T. Hislop, took the opportunity to remark that he could not take into account for leniency the fact that the soldier had been "in liquor". On the contrary, the General considered that this added to the offence.

On 5th July, 1815, Private Kailawe, 84th Regiment, was ordered one thousand lashes for mutiny, having threatened to shoot Lieutenant-Colonel Campbell, his Commanding Officer, and having offered a double Fanam to any man who would bring him a ball cartridge with which to do it, and declaring if nobody would give him a ball cartridge, he would shoot the Colonel "at the first opportunity with a button of his jacket".

Private J. Keenon, 25th Light Dragoons, was on 20th October, 1815, found guilty of the following charge, and was ordered one thousand lashes : He deliberately loaded a pistol with a ball cartridge, and whilst a Sergeant forced the pistol from him, said, "It is a good job that you caught me, I intended it for you, I would have given you your supper off it". Keenon was then placed as a prisoner in the rear-guard and again loaded a pistol with a view to taking his own life. This was made an additional charge at the trial—*to which was added the charge of wasting ammunition delivered out to him* ! As well as the whipping Keenon was drummed out of His Majesty's Service.

On 30th April, 1816, Private Terence Dunn, 84th Regiment, was found guilty of using traitorous and disrespectful expressions against the King, and also, whilst being held prisoner, against certain officers. He was sentenced to receive one thousand lashes, which sentence was confirmed.

Two months before, on 28th February, 1816, Private Patrick Hand, Royal Scots, was ordered one thousand lashes for desertion and breaking from confinement. Around this period courts martial were busy passing sentences of death, transportation for seven or fourteen years, and to solitary confinement of from a month to two years.

On 9th October, 1817, Corporal John Hatfield Merry, for having refused a march, and for having accused ten privates of his regiment by which they were unjustly arrested, was ordered to be reduced to the ranks and then to be flogged to the tune of five hundred and fifty lashes.

12th March, 1817. 67th Regiment of Foot. Privates John Lockney, John Murphy, one thousand lashes each; Privates Matthews, Thompson and John Rogers, eight hundred lashes each, for desertion; the first two having also made away with ammunition. Matross Wm. Clarke (1816), Horse Artillery, one thousand lashes for taking with him a pair of leather pantaloons, the property of Matross Young, and selling them to Private

Butler of the 67th Regiment, for various desertions, and forcing a sentry.

On 22nd January, 1818, Private Roger M'Mahon, Royal Scots, was found guilty of quitting the ranks, advancing fifty paces, turning round, and, facing the Company, attempting to fire his loaded firelock at it until secured. He was ordered one thousand lashes, but the drumming from the Service was not confirmed by Lieutenant-Colonel Hislop.

An interesting case occurs on 24th November, 1818. Private Charles Donnelly of the 69th Regiment was accused on four charges; "of going to the quarters of Captain Hall and asking disrespectfully for leave, and of demanding leave for his friends; for refusing to go to his quarters and for saying that if his friend, McKenzie, was not given leave, he would go to another officer who would give the desired leave; for making use of threatening language to the Corporal who was ordered to take him to his quarters by Captain Hall; for saying that he would be damned if he would be confined by Captain Hall, by the Corporal, or by anyone else, upon which Captain Hall wrested from him a bayonet he had grabbed; for calling Captain Hall a damned liar and refusing to go to the guard-house when ordered, and then striking the Corporal of the Guard; for threatening the Corporal of the Guard when taking him to the guard-house, and for saying that he would shoot the first bugger of the regiment he met with, after he was released". Private Donnelly was found guilty, and he was sentenced to receive one thousand lashes *alternately on his bare back and breech.*

On the 22nd March, 1820, for having wantonly kicked the Commanding Officer at the head of the parade, and for using disrespectful words to him, and for having kicked and otherwise ill-treated the N.C.O. whilst under arrest, Private Thomas Casey, 85th Regiment, was ordered one thousand lashes, the court regretting it had not the power to order transportation.

They did not award death as they thought the prisoner might have an infirmity of mind caused by a previous injury. Another interesting sentence was that of Gunner Scarrott who received one thousand lashes and was "transported as a felon for fourteen years, thereafter to be at the disposal of His Majesty for service as a soldier for life wherever His Majesty should think fit".

On 23rd December, 1820, a private was sentenced to one thousand lashes for having stabbed Corporal Lennox with a bayonet. 59th Regiment.

In the same year, Matross James Dixon, of the Horse Artillery, was sentenced to one thousand five hundred lashes for desertion. The Commander-in-Chief pointed out on this occasion the inexpediency of awarding punishment which could never be inflicted, and ordered the soldier to receive five hundred lashes.

On 25th January, 1821, Private John Buxton was ordered one thousand lashes for desertion.

It is of interest to note that the following were flogged in India on the dates below : —

Private Thomas Crooke, 34th Regiment. 23rd January, 1817. Mutiny. One thousand lashes.

Private Francis Blincoe. 4th October, 1817. One thousand lashes.

Private Dennis Donnovan, 59th Regiment. 23rd December, 1820. Mutiny. One thousand lashes.

Matross Geo. Williams, H. C. Artillery. 14th March, 1816. Drunk and absent on sentry. Seven hundred lashes.

Private Anthony Kirby, 67th Regiment. 1814. Various mutinous acts. Five hundred lashes.

Matross Richard Moran, Bengal Horse Artillery. 26th January. Desertion. Nine hundred lashes.

Gunner Michael Fallen, Horse Brigade. 8th November, 1819. Eight hundred lashes and stoppages for desertion and making away with his necessaries.

Private Joseph Gladhall. 18th May, 1819. Five hundred lashes for deserting and for making away with his arms, etc.

Trumpeter T. Whittle. 30th October, 1816. Eight hundred lashes for desertion and for taking a helmet with him.

Private Edwd. Gillman. 17th April, 1819. Desertion. Five hundred lashes.

Private Henry White, Madras Regiment. 29th April, 1819. Desertion. Five hundred lashes.

Private Wm. Flaherty. 29th August, 1820. Eight hundred lashes for desertion.

Private James Light, alias Field. "For deserting and enlisting into another regiment. Eight hundred lashes *and to be marked on the left side two inches below the armpit with the letter "D", such letter not to be less than half an inch long, and to be marked on the skin, with some ink or powder, so as to be visible and conspicuous and not liable to be obliterated.*"

Private J. Gray, 34th Regiment. 20th October, 1815. Desertion. Eight hundred lashes.

Private Wm. Wellington, Madras European Regiment. 17th April, 1819. Desertion. Five hundred lashes.

Private Hugh McDonald, Madras European Regiment. 18th May, 1819. Desertion. Five hundred lashes. (*Half the punishment remitted as prisoner was advanced in years.*)

Privates Wm. Lewis and Michael Kelly. 1816. Eight hundred lashes each for desertion.

Privates W. Harold, D. Frew, H. Groves. 15th March, 1816. Seven hundred lashes each for desertion.

Private John Latimore. 12th April, 1819. Deserting *and giving himself up nine months later.* Seven hundred and fifty lashes.

Matross R. Thomas, Horse Artillery. *Attempting* to desert. Eight hundred lashes.

G

II.

The early nineteenth century, as we have shown, was very whip-conscious, and from voluminous records of blood-letting that must have far exceeded action-wounds, we have chosen the following : —

On 14th May, 1819, Private Wm. Cook, of the 90th Regiment, claimed Private Edward West (alias James Merrett), of the 9th Lancers, for a deserter from the 20th L.D. They were found guilty after statements by them had been totally disproved, and the story had been proven as a plan got up between them to get the reward offered by the Army for recovering deserters. H.R.H. The Commander-in-Chief ordered the sentences and facts to be read at the head of every regiment. At which times the two men were rending the air with their cries as the first of five hundred lashes each were descending on their bare backs.

Gunner Francis Thomas, Regiment of Artillery. 10th April, 1819. Repeatedly absenting himself from his corps. Five hundred lashes.

Matross Dennis Burke. Absence without leave, but desertion not proven. 1813. Four hundred lashes. Punishment remitted.

For leaving their posts without being regularly relieved, Private Daniel Haley, 47th Regiment, was ordered one thousand lashes, in 1817; Private James Kirwan received one thousand lashes a year later for the same offence (67th Foot); and Matross J. Murphy, Horse Artillery, in 1816, was given eight hundred lashes for the same offence.

Private Michael Casy, 89th Regiment. 31st March, 1816, was ordered one thousand lashes for wounding himself intentionally in the left hand, and with the theft of one musket ball. After leaving hospital he was to be drummed from the Service.

Private Jeremiah Lennon, Royal Scots, 28th

February, 1816, for the same offence, also received a sentence of one thousand lashes.

Private John Dunnon, 65th Foot, 31st January, 1816, repeatedly refused to obey the orders of Lieutenant R. Sutherland. He then followed the Lieutenant into his tent and there struck him violently in the face. Dunnon was ordered one thousand lashes.

Private Michael Maher, 67th Regiment, fired a loaded musket at Colour-Sergeant Black. On 28th September, 1820, he was given one thousand lashes.

Private Pat. Gilling, 67th Regiment, having absented himself without leave, together with a stolen brass trumpet, and two brass tumboas and a brass dish, and for having in his possession a white jacket, a white cap and three white shirts, and knowing them to have been stolen, at last found himself tied up with a bared back, about to receive the first of one thousand lashes with the cat.

Private Patrick Moone, 89th Regiment, at Trichinopoly, 20th November, 1818, violently assaulted a Sepoy in another regiment, and then stabbed him several times. This being "contrary to good order and discipline", Private Moone was ordered nine hundred lashes on his bare back.

Private Bradley, 59th Regiment, on 15th February, 1816, violently threw down his possessions, refused to obey orders, and threatened to strike an officer in the execution of his duty, and also broke his musket. For all of which temperamental outburst, Private Bradley found himself worse off with a sentence of eight hundred lashes.

Private Gilbert Kane, of the Buffs, 30th April, 1813, cut off one of his fingers, near Dublin. He received a sentence of seven hundred lashes, but did not get himself out of the Army—his original intention !

Private James Banco, Galway Regiment, in September, 1814, knocked down and violently assaulted Mrs. Ann Mills on the highway near Dover. Her cries for

help brought her husband, who was also attacked by
Banco. Private Banco received six hundred lashes.
(*What would the "cosh-boys" of our days say to such a
sentence?*)

Private Patrick Murphy, 89th Regiment. 6th
January, 1819. Nine hundred lashes for taking a firelock and firing it at four other privates.

Sentences had not lightened at the end of the first
quarter of the nineteenth century, and while Victoria
was still a child man's severity unto man was as inhuman
as it had ever been; though now better cloaked in the
paraphernalia accompanying Justice, sheer brutality of
sadistic expression was still the prerogative of military
authority a little over one hundred years ago.

In a book published for official use in 1825, the
following examples are quoted *as a guide* at General
Regimental Courts Martial :—

Shooting to death an N.C.O. in the execution of his
duty. Sentence : DEATH.

Stabbing an N.C.O., etc. Sentence : Death or two
years Solitary plus one thousand lashes.

Presenting and snapping a loaded pistol. Sentence :
Death, or twelve, or six months Solitary.

Striking his superior officer with his fist. Sentence :
Death, or one thousand lashes.

Charging at his superior officer with his bayonet.
Sentence : One thousand lashes.

Attacking a guard, etc., with drawn sword. Sentence : Twelve months' Solitary.

Attempting to draw his sword on his Commanding
Officer. Sentence : Cashiered.

Drawing and refusing to put up his sword. Sentence : One thousand lashes.

Attempting to strike, etc. Sentence : Eight hundred lashes.

Having used violence, etc. Sentence : Two years'
solitary confinement.

Threatening to shoot, etc. Sentence: Seven hundred lashes.

Refusing to obey orders on parade. Sentence: One thousand five hundred, one thousand two hundred, eight hundred lashes.

Refusing to cross at a ferry. Sentence: Three hundred lashes.

In this history, we are mainly concerned with corporal punishment, and we give, in the following pages, only those cases which deal with the corporal punishment sentences quoted above, to which have been added one or two others taken from the same source; together with any remarks made by official circles and considered appropriate.

III

SUNDRY CASES OF FLOGGING IN THE BRITISH ARMY IN INDIA, 1810-1825

CASE 1. At a court martial in Berhampore, on the 7th December, 1821, Private M. O'Brien, H.M.'s 17th Regiment, was arraigned upon this charge:—

"M. O'Brien, private of H.M.'s 17th Foot, charged with having at Berhampore on the night of the 13th June last, used the following mutinous expressions to Captain Halfhide, the captain of his company, in the execution of his office—'I know what I have done, I have killed two men—and had I completed my threats, and taken away your life also, I would have glorified in it, and died happy', and having further said, 'Captain Halfhide, I can never forgive you as long as I have life, I will never forgive you', or words to the above effect—he, M. O'Brien, having at the same time been seized, accused of having just stabbed with a bayonet, Sergeant Aylward and Private Grattage of his own corps."

Upon which charge the court came to the following decision. Finding: Guilty. Sentence: To receive nine hundred lashes on his bare back, and in the usual manner. Approved and confirmed. (Signed) Hastings.

CASE 2. G.O.C. Madras. 25th February, 1811. Crime. T. Crooke, private soldier, H.M.'s 34th Regiment, was arraigned on the following charges : —

"For mutiny, in having, when under arms, on the evening of the 9th November, 1810, rushed out of the ranks, and with his arms in his hands, and his bayonet fixed, assaulted and stabbed Sergeant J. Hethershaw, of the said regiment, he, the said Sergeant, being then in the execution of his office."

Finding : Guilty. Sentence : To receive one thousand lashes on his bare back with a cat-o'-nine-tails.

At a later date, the court assembled to order; a letter was read from the Adjutant-General of the Army to the President of the Court, informing him that H.E. the Commander-in-Chief had directed a revision of their sentence : —

"Sir, I am directed by H.E. the Com.-in-Chief to inform you that he has received with the greatest surprise and concern, the opinion and sentence of the gen.-mar. of which you are the president, assembled for the trial of private soldier T. Crooke, of H.M.'s 34th Regt., which his duty to the Service will not permit him to approve, and which he cannot confirm without directing the court to revise their sentence, and warning them of the dangerous consequences that must result to the Army from such mistaken lenity. It has never occurred to the Com.-in-Chief to be acquainted with so unprovoked and outrageous an act of mutiny, or one which calls so imperiously for capital punishment as the present. The prisoner immediately on duty under the Sergeant's command, rushed from the ranks and stabs him with a bayonet, without any further provocation than his having ordered him into confinement for repeated irregularity. If such a proceeding is suffered to pass without the severest punishment, the discipline of the

Army must receive a blow which may, before long, recoil on the members themselves; H.E. the Com.-in-Chief, therefore, warns the court, if they regard the Service, and as they value their honour, not to let a mistaken pride prevent their altering the sentence, if, on further reflection, they are convinced of the aggravated guilt of the prisoner and the necessity of an example. The only reason which gives the least colour to so lenient a sentence (for drunkenness can never be admitted as an excuse), must be found in the character given to the prisoner : but the Com.-in-Chief reminds the court, that it cannot alter the nature of the sentence, which should follow the commission of it; it can alone have weight with the authority vested by mil. law with the power to remit the sentence, a gen. ct. mar. is bound to give, according to the evidence and nature of the crime. The recommendation of a gen. ct. mar. will always be attentively considered by that authority, and when duty will must always joyfully be acceded to.

(signed) T. H. S. Conway, Adj.-Gen."

"Revised Sentence : The court having reconsidered the evidence brought before them, adhere to their former opinion.

(signed) S. Auchmuty, Lieut.-Gen."

So Private Crooke received his thousand lashes, with the cat-o'-nine-tails.

CASE 3. "G.O.C.C. 22nd November, 1815. D. Rooney (another Irishman), private soldier, in the 1st Battn. H.M.'s 59th Regt. confined by Sergeant Berwick, of the same regt., for an Act of (the most daring and outrageous) mutiny, in having on the morning parade of his com. at Ft. Wm., on Tuesday, the 17th October, 1815, threatened the life of Serj. T. Berwick of the same com. whilst he, the serj., was in the execution of his duty, and attempting immediately to put the same threat into execution, by charging the serj., aforesaid, with a musket and fixed bayonet, with the evident intention of putting him to death, as appeared by his own threatening declaration afterwards to the men who took him to the guard-house.''

Finding: Guilty, except of the words in brackets. Sentence: To receive one thousand lashes.

Remarks by the Commander-in-Chief: ''The conduct of the prisoner has been so atrocious, and the crime . . . so henious that the Com.-in-Chief (though with infinite reluctance and regret) feels it to be his bounden duty . . . that the sentence be carried into execution. An outrage of such magnitude . . . this unfortunate and melancholy instance . . . Col. East will be pleased to order the sentence to be carried into execution, in the presence of the 1st Btn. 8th Regt.''.

CASE 4. C.O.C.C. Bombay. 26th December, 1816. Crime: Sergeant-Major Wm. Whiting, of the 1st Battalion 8th Regiment, N.I., on the following charge (brought by the Commanding Officer):—

''For mutinous conduct, on the evening of the 12th inst., in striking me (his Commanding Officer) with a stick, when directing him to be taken to the quarter guard, for irregular behaviour.''

Finding: Guilty. Sentence: To be reduced to the ranks, and to receive one thousand lashes.

Approved and confirmed:

(signed) M. Nightingall, Lieutenant-General.

Remarks by the Commander-in-Chief: ''The conduct of the prisoner has been so atrocious, and the crime . . . so henious that the Com.-in-Chief (though with infinite reluctance and regret) feels it to be his bounden duty . . . that the sentence be carried into execution. An outrage of such magnitude . . . this unfortunate and melancholy instance . . . Col. East will be pleased to order the sentence to be carried into execution, in the presence of the 1st Bat. 6th Regt. . . .''

It would seem from the last two cases, though thirteen months apart, that the Commander-in-Chief had so often to confirm ''with reluctance and regret'' the findings of courts martial under his jurisdiction that

FLOGGING IN THE ARMY IN INDIA

[*Face page* 90]

in such "unfortunate" and "melancholy" instances only an exact repetition of his sentiments would be suitable when addressed to the 1st Battalion.

CASE 5. At a general court martial, at Berhampore, on 17th December, 1821, Private J. Bailey, H.M.'s 17th Regiment, was arraigned upon the undermentioned charges : —

First. "For highly disrespectful and mutinous conduct and language to me on the 14th November, 1821, in saying 'that he did not care a damn for the gen. ct. mar. by which he was to be tried, more than he cared for me or my command over him, and that I might go and be damn'd'."

Second. "For mutinous conduct in attempting to strike Sejt. W. Barker of the same comp., while in the execution of his duty on the 14th November, 1821, when escorting or going to escort the prisoner J. Bailey, from the cantonment to the guard-house."

Finding : On first charge, guilty; second charge, guilty; inasmuch as having thrown a stone or brick at Sergeant Barker while escorting the prisoner to the guard-house. Sentence : To receive a punishment of eight hundred lashes on the bare back, and in the usual manner.

Approved and confirmed : (signed) Hastings.

It will be noted that in the above sentence, the words, *"on the bare back, and in the usual manner"*, are additional to other examples given in these cases. This is because as late as 1821, Commanding Officers were giving the lash from time to time in any. manner they thought most fitting . . . frequently on the bare posteriors, often a stroke across the back and the next stroke across the buttocks. Several orders were made that this carrying out of a sentence was not to take place, and that the bare back (from the shoulders to just above the waist) was the official place to whip. The words "in the usual manner" referred to the method of tying-up, which was to be by cord round the wrists, the wrists

then drawn up above the head, the ankles tied to the
ladder, halberds (or whatever was in use as a block),
with the feet about a foot or a foot and a half apart; in
addition, a cord was passed round each leg above the
knee and secured to the block, both to stop the writhings
of the prisoner and to make the Drummer's aim more
precise.

CASE 6. In 1822, Buldayo Sing, for the crime of
deserting his post whilst on sentry, and of having taken
a box containing jewels, silver and gold worth three
hundred and fifty rupees, was found guilty. He was
ordered "to receive nine hundred lashes with a cat-o'-
nine-tails on his naked back in the usual manner. After
receiving the foregoing punishment, to be turned out of
the company with disgrace, with his coat turned, and a
halter round his neck, after which he was to be stripped
of his uniform, and turned from the barracks".

Many are the sentences of transportation to New
South Wales for periods of seven years, and for life.
The Commander-in-Chief, in a circular to the troops
about this period, reminds them that a sentence of
transportation to New South Wales entails working in
irons by day. When one considered these men, working
in the heat of the New South Wales summer, almost
stripped, building roads, encampments, and working in
the fields, under the constant eye of the overseer and the
even more constant bite of the whip across their back
and legs, one can well understand what has made the
Australians, descended from these men, the tough
fighting men we know to-day. Amongst those transported from India to New South Wales in 1817, were
Private T. Graley, for maiming himself with a knife to
avoid military service and for deserting, and Private J.
Forbes, also for deserting.

At Nagpore, in 1823, Private G. Renwick was found
guilty of breaking open the box of the Pay-Sergeant,
and stealing ninety-two rupees. For this he was sentenced to receive six hundred and twenty lashes on his

bare back. This is an extraordinary number, and might conceivably have been arrived at by the system of courts martial in those days when the average number of strokes of all five members was taken as the number of lashes to be inflicted. Mathematicians will, doubtless, be able to work out how six hundred and twenty is arrived at.

In 1821, one Benick, Sirdar-bearer to Major B——— of the Horse Artillery Brigade, threw some water over the Major, slapped his face, and used what is described as "highly improper language". The Major's face might have been red after the slaps, but so was Benick's back after five hundred lashes !

Private J. Dunnon, of H.M.'s 65th Regiment, was arraigned for coming to the tent door of Lieutenant R. S. ——— and, without any reason, following him into the tent although ordered to go back to his own lines, and violently striking him in the face, the whole of such conduct being utterly subversive to military discipline. The sentence was that Dunnon should receive one thousand lashes on his bare back, with a cat-o'-nine-tails, at such time and place as the Commanding Officer of the field force should be pleased to direct.

Private M. Maher, of H.M.'s 67th Regiment, accused of disorderly and insubordinate conduct, deliberately firing a loaded musket at a Colour-Sergeant, and for saying to Sergeant-Major J., "I am sorry I was not placed sentry at the back of your hut, for I would have shot you and I will do it yet"—or words to that effect. However, the shooting had to wait, for Private Maher found himself a few days later lying on his front in hospital, whilst surgeons dressed his back, which had received five hundred and fifty lashes with a cat, of a one thousand lash sentence.

Private P. Gilling also found himself in trouble. He was accused, in 1820, at a general court martial, of having in his possession three white shirts, one white cap cover, one white jacket, and with being absent from his quarters on the night of 9th July, 1820. Private Pat Gilling was sentenced to one thousand lashes.

IV

As a contrast to the severity usual in the early nineteenth century, we are pleased to quote this recorded exception : —

On 25th September, 1812, T. Sloan, J. Allisen, R. Scott, and A. Wallace, of the Dumfriesshire militia, and J. Pugh and D. Evans of the Montgomery militia, and T. Mitchell of the Westmorland militia, together with S. Newton of the Nottingham militia and W. Graham of the Northumberland militia, were charged with mutinous conduct by refusing to go to the Island of Sheppey, or to cross the passage at the King's Ferry, being an express violation of their duty as soldiers and contrary to the Articles of War. They were found guilty and each sentenced to receive three hundred lashes.

The court, taking into consideration that they afterwards agreed to go to the Island, and in view of the fact that they thought the Island of Sheppey was one of His Majesty's islands beyond the seas, forgave them their punishment. The militia were not compelled to serve out of the kingdom.

An interesting case was tried in 1814, when a private was charged with : —

First. "Highly unsoldierlike and outrageous conduct, about the hours of ten and eleven o'clock on 14th September, on the King's Highway, in Kent, by violently assaulting and repeatedly knocking down Mrs. A. M. ———, wife of W. M. ———; attempting, at the same time, by his brutal and violent conduct, to force the said Mrs. A. M. ——— into a compliance with his wishes to be carnally connected with her, and further by bruising and wounding the said Mrs. A. M. ——— with the socket of his bayonet in various endeavours to perpetuate his horrid and unlawful intentions; such conduct being injurious to the peace of H.M.'s subjects, subversive of good order and military discipline, and a breach of the Arts. of War."

Second. "For highly outrageous and unsoldierlike conduct, in repeatedly striking and knocking down W. M., husband of Mrs. A. M., . . . and endeavouring thereby to stop W. M. from the rescue of his wife, from the brutal treatment offered to her by him."

Third. "For violently assaulting P. P., who came to the rescue, etc."

Fourth. "For being absent without leave from his post."

The sentence was six hundred lashes, every one of which was taken in full consciousness upon the bare back by the rapacious private. This case is conspicuous in its similarity to crimes reported weekly in the "sensational" Press of our day; and also conspicuous in the *difference* between sentences of 1814 and now.

V

The Articles of War at the beginning of the nineteenth century, were both very precise and very elastic. By changing a word, or by adding, or leaving out a specific charge, the Colonel was able to direct, by remote control, whether the man, if found guilty, was to be lashed, lashed and imprisoned, transported with or without the letter "D" tattooed into his left side, etc.

The table below will give the reader an idea : —

1. Deserting and going over to, and entering into the service of the enemy : DEATH.

2. Deserting in front of the enemy with his horse, arms, etc. : DEATH.

3. Deserting with his arms, etc., and joining a rebel chieftain : DEATH.

4. Deserting during an action : Nine hundred lashes and dismissed the Service.

5. Deserting when on service : DEATH.

6. Deserting when sentries, and carrying off money placed under their charge : DEATH, or nine hundred lashes and drummed out of the regiment.

7. Deserting from an escort in charge of a state prisoner : DEATH.

8. Deserting when on guard : One thousand five hundred lashes.

9. Deserting when under orders for service : One thousand lashes.

10. Deserting when having been pardoned a few days earlier for the same offence : DEATH.

11. Deserting and again breaking from confinement : Transported for seven years.

12. Combination (and oath of secrecy) to desert, and deserting : DEATH, or one thousand five hundred lashes.

13. Deserting, having before deserted : Transported as a felon for life, or/and nine hundred lashes.

14. Deserting, having before been absent without leave : Eight hundred lashes.

15. Deserting, and maiming himself : Transported for life.

16. Deserting and making away with regiment coats, etc. : Nine hundred and fifty lashes and stoppages.

17. Deserting and trying to get back to England : Six months' Solitary.

18. Deserting and proceeding to another Presidency : Eight hundred lashes.

19. Deserting and not returning until brought back a prisoner : Dismissed the Service; or transported for seven years, or seven hundred and fifty to nine hundred lashes.

20. Deserting and enlisting in another regiment : Eight hundred lashes and mark "D".

21. Deserting and giving himself up : Seven hundred and fifty lashes.

22. Quitting his corps with intention to desert : Eight hundred lashes.

23. Quitting his post when sentry, with intention to desert : Five months' Solitary.

24. Falsely claiming a soldier as a deserter from another regiment : Five hundred lashes. (Rewards were given at this time for information leading to the arrest of a deserter, but woe betide the skin of a man who tried to obtain the reward falsely.)

25. Entering into an illegal arrangement with a soldier to claim him as a deserter : Five hundred lashes. (It is not quite clear what happens here, unless it be that both soldiers share the reward and that the alleged deserter takes a flogging in addition to his half share— if they are neither of them caught. In the latter case, they both received five hundred each.)

* * * *

"There is an endless merit in a man's knowing when to have done."
                                    Carlyle.

"None know but they who feel the smart."
                                    Sir J. Denham.

CHAPTER THREE

CORPORAL PUNISHMENT IN THE ROYAL NAVY

The type of men who, as a general rule, enlisted for service in the Royal Navy, and the conditions under which they lived and fought from the mid-seventeenth century to the end of the nineteenth century were such that "discipline" was, in fact, nothing less than fear of death or consideration of skin. When it is remembered that quite a considerable proportion of sailors were far from being volunteers during most of the years above under review, but were actually "pressed" most brutally and with violent trickery into service under the Crown, it will be readily appreciated that order and discipline were maintained largely and by fear of the punishments given for misbehaviour; and the most frequent was, of course, the whip.

Flogging at sea was a far more impressive experience for everyone concerned than it was on the battle-field and barrack-square. It was a more *intimate* punishment, taking place in a much smaller area, the spectators being closer to the man being whipped, more *related* to him as ship-mates than the average regiment can ever be to any one member of it.

I

The first ordinance, or statute, for the government of the Navy, originated with the Long Parliament, and a very complete system for trial by councils of war was organised by the Admirals and Generals of the fleet in the service of the Commonwealth.

Fleets fitted out from the revenue of the State were unknown in the early ages of the monarchy, and it was the Cinque Ports who raised and fitted out the greater part of both ships and men. The Commanding Officers were appointed by the king and the feudal levies, who formed the military force of the realm, were embarked as soldiers and did good service. The terms of service and the compensating immunities of the Cinque Ports were accurately defined by Royal Charter; the earliest known being those of Edward the Confessor and William the Conqueror. Their liberties were confirmed by the Great Charter, and the Charter of Edward I.

The first great battle at sea between England and France was fought by the men of the Cinque Ports in 1217, and is remarkable for the bold spirit which has ever moved the English sailor, however inferior in force. The office of Lord High Admiral was of a later date, when Henry IV appointed Beaufort, Duke of Exeter, to be Admiral of the Fleets of England and Ireland. New regulations for the maintenance of discipline in the Navy were introduced by Charles II. In the following pages will be found a survey of corporal punishments, together with sentences, personal narratives, customs, laws, and the instruments used in the punishments.

There was no standing Navy during the thirteenth, fourteenth, fifteenth and part of the sixteenth centuries, so there was no fixed code of naval law.

Prudent, avaricious, sagacious, money-short Henry VII, to avoid the expense of continually hiring and raising ships, ordered the "Great Harry". The cost was £14,000; it had three masts, and was the wonder of the day. This must be considered England's first man-of-war.

Henry VIII, often at war, founded the dockyards at Woolwich, Deptford and Chatham. He built the first man-of-war to be fitted with port holes for cannons, the "Henri Grace de Dieu", one thousand tons, three hundred and forty-nine soldiers, three hundred and one mariners and fifty gunners. Drake, Hawkins, Raleigh, Frobisher, followed in Elizabeth's reign. The Lord

H

High Admiral still ruled. At this period the word "flogging" was unknown, but we have it on good authority that "whipping took place amongst the sailors for petty crimes committed amongst themselves", and at this period "starting" was practised.

King James advanced his favourite, Buckingham, to the post of Lord High Admiral, with a council of men of rank with great naval experience to guide and help him. This is the origin of the Board of Admiralty.

In 1635-37, Charles I greatly increased the Navy and, in 1637, launched Pett's "Sovereign of the Seas", one thousand six hundred and thirty-seven tons, and "not paralleled in the Christian world". Shortly after Buckingham's death the office of Lord High Admiral was first put in commission, all the great officers being named as Commissioners. The Admirals and Captains of the Fleet were told to punish according to the crime committed, and punishments suggested to them were putting a culprit in the billbows during leisure; keeping the man fasting; ducking at the yard-arm, or hauling from yard-arm to yard-arm under the ship's keel; or making fast to the capstan and whipping them there; or at the capstan and mainmast hang weights about their necks until "their necks and hearts be ready to break"; or to gag or scrape their tongues for blasphemy or swearing.

We are now in 1645 and the Long Parliament framed the first laws for the government of the Navy. In 1648 and 1653 further orders were made. In Cromwell's time the fleet was increased to one hundred and fifty ships. At the Restoration the Duke of York was appointed High Admiral.

The Articles of War of 1661 commenced the discipline we know to-day, with court martial and a Naval Code for trying offenders. In 1673 the Duke of York resigned and a Board of Admiralty was constituted. In 1707 Prince George of Denmark was Lord High Admiral. In 1708 the office of Lord High Admiral was again put into commission; since which period it has continued to be executed by Lords Commissioners of the Admiralty. In 1827 H.R.H. the Duke of Clarence was appointed with a council of four members to assist him.

In 1747 the Board of Admiralty established uniforms for naval officers.

In 1749 "the laws relating to the government of His Majesty's ships, vessels, and forces by sea", were consolidated.

In 1797 two Acts were passed for the suppression of mutiny, at a time when the mouth of the Thames was blocked by our own Fleet.

1797 was the height of what might be named, "the flogging decade". The Navy had grown more quickly than the rules needed to control it, and sentences of duckings, whippings and milder punishments had grown into running the gauntlet and floggings of such barbarous ferocity that they often brought death soon afterwards.

It will be noted that in this volume, on occasions the words "ruling at this time", appear. This is due to a General Order having been issued prior to a revision, or to a newly worded and edited edition of the Articles of War, or the Printed Instructions.

For instance, in 1793, the current Printed Instructions, under the head of Rules and Discipline, etc., stated that a Captain was not to punish a seaman beyond twelve lashes upon his bare back, with a cat-o'-nine-tails; but if the fault deserved a greater punishment, he was to apply for a court martial.

But Captains frequently punished by inflicting two or three dozen lashes *at a time*, when the offence was attended with aggravating circumstances, or where it was of such a nature as to fall under different articles. And, upon this latter instruction a Captain might give three dozen for drunkenness. It was justifiable, however, only from ancient usage and practice in the Navy, and it was considered lenient for a Captain to order three dozen rather than bring an offender to a court martial—where he might get six times as many lashes.

In 1804, on board the "Explosion", John Brown, a gunner, having got drunk, was given one dozen lashes by the Captain next morning. Here are some examples of courts martial in 1806 : —

"Sentence of a court martial on twenty seamen belonging to His Majesty's ship 'Narcissus' for making several mutinous assemblies, and uttering words of sedition and mutiny. That Hamilton Wood, Thomas Crandon, Josiah Marshall, Francis Rae, Owen Cooper, and Thomas Splitman be hanged by the neck until they are dead, at the yard-arms of His Majesty's ship 'Narcissus', at such time as the Commander-in-Chief of His Majesty's ships and vessels at the port shall direct, and the body of the said Hamilton Wood to be afterwards hung in chains, in the most conspicuous place the Commander-in-Chief shall think proper to direct. That Robert Wisely shall receive five hundred lashes, and Peter Delaney shall receive two hundred lashes with a cat-o'-nine-tails on their bare backs, alongside of such ships and at such times, in such proportions as the Commander-in-Chief shall think proper." The remainder of the men were acquitted. This court martial took place aboard the "Assurance", in the North River, New York, and the court met eight times before giving the sentences.

In 1783, at Plymouth, a court martial proceeded to try William Owen, a seaman belonging to H.M.S. "Albion", for having abused in the grossest and most offensive terms Sir Geo. Home, Second-Lieutenant of that ship and for having quitted the yaul to which he belonged, without the permission of the coxswain, and not returning to him on his commanding him to do so, and having heard the witnesses produce on the part of the Crown in support of the charge and what the prisoner had to allege in his defence, the court "do sentence the said William Owen to receive fifty lashes on his bare back".

In the eighteenth and nineteenth centuries, the environment of the typical man-of-war, the wooden hulk below, the flapping sails above, the huge "immense, uncaring sea" all about, the isolation from land, kith and kin, gave to punishment parades on deck a dramatic and impressionable quality that seared itself as effectively into the brains of the spectators of the flogging as did the cat-o'-nine-tails into the naked back of the man lashed to the taut rigging or grating.

Vice-Admiral Sir William Kennedy, K.C.B., in his reminiscences, *Hurrah for the Life of a Sailor* (1900), gives many instances of flogging and whipping at sea. The crews, Kennedy states, were picked up anyhow, longshore loafers, jail-birds, and suchlike, with a sprinkling of good seamen amongst them, and "it took a year of the first commission to knock them into shape". At this time, also sent to the gunroom, where Kennedy was then a midshipman, were older midshipmen—throw-outs from the examination room, and generally bullies and wasters.

They were all drunkards, and were turned out of the Service before the ship went to sea. But not before they had put Kennedy and the other eight middies aboard through their own particular brand of fun. This was to make them sit on chairs and hit each other; the next part of the programme being a fox-hunt, in which the middies were made to chase one another, slashing the while, with hair brushes, and other weapons supplied. During this amusement, the bullies looked on over tumblers of grog. The proceedings were usually brought to a conclusion by prayer, the middies being made to kneel and pray in a loud voice that the bullies should pass their exams.

On one occasion Kennedy and four of his friends

knocked down the chief bully as he was leaving the gun-room, bound him down to iron bolts in the deck spread-eagle fashion and gave him a thrashing that put him on the sick list for a fortnight. He was whipped with ropes, knotted at the end, "After every dozen, administered with thése ropes, or a sword scabbard, we asked him if he would leave us alone in future; but being answered with oaths, the punishment was continued until he had received thirteen dozen, when he fainted and was cast off. This quieted the scoundrel for a bit, but he had to have another dose. This time he armed himself with the office rule, with which he felled one of our party like an ox; but we were on him like tiger cats, and gave him such a dressing that he was *hors de combat* for many a day".

In those days (1851) discipline was maintained with a severity *unimaginable* a hundred years later.

Kennedy reports that half a launch's crew received forty-eight lashes for drunkenness, and the gunroom steward who served them, received the same. He says that the right to flog was grossly abused, and he was pleased to see it eventually curtailed.

It is noteworthy that fifty years ago, when corporal punishment was debated as heatedly as it is to-day, Kennedy gives it as his considered opinion that no one of sense and proportion can object to flogging males responsible for cowardly attacks on women or aged folk, any more than (in his day) people could object to birch-ing in schools.

The first court martial in the Royal Navy that we can find is about the time of the Revolution of 1688. In 1680 three sailors of the "Hampshire" were condemned on Herbert's flagship, the "Bristol", in Cadiz Bay, for disobedience to the orders of the master. They were ordered to draw lots, and the loser had to receive fifty lashes on his bare back with a cat-o'-nine-tails. At Tangier, Thomas Woodgrean was sentenced to receive ten lashes alongside the "Bristol" and five beside every

PUNISHING A SAILOR THIEF IN THE NAVY, c. 1900

other ship in the squadron, a paper declaring his fault was to be hung round his neck, and he was to be towed ashore at the stern of a boat, for scandalously and falsely accusing his Captain of cowardice in action, and in 1681, William Jenkins, a sailor on the "Adventure", was ordered to be flogged for scandalous words about Captain Wheeler of the "Nonsuch".

1698. Mutiny on board H.M.S. "Speedwell" : "Thursday last, one Beer, and two others, lately brought from the West Indies, were tried on board the 'Restauration' at Spithead, for endeavouring, with several others, to seize the 'Speedwell', man-of-war, and turn pyrates; and being found guilty, the first was executed, and the other two whipped from ship to ship".

1745. Complaint from men of H.M.S. "Leopard" : To the Lords Commissioners of the Admiralty. The case of the oppressed seamen turned over from H.M.S. "Newcastle", and the rest of the seamen aboard the "Leopard" :

"On 8th December, 1744, they were ordered to take their hammocks only and go aboard the 'Leopard'; were not allowed to return to the 'Newcastle' to get their clothes and other necessaries, and were so sent on a cruise in the middle of winter; the ship was sent to the Mediterranean and they were kept cruising off Cape Nola, without their clothes in the depth of winter, under the snowy mountains of Piedmont. When they were but two nights on board, having been all day at hard work, the midshipmen came in the middle of the night and cut several of them down, letting their own ship's company lie still. The Lieutenants were in the habit of calling them 'mutinous dogs, villains, rascals and other such vile epithets'. When the watch was hoisting the main top sail, the First Lieutenant came into the waist with a stick in his hand, and beat the men fore and aft, cursing them and saying, 'you mutinous dogs, you are the "Newcastle", but I will let you know you are on board the "Leopard" now'. For slight or no offence, the Second Lieutenant would order them to be coped (cobbed) with a board upward of an inch thick. The Boatswain, not thinking a stick made out of an ash oar strong enough to beat men with, ordered his yeomen to get about three feet of two and a half inch rope; which he wormed and moulded snake-fashion with new twine, on purpose to beat the men."

II

Writing in *Macmillan's Magazine*, 1898, an ex-naval officer describes *Discipline in the Old Navy*.

"In the old Navy the flogging of grown men with the cat was common . . ."

"Flogging was an old-established custom, and it is noteworthy that at the great mutinies, at Spithead, Plymouth, and the Cape, the men did not protest against it, and even inflicted it themselves upon ill-behaved members of the mutinous crews."

By the *Rules of Discipline and Good Government to be Observed on Board His Majesty's Ships of War*, dated 1730, no Captain could inflict more than twelve lashes. But this had been modified by the time of the American War, and Captains were in the habit of awarding up to forty-eight lashes. The offences thus punished were drunkenness, theft, insubordination, malingering, and slackness in performing duty. The sentences and the number of punishments varied greatly with different Captains, and there was an old saying "as many Captains, so many navies". Thus seamen had a real grievance, for what was tolerated in one ship might be severely punished in another. This irregularity and capriciousness were bad in every way. The Captain was omnipotent; complaints, as the courts martial show, were rarely successful, and only too often drew down upon those who made them yet severer penalties.

Deaths from flogging by the Captain were not unknown : "A man in the 'Theseus' was severely and repeatedly punished till at last he could not walk. He was, however, brought on deck in this weak condition, laid upon a gun, as he could not stand, and again flogged. He died almost immediately afterwards, and being buried on shore, an inquest was held and a verdict of wilful murder returned". The Captain does not seem to have suffered, and the ship's surgeon swore that the case appeared so lenient that his attendance was not required. "To see men lose their lives for petty matters, this is a thing God will reckon for," said Cromwell, but our country had forgotten his saying.

How frequent were these floggings can be proved by an examination of ships' logs. (See pp. 150 to 158.)

When a man was flogged by the Captain, he was tied up to the gratings, which were in action placed over the hatchways, but which were at other times kept in the gangways, or narrow passages on each side of the ship from the quarter-deck to the forecastle. He was stripped to the waist; the crew were turned up to witness his punishment; and then the lashes were laid on by the Boatswain's mate, a big, strong man. There were two kinds of cat, a special one which inflicted severer torture being used for thieves. Occasionally brutal Captains pickled the cat in salt, but such practices were reprobated and censured.

Baron Ompteda, a Colonel of the King's German Legion, has left us a curious picture of discipline on board one of our smaller ships in 1809. He says in his letters : —

"A rapid alteration of sails (change of tack) became necessary. Either by want of skill or ill-humour, the manoeuvre was badly executed. The Lieutenant came down in great wrath, and desired to know the names of those who were in fault. No one wanted to give them. 'Very well,' said he, 'if nobody is to blame, you are all to blame, and I'll treat you accordingly.' And he had them all on deck, one after another, and treated each to three dozen with a rope's end (cat?) . . . In one of the battalion journals the remark is found relative to the effect of this punishment : 'Twelve lashes on board ship are equal to one hundred and fifty lashes in the Army, on account of the thicker rope and stronger arm'."

Here, then, we have something like half the crew flogged. Thiebault, a careful observer, on his passage to France from Portugal in a British ship, the "Fylla", gives a similar picture : —

"As for the discipline, it was severe to the point of cruelty. The least fault was punished with lashes of the cat, which drew blood from those who suffered. The morning was dedicated to these punishments, and as there was never a day which was not marked by three or four of these executions, I was tortured on waking by the shrieks of the unhappy culprits . . . And when I left the 'Fylla' there were more than seventy floggings to be divided among the crew, composed of one hundred and forty men."

The floggings by Captains were terrible enough in all conscience; but what shall we say of the far more dreadful flogging round the Fleet inflicted by courts martial? For here the limit to the number of lashes was only the endurance of the human frame, and in the opinion of Captain Marryat the punishment was worse than death itself. The sentence was pronounced in these words : —

"We adjudge him to be punished by receiving —— lashes on his bare back, with a cat-o'-nine-tails, alongside such of His Majesty's ships at such time and in such proportions as the Commander-in-Chief shall think fit to direct." The prisoner was towed in a boat from one ship to another, and flogged beside each, the whole crew being sent up the rigging to witness his punishment. The Captain of the ship alongside which the man was flogged saw that the blows were laid on with vigour, and there is an incidental mention in the courts martial of a case where four blows were ordered not to be counted, *because not given hard enough.* The heaviest sentence which we have been able to discover is one of five hundred lashes, equal, we are assured, to two thousand lashes with the military "cat"!

III

Most used of punishments not to be found in Rules of Discipline or the Articles of War, but which had grown up with the Service, was that of "Starting". This was the use of ropes' ends and canes to beat the men with if they were slow or slack in doing their duties. A big, tough seaman could be beaten at will by the newest and youngest of midshipmen if he failed to "jump to it". One instance is of a Lieutenant (dismissed the Service on this occasion) who beat a seaman savagely on the bare back with a two-and-a-half inch rope. The rope was thirty inches long and the seaman was given more than two dozen blows. This Lieutenant ended his day's work by knocking down with his fist another seaman and then ropes'-ending him.

But here is another side to the story taken from Ross's *Life of Saumarez* : Captain Caulfield of the "Grampus" had laid it down that no ropes' ends or canes should be carried by his officers. The "Grampus" was at anchor when the call was given that a prize was sailing towards the ship. The master, who sprang forward, called aloud, "Veer away the small blower-cable or she'll be on board of us!" The pause which had been made in the Captain's speech was broken by orders from him to veer away the cable quickly. "Down, my lads, veer away!" was repeated by every officer; but the men, not aware of the fatal consequences, and knowing they could not, after what the captain had said, be "started", moved very leisurely to perform their duty, which, to save the ship, it was absolutely necessary should be done with the utmost alacrity. To save the ship, the Captain shouted to the officers to start the men. But they had no canes! He saved the situation himself by leaping down among the men, and with the end of the thickest rope he could find, became the transgressor of his own laws, of the absurdity of which he was now fully convinced.

The memoirs of seamen of the 1780-1815 period are filled with stories of arbitrary punishments, many of them interesting, all of them tinged with cruelty. Occasionally the men complained. Occasionally they proved their cases, but too often their complaints were dismissed as frivolous. Tying a man up to the rigging is often found, as is spread-eagling a man to the rigging, stripped to the waist, in a blizzard. The last man up and the last man down the rigging were frequently lashed, and this led to many a fatal accident in the rush not to be "last man". One Captain tied a sailor over a gun and ordered the Boatswain to "lash that man until his behind is as flat as his back"; it is recorded that the man received more than six hundred strokes on his bared buttocks with the cat-o'-nine-tails before being taken down in a state of collapse.

The tying a man over a gun became known as "Kissing the gunner's daughter". It was an everyday occurrence, but the men, contrary to the example given, wore thin trousers and were beaten with ropes' ends.

Making a man "ride the spanker-boom sitting on a wet swab";* tying a seaman's hands, extended, to the Boatswain's handspike laid across his back, to each end of which a twelve pound shot had been fastened; tying two men up to the rigging by their left hands, and compelling them to beat each other with a one-and-a-half inch rope in the right, are some of the curious punishments we find. The three last were employed by the Captain of the "Rattlesnake" who was dismissed the Service. The mutiny at the Cape, where was stationed this ship, made some attention to seamen's grievances necessary, or, from other records, he might have merely been reprimanded. Captain Mackenzie had blown a

* The swab was of gunpowder and caused an unbearable and maddening itching and smarting.

FLOGGING IN THE NAVY, TIED TO THE GRATING

[*Face page* 110

marine from a gun on the West Coast of Africa at an
earlier date. The marine had tried to bore a hole
through the ship's bottom. (The Captain received a
Royal Pardon.)

Perhaps the best known, because to the "land-
lubber" the most "salty" and dramatic, was the punishment called "keel-hauling". Authors blandly state that
"keel-hauling was never much used in the Navy of this
country, but was a Dutch punishment". They are
entirely wrong, and had their research taken them back
to the early periods after the Revolution, they would
find themselves in a whole series of keel-hauling, and
this is why, supposedly, writers of books on these subjects, have dismissed the punishment as a foreign one.
It was still being used in the Dutch navy as late as 1806,
but there is no trace of it in English records after 1770.
Here is a description of keel-hauling an English sailor in
1710 (the sentence had been passed on the man for
blasphemy).

"The sailor was ordered to strip off all his clothes
except for a strip of cloth round his loins. He was suspended by blocks and pullies, and these were fastened
to the opposite extremities of the main yard, and a
weight of lead or iron was hung upon his legs to sink him
to a competent depth. By this apparatus he was drawn
close up to the yard-arm, and thence let fall suddenly
into the sea; where, passing under the ship's bottom, he
was hoisted up on the opposite side of the ship. And
this, after sufficient intervals of breathing, was repeated
two or three times."

If the unlucky sailor was drawn too near the ship's
bottom, his flesh was torn and scratched by barnacles
and such like, which, no doubt, was why he was stripped
before the punishment. Uncleanliness and scandalous
actions were the other crimes for which keel-hauling
was the punishment.

Running the gauntlet was also occasionally executed
at sea.

112   UNDER THE LASH

On the 12th October, 1762, John Brown, J. Johnson, and John Bryan, seamen belonging to the "Ocean", were tried for stealing a purse of money belonging to a man in the ship. John Bryan was sentenced to run the gauntlet on board the said ship one round, the second named, thrice, and John Brown four times.

"The whole ship's crew is ranged in two rows, standing face to face on both sides of the deck, so as to form a line, whereby to go *forward*, on one side, and return *aft* on the other; each person being furnished with a small twisted cord, or spun-yarn, called a *knittle*, having two or three knots upon it. The delinquent is then stripped naked above the waist and compelled to march forward, in ordinary or quick time, between the two rows of men, and aft on the other side, a certain number of times, rarely exceeding three, during which every person gives him a stripe with his knittle as he passes along. Although the punishment be termed running the gauntlet, yet in the Navy the delinquent is never permitted to *run* between the ranks of his executioners, because it is usual to compel him to march in ordinary or in quick time, preceded by the Master-at-Arms, with a drawn sword pointed in the rear towards him, while the Corporal follows him behind at a proper distance with another drawn sword; or, instead of the Corporal, it is sometimes usual to cause the Boatswain's Mate to follow him, furnished with a cat-o'-nine-tails, but he never applies the lash of it in the march, unless the offender retrograde."

With ducking, spread-eagling, and other punishments of its own, the Navy did not often use the gauntlet; mainly, we suspect, because there was not a sufficiency of room aboard to carry out the punishment properly.

However, when it was ordered, the sailors used "knittles", which looked like ten-inch lengths of knitted cords with a knot at the end. These bruised more than they cut, and in the early days of the Navy may be said to have been the true beginning of flogging; for Captains, *and there was never anybody so absolute as the Captain of a Navy ship in the eighteenth century,* used them unmercifully and in several ways. Most frequent were variations on the gauntlet theme, and we have examples of sailors stripped and tied over barrels and gun barrels and capstans, whilst parties of their mates were ordered to lay into them with knittles or ropes' ends.

We read of one Captain who delighted in the "lower discipline" and for the least fault would have the culprit tied up, his trousers lowered, and a hundred lashes with the cat delivered by a hefty Boatswain.

On other occasions the man was tied down over a capstan—a most uncomfortable position—whilst his shipmates were ordered to lay-on with all their strength under threat of a similar fate. The convulsions of the unhappy victim, his hams raised in the air, can well be imagined. It was excesses of this sort which lead to the gradual introduction into the Navy of controls, until to-day, with our King's Regulations and Admiralty Instructions, little, or nothing, remains unindexed.

A frequent punishment of the seventeenth and eighteenth centuries was *The Capstein.* The punishment at the capstein is when "a capstein bar being thrust through the hole of the barrel, the offender's arms are extended at the full length crosswise, and so tied to the bar, having sometimes a basket of bullets, or some other like weight hanging by his neck; in which posture he continues till he be brought either to confess some plot or crime, whereof he is frequently suspected; or that he receives such punishment as the Captain will have him endure".

The punishment by *The Bilboes,* is when "a delinquent is laid in irons, or a kind of stocks that they use for the purpose and which are more or less ponderous, as the quality of the offence is, that is proved against the offending patient".

"The ducking at the main yard-arm is when a male-
factor, by having ropes fastened under his arms, and
about his middle, and under his breech, is thus hoisted
up to the end of the yard, from whence he is violently
let fall into the sea, sometimes twice, sometimes three,
sometimes several times, one after another; and if the
offence be foul, he is also drawn underneath the very
keel of the ship, and being thus under water, a great
piece is given fire, unto right over his head, as well to
astonish him the more with the thunder thereof, with
proveth much offensive to him, as to give warning to all
others to look out and beware." As for petty pilferings,
and the like of that nature, they were generally punished
with the whip; "the offender being to that purpose made
fast to the capstein; and the knaveries of the ship's boys
are pay'd by the Boatswain with the rod; and commonly
this execution is done on the Munday mornings; and is
so frequently in use that some meer seamen believe in
earnest that they shall not have a fair wind unless the
boys be duely 'brought to the chest', that is be whipped
every Munday morning".

The famous naval mutinies of 1797 were not so much
due to excessive punishments as to the horrible conditions under which the men lived. There were, however, examples of excessive and cruel punishment
aboard the ships "Nymphe" and "Marlborough". On
the "Nymphe" the complaints were against the Lieutenants and against the First Lieutenant, Irwin, in
particular. The punishment of a seaman, by his order,
for silent contempt, has passed into history : —

George Verrey, a seaman of the "Nymphe", was
seen to smile at the end of a flogging. Irwin noticed the
smile and decided the flogging had not had the desired
effect. Verrey was therefore given a further three dozen
lashes across his back. Irwin also beat him about the
head with a speaking trumpet.

The Captain of the "Marlborough" also used his

speaking trumpet with such violence that the mouth-piece was broken and necessitated a metal replacement being fitted.

The Lieutenants of the "Nymphe" also whipped the men themselves when the Boatswains' mates did not lash strongly enough for their liking. On one occasion a man had been sent up the rigging, but did not climb fast enough for the Lieutenant. A second man was sent up to bring him down. This man's climbing also did not satisfy the Lieutenant, and both men were ordered twelve lashes. When the "Nymphe" was in action at Brest, says the report of Colpoys, several seamen were beaten at their quarters. Lieutenant Compton of the "Minitaur" often punished the men with "starting", for the slightest offence, and the men of the "Amphitrite" brought similar charges against their First Lieutenant.

"Our First Lieutenant," the seamen said, "he is a most Cruel and Barberous man, Beating some at times until they are not able to stand, and not allowing them the satisfaction to cry out. If your honr. be pleased to look Round you may find many ships that Want men and as we want another ship by grantg. one Wee will Remain In duty Bound to Remain

Your ever lasting Servants and petitioners,

Ship's Company of the 'Amphitrite.' "

Gagging is described by Dr. Burney as a mode of punishment used in the Navy to prevent insolent language during confinement for drunkenness or other misconduct.

The infliction of this punishment, or "measure of restraint", is thus described by a Medical Officer of the Navy : —

"I have," wrote Dr. Forbes, "seen gagging per-formed in the following manner : A piece of wood or iron, various in diameter and length, is introduced into the mouth, exactly in the way a bit is introduced into the mouth of a horse, so that a portion of it shall project

I

from each side. It is retained in this position by means of a cord passed over the projecting extremities and behind the head. As the operation is one which is seldom proposed but when gentler means have failed to procure a cessation of outrageous conduct, it will naturally be concluded that it is one which is never voluntarily submitted to. Against the drunk man's efforts, accordingly, to keep his mouth shut, considerable force must generally be employed before the business can be properly accomplished."

In the year 1815, Captain J. T., of His Majesty's sloop M——— was tried by a court martial on charges of cruelty and oppression. The first charge stated, that "Thomas Payne, belonging to His Majesty's sloop M———, had suffered a dislocation of the jaw, from the severe punishment of gagging, inflicted on him by direction of Captain J. T.".

The pieces of wood with which Payne was successively gagged were of fir, about six or seven inches long, and of the thickness of the finger or thumb. Payne bit through one or more pieces of wood successively; and when he had bitten through the third piece, he appeared to have hurt himself, and upon examination by the Surgeon, it was found that his jaw was completely dislocated. The dislocation was shortly after reduced; but next day, or the day after, the Surgeon discovered that the jaw was again in a state of dislocation, and his repeated attempts to reduce it were ineffectual. "The distortion and disfigurement of countenance were disgusting and humiliating, conveying the impression of idiotism."

The decision of the court was as follows : "The court is of opinion that the dislocation of Thomas Payne's jaw was occasioned by his own violence in biting the piece of wood through, and *by a facility which he had of putting the jaw out and in himself*, and not from the severe punishment of gagging".

The Captain was accordingly fully acquitted.

A witness at the trial stated, that he had usually seen "the pumpbolt", the iron bolt on which the handle of the ship's pump works, "bayonet and drum-stick", used for the purpose of a gag.

Spread-Eagle.—"This punishment I have seen inflicted on a man while he was in a state of inebrity. The culprit is placed upon the standing rigging of the mizenmast, his feet and arms being stretched wide and secured. In this state he remains until the officer of watch directs him to be taken down."

The Wooden Collar.—"This instrument of punishment appears to be a modification of the Chinese kea, or cangue, a portable pillory, consisting of two thick pieces of wood, hollow in the middle, so as to fit the neck of an offender, and about two feet broad. On the upper surface of the collar shot are fixed, by which means the instrument is heavy or light, according to the nature of the crime or the pleasure of the Commanding Officer; generally it is about sixty pounds weight. The delinquent is to wear the instrument on deck, or in some public place of a ship."

Barrel-Pillory.—"Another species of pillory has lately (in 1840) been adopted in the Navy as a punishment, which, according to report, has effectually supplanted flogging. Two large barrels are placed on the quarter-deck, in which the culprits are placed for several hours during the day, wearing a cap not unlike that used in some schools, and designated the fool's cap. In front of the cask is written the nature of the offence committed, and in this manner they are subjected to the gaze of the curious who visit the ship, as well as the ridicule of their comrades."

Carrying a Capstan Bar.—"This punishment consists in a man being obliged to carry a heavy beam of wood, and to walk fore and aft upon the weather gangway, for the period of a watch, or about four hours."

Black List.—This list is composed of men who have been guilty of venial offences, commonly some trivial neglect of duty, and are placed on the black list of the First Lieutenant. "The ingenuity of officers to punish in this manner, rather than resort to the cat, has been most amply exemplified of late years (1845). The author of *The Life of a Sailor* informs us, that 'he knew a Captain who made the black-list men, when the duty was over for the day, carry their hammocks on their shoulders up and down the quarter-deck, at every six feet placing a rope about three feet from the deck, and making these poor devils, who followed one another like sheep, step over each rope. The exertion required, and the consequent fatigue experienced, is beyond all calculation'."

The original Articles of War were issued by Charles the Second's first Parliament. The Articles were revised in 1778. It is noticeable that in the 1797 mutiny, the mutineers did not find serious fault with the punishment code, which was similar to that on land. There must have been in the Nore Fleet many sober and honest men, and any relaxation of discipline would have been entirely to the disadvantage of such men, for it would have set a premium on indolence and disorder. The delegates of the Nore Fleet actually showed their approval of the correction, by floggings and duckings of their own authority. A seaman of the "Pompee" was flogged severely for bringing spirits on board.

The men of the "Nassau" had said that their Captain was a tyrant and that the next in cruelty was their Second Lieutenant, who would make them strip in the night and give them two or three dozen with a rope's end or a rattan. Another man on another ship received two dozen for not having his name sewn on his hammock. Most harrowing of all the tales from the 1797 mutiny is that of the "Hermione", which was in the West Indies at that time. That ship had the toughest of tough crews, and it was said that they laughed at two dozen with the cat. Be that as it may, Captain Pigot of the "Hermione" always flogged the last man down from the yards. Two

A PAGE FROM THE LOG-BOOK OF H.M.S. "IMMORTALITÉ,"
OFF THE RIO GRANDE, FEB. 1863.
Recording the punishment of Isaac Alger (Boy, 2nd-class)
with 36 lashes.

[*Face page* 118

topmen anxious to avoid the usual flogging, hurried so much that they both fell and broke their limbs.

Pigot immediately ordered that the men should be thrown overboard, which, in fear, other sailors did. That night the sailors rose and murdered the Captain and many of the other officers.

How pleasant, then, to read of a petition from the men of the "Vestal" in the shape of a round-robin in a circle, each man writing towards the centre to avoid priority, saying : —

"We, the men of the 'Vestal', having heard that Captain MacDougall . . . has been appointed to the 'Asia', would be very happy to sail along with him."

Admiral Duncan was so loved that his men declared themselves ready to do anything for him down to the shedding of their blood. The men of the "Weazle" wrote that their Lieutenant used to come aboard drunk and then amused himself by choosing men to strip, seizing them up to the rigging and beating them with a rope's end "till we almost expire".

When the mutiny came to an end, the leader, Parker, was hanged of necessity. In the twenty-six ships, four hundred and twelve men were court martialled, fifty-nine sentenced to death, twenty-nine actually executed, twenty-nine imprisoned, the rest were pardoned except for nine who were flogged; the floggings ranged from forty to three hundred and eighty lashes, the latter being inflicted on a seaman of the "Monmouth".

From the above the reader will have reconstructed a picture of life at sea under the Crown during the seventeenth and eighteenth centuries. That men could, and did act so heroically, and with such a lasting impression on history, and carry England's flag to every corner of the earth under such discipline and conditions of service above and below deck, speaks "volumes".

CHAPTER FOUR

CORPORAL PUNISHMENT IN THE ROYAL
NAVY—*continued*

There were Captains who moderated their use of the lash, some—like Captain Collingwood—who avowedly hated punishment by whipping, but it was nevertheless as true on the sea as it was on land, that discipline was mainly kept by fear of the lash.

It must also be borne in mind that it was only due to the smaller number of men aboard each ship than in a regiment, and due to the fact that replacements at sea in emergency were impossible, and also to the high intrinsic value of every man aboard, that the punish ments given at sea were very seldom as incapacitating as they were in the barrack-square.

Here is a rare contemporary record of punishment at sea, under the Crown, in the late eighteenth century : —

"Sketch of the Punishments to which Common Seamen and Marines are liable in the Royal Navy. By a Surgeon's Mate of 1803.

"In the twenty-second year of the reign of George II, an Act was passed, entitled, 'An Act for amending, explaining, and reducing into one Act of Parliament, the laws relating to the government of His Majesty's ships, vessels, and forces by sea'; and in the nineteenth year of George III another Act was passed, which modified and amended the Act passed in the former reign (1784). These two Acts of Parliament contain, with the requisite modifications, all the rules, articles, and orders, for the regulating and better government of His Majesty's ships, vessels, and forces by sea.

"In the naval penal code above mentioned, there are nine articles, or branches of articles, which refer to common seamen and which, on conviction, expressly inflict _death, without alternative, or leaving any discretionary power to the members of a court martial to award a milder punishment; and there are about twelve articles which inflict the punishment of death or 'such other punishment as the nature and degree of an offence shall be found to deserve', and which a court in its discretion may award.

"In about ten other articles the word death is omitted, and the punishment to which a man may be sentenced is left, both in kind and degree, wholly to the discretion of a court martial; and as these articles are for the punishment of offences not of so flagrant a nature as in the former two classes of articles, it may be presumed that the Legislature meant to exclude the power of a court martial to inflict a capital punishment for any of the offences therein specified. In these cases it is left wholly to the discretion of a court martial to discriminate the shades of guilt, and to inflict a punishment, in quality and amount proportionate, in their opinion, not affecting life and limb.

"In early times, and even during the last century, it would appear that punishments were more severe and certain than during the last thirty years. It was not then uncommon for an offender, guilty of desertion, to be adjudged to suffer death, or to be punished with five hundred lashes. By the records of courts martial, it appears that the sentences awarded at one time varied from one dozen to one thousand lashes. The punishments which it is in the power of naval courts martial to inflict, are various in their nature and degree. They are from death, the greatest and highest, descending in various shades down to mild reprimand and gentle admonition."

By the 36th Article of War it was declared, "that all other crimes not capital, committed by any person or persons in the fleet, which are not mentioned in this Act, or for which no punishment is hereby directed to be inflicted, shall be punished according to the laws in such cases used at sea". For anomalous offences the old standing customs and usage of the Service were directed to be resorted to as a kind of unwritten or common law, which supplied the place of express statutes. A case which was tried in the Court of Common Pleas will illustrate the above. The action was brought for an act of violence upon the person of the plaintiff (a midshipman) in consequence of his disobedience of an order of the defendant, his Commanding Officer, who ordered him to the mast-head as a punishment, according to the usage of the Service. The judge observed that the custom of the Service justified the order, and rendered the punishment legal; therefore, the disobeying such legal order justified the measures taken to enforce it, or put it into execution. The jury, without hesitation, returned a verdict for the defendant.

Early in the month of March, 1797, a mutiny broke out in the fleet at Portsmouth, the principal subjects of discontent among the seamen being the smallness of their pay, and of the Greenwich pensions; the very unequal distribution of prize money; the excessive harshness and severity of the discipline; and the haughty and tyrannical behaviour of many of the officers. The seamen obtained all their demands, and forthwith returned to their duty. Among the officers charged with oppression, and discarded by the men, there were one Admiral, four Captains, twenty-nine Lieutenants, seventeen Masters' Mates, twenty-five Midshipmen, five Captains of Marines, three Lieutenants of Marines, four Surgeons, and about thirteen Petty Officers. The men refused to receive on board those tyrannical officers, whom they had sent on shore; and Lord Howe, who had been commissioned to settle all matters of dispute, found himself obliged to comply with the decided resolution of the men. It is to be regretted, that previous care had not been taken to prevent discontent, by remedying the undeniable evils of which the seamen complained, but from this mutiny, however, may be dated the most rapid improvement in the management and condition of our sailors, with a proportionate improvement in the discipline and spirit of the men, and the gallantry of the officers.

About the middle of May, 1797, a mutiny broke out at the Nore, and the mutineers petitioned against the naval code, the eighth article of their list of grievances being an affirmation "That the Articles of War, as now enforced, require various alterations, several of which to be expunged therefrom, etc., etc.", thereby expressing an opinion, that the system of discipline and the Articles of War were unnecessarily severe and required relaxation, in order to disabuse seamen in general of the prejudice against the Navy. In the letter which the mutineers at the Nore forwarded to the King, through Lord Northesk, they petitioned or urged, "that no punishment should be inflicted on board a King's ship, until the offender had been previously tried and convicted by a jury of seamen".

Courts martial in the Navy were ordered either by the Admiralty or by the Commanding Officer of a station. The punishments to which seamen were liable by the sentence of a court martial at the beginning of the nineteenth century were as follows : —

1. Death. 2. Flogging round the Fleet.

The punishments frequently inflicted at the discretion of a Captain or Commanding Officer, and which nothing but the usage of the Service appears to have authorised, were : —

1. Flogging at the Gangway. 2. Running the Gauntlet. 3. Starting. 4. Keel-hauling. 5. Ducking. 6. Gagging. 7. The Spread-Eagle. 8. The Wooden Collar. 9. The Barrel-Pillory. 10. Carrying a Capstan Bar. 11. The Black List.

Execution of the sentence of death : —

"The fatal morning is arrived—the signal of death is already displayed—the assemblage of boats, manned and armed, surround the ship appointed for the execution.

The crews of the respective ships are arranged on deck, and after hearing the Articles of War read, and being made acquainted with the crime for which the punishment is inflicted, await, with silent dread and expectation, the awful moment. At length a gun is fired (the signal to rouse attention), and at the same instant the unhappy victim, who has violated the laws of his country, is run up by the neck to the yard-arm; the whole spectacle being intended as a warning to deter others from the commission of similar crimes." (*Principles and Practice of Naval and Military Courts Martial*, by John M'Arthur.)

Execution of the sentence of corporal punishment. Flogging round the Fleet.—"In carrying the sentences of naval courts martial for corporal punishment into execution, the Admiral or Commanding Officer of the station issues orders to the Captain of the flag, or other particular ship, to make the signal for the boats of the squadron to assemble, manned and armed, on the day appointed, to attend the punishment, and likewise orders the other Captains to send a Lieutenant, with a boat manned and armed, from their respective ships, to attend and assist thereat.

"An order is at the same time issued to the Captain or Commander of the ship to which the prisoner belongs (accompanied with a copy of the sentence), directing him to cause the punishment to be inflicted alongside of the different ships, in the manner, and in such proportions, as therein specified. Directions are at the same time given to the Captain to cause the Surgeon of his ship to attend in the boat, with the Lieutenant, as well as one of his mates, in the launch with the prisoner, for the purpose of judging of the prisoner's ability to bear all his punishment, the Surgeon being authorised to recommend that the punishment should be suspended when he conceives the prisoner is not able to bear more without endangering his life.

"The Provost-Marshal or Master-at-Arms attends

the punishment, and he reads publicly the sentence of the court martial alongside of each ship respectively.

"The delinquent having been put into a launch, attended by a Surgeon's Mate (now denominated an Assistant Surgeon), he is forthwith stripped naked to the waist, and tied up with his arms extended upon a frame of wood, when he receives a specified number of lashes. The Master-at-Arms stands beside him with a drawn sword, and reckons the lashes as they are inflicted. A drummer and fifer stand in the bow; a Lieutenant and the Surgeon of the ship accompanying the launch in another boat. The whole flotilla of boats then fall into line, taking in tow the launch containing the culprit. The fifer strikes up the *Rogue's March*, accompanied by the drum, muffled, and the procession moves on at a slow rate, following a light gig, called the dispatch-boat, which goes forward to announce the delinquent's approach to those ships where he is to receive his punishment. The prisoner having reached the ship, the crew cover the sides and channels upon that side where the procession has halted. The sentence of the court martial is read aloud, after which two Boatswain's Mates are sent from the ship, who inflict that portion of the punishment which has been directed to be given alongside each ship, the amount of lashes being divided among the number of ships belonging to the Fleet. A blanket is then thrown over the man's shoulders, the flotilla of boats again takes the launch in tow, the music strikes up, the dispatch-boat proceeds to the next ship as before, and thus the culprit is slowly dragged from one vessel to another, for a period extending sometimes to several hours, till the sentence has been carried into effect, or the punishment suspended by the recommendation of the Surgeon."

Here we include an account of this mode of flogging round the Fleet, recorded by two naval officers :—

"In the year 1811, when Admiral Sir C. Cotton commanded the Mediterranean Fleet, a seaman belonging to a frigate was sentenced to be flogged round the Fleet, and the punishment was accordingly inflicted at Port Mahon, in the Island of Minorca. This harbour has such deep water, that even the largest ships lie moored close to the rocks and quays. Attracted by the cavalcade of boats, the music, and above all, by the cries of the criminal, thousands of the inhabitants crowded to the shore to witness the scene. When these spectators noticed that the punishment was alternately suspended and renewed, so as to produce more acute pain, they exclaimed loudly against British cruelty. 'You boast of humanity,' said an aged monk to the writer, 'What is there in all the tortures that your nation truely or falsely impute to the tribunal of the Inquisition more protracted or inhuman than this proceeding? Why do you suspend the lashes but to increase the agony? The culprit has already fainted twice, yet your Surgeon authorises a continuance of the whipping. Is not the poor wretch's back entirely flayed from his neck to his loins? Yet the scourging still goes on, and will frequently be suspended and renewed again before the sentence is fulfilled. What worse torture than this could disgrace the prisons of the Inquisition, or even the dungeons of Algiers?' Some attempt was made to deprecate this censure, by explaining that the difference consisted in the British seaman having had a fair and open trial, confronted with his accusers and with the witnesses; yet, whatever advantages might have attended his trial, it was impossible to deny that his punishment was altogether cruel and indefensible." (*United Service Journal*, 1830.)

Moral virtue could also be adjudged and punished as military vice. The following example appears to be a conversion of this kind : —

"In the year 1805, an impressed seaman, belonging to a ship in the West Indies, received a letter from his father announcing his being in a rapid decline, and desiring his son to hasten home. The young seaman determined to run all risks. He deserted from a watering party, but was retaken and slightly punished. He again fled from the ship, was brought back, and received a more severe flogging. Being detected in the third attempt to escape, he was brought before a court martial, which, according to the Articles of War, might have adjudged the culprit to be hung at the yard-arm. Taking, however, into consideration the youth of the prisoner, and his having been recently impressed into the Service, together with the account he gave of his motive for deserting, the court sentenced him to be flogged round the Fleet, and to receive four hundred lashes on board or alongside of such ships as the Commander-in-Chief might appoint. The Admiral remitted one-fourth of the punishment, and the remaining three hundred lashes were ordered forthwith to be inflicted.

"The fatal morning at length arrived. The young man's back, which had scarcely healed since his former floggings, was quickly laid raw beneath the sharp strokes of the whip-cord. Possibly, the torture might have been endured but for the intervals in which it was suspended between one ship and another. By these cruel interruptions the benumbed flesh was repeatedly restored to sensation, and the miserable culprit frequently fainted under excess of suffering. The attending Surgeon, distressed at the scene, knew not how to determine for the best. It appeared less humane to suspend than to continue the punishment, because, as the sentence must be executed, there seemed real mercy in inflicting the whole number of lashes at once. (The authority of the Admiral is required to remit a portion of a sentence awarded by a court martial in this country.) At length, however, the back became so badly lacerated, that the flesh quivered under every stroke of the whip— the head of the sufferer fell senseless upon his bosom— the punishment was suspended—the criminal removed to the hospital, where the heat of a tropical climate produced gangrene, and in two days after he expired."

We note that, in this instance, the author thinks "blame could hardly attach to any person. The Captain did not bring the culprit to trial till his third offence—the court martial commuted the capital penalty—the Admiral mitigated the severity of the sentence—a skilful and humane Surgeon superintended the punishment—every spectator shed tears of pity—and yet a comparatively innocent being was openly tortured to death, under the authority of an inhuman and antiquated custom".

Sir Robert Steele, who served as a Marine Officer, after stating the circumstances of seven men belonging to the "Edgar" having been sentenced "to go through the Fleet", describes the consequences of that terrible punishment : —

"I believe no man has ever been known to hold up his head after going through the Fleet. The heavy launch is fitted with a triangle, to which the wretch is tied, as if to a cross. It takes some hours to row (sometimes against wind and tide) through the Fleet. The torture is, therefore, protracted till, to use a sailor's phrase, 'their very soul is cut out'. After this dreadful sentence they almost always die."

"It was at a few minutes before eight o'clock in the morning, when the First Lieutenant of the ship ordered me to take charge of the launch, and see the punishment carried into effect. Had he given me orders to mount the sides of an enemy's frigate, at the head of a launch's crew, it would not have distressed me half so much, as I might have considered that my good luck might bring me a Lieutenant's commission; but here was a service devoid of honour and full of painful consequences, from which, however, there was no chance of escape. I must needs obey; and the heaviest, bitterest hour of my life was when I stepped into the boat to superintend the infliction of *five hundred lashes* on the back of poor Evan Evans, a half-idiot Welshman. The men on board were ordered up to the rigging, so that every person on board might see the whole operation. The Captain, taking off his hat, which was followed by all on board and in the boats, which were lying on their oars within earshot, then proceeded to read the sentence of the court martial. This effected, the Boatswain of the ship himself stepped into the launch; the blanket was removed from the culprit's shoulders, and he, the Boatswain, inflicted the first twelve lashes. The poor fellow screamed and groaned, and struggled; but all this, like the struggles of the dying sheep under the knife of the butcher, passed unheeded. The Boatswain returned on board, and two Boatswain's Mates came down and completed the number of fifty lashes. The blanket was immediately thrown over his shoulders; the people were piped down out of the rigging; I gave the word of command to shove off, and the boats which took the launch in tow began to row towards the Admiral's ship, the drummer striking up the 'Rogue's March'. The origin of this idea of having music in the boat was, no doubt, to drown the groans of the sufferer, lest the ordinary feelings of humanity should revolt against the barbarous practice of so mutilating the body of a fellow-creature. A quarter of an hour elapsed, during which the poor Welshman's groans mixed with the vile sounds of the drum, and we were again alongside of a large two-decked ship, the men of which exhibited themselves in the rigging on our approach. The towing-boats lay on their oars; we hooked on to the ship, and three stout fellows jumped into the launch, each with a new cat-o'-nine-tails ready in their hand, prepared to expend his strength on the back of the sufferer. The First Lieutenant of the ship came to the gangway. I handed him a copy of the sentence, which he read aloud to the crew, and the Boatswain's Mates removed their jackets ready for the infliction. The cats, as I have just observed, were new, their lashes or tails were made of strong white cord, just the thickness of a common quill, and the glue, or size, which is worked into the cord, had not been removed by soaking in water. They curdled up, and were literally almost as stiff as wires. As officer of the boat I objected to their being used for the first time on the poor man, and others were procured which had told many a tale of suffering. He looked at me gratefully, and said, in a weak voice, 'Thank ye, Sir'. The blanket was removed, and I observed the poor fellow shudder as the cold air struck the bleeding sore on his flesh; the next moment a heavy lash fell upon it, and his screams were agonising. He received a dozen lashes, and then began to cry for water. The punishment was stopped till he had taken some. He afterwards told me that at this period the thirst he felt became intense, and that each lash caused *a violent burning pain at his heart,* and seemed to fall like the blows of a large stick on his body, but that the flesh was too *dead* to feel that stinging smart he felt at first and when the flogging was renewed. *The same scene was repeated alongside two other ships,* with the like interval of misery to the sufferer and of disgust and vexation to myself. My reflections, indeed, were painful enough; for I utterly condemned myself for ever becoming one of the many unfeeling wretches who were so seriously occupied in torturing this poor wretch. Perhaps many others felt as disgusted as I did.

"*Two hundred lashes* had now been inflicted with a cat-o'-nine-tails, or EIGHTEEN HUNDRED STROKES with a cord of the thickness of a quill. The flesh, from the nape of the neck to below the shoulder-blades, was one deep purple mass, from which the blood oozed slowly at every stroke; a low groan escaped, and the flesh quivered with a sort of convulsive twitch, the eyes were closed, and the poor man began to faint. Water was administered, and pungent salts applied to his nostrils, which presently revived him in a slight degree. At this period I gave the Doctor a hint, by asking the Master-at-Arms, in a loud tone, how many lashes the prisoner had received. 'Two hundred lashes, exactly, Sir,' was the reply. I knew this very well, but it answered the

"STARTING" WITH A ROPE'S END

[Face page 130

purpose; for I saw the Doctor look at me, and then ordered him to be taken down. This was instantly done, and I ordered a fast boat, in the vicinity, to take him on board. The poor fellow was laid on some blankets in the stern-sheets, the sails hoisted, and in a quarter of an hour he was in his hammock in the sick berth, and the Doctors were engaged dressing his wounds. *Five weeks* after this I was again compelled to superintend a further mutilation of the back of poor Evans. This time he looked more miserable than ever; his frame was shrunken and his cheeks fallen, and, when his shirt was removed, *I observed that the wounds were barely healed over*, and that all about the sides of them there were dark discolourations, which indicated a state of disease. I was surprised that the medical men allowed him to be taken out again for punishment. The first six lashes, given by the arm of a herculean Irishman, brought the blood spurting out from his old wounds, *and then almost every blow brought away morsels of skin and flesh.** It would disgust the reader to detail this second flogging. Suffice it to say the poor fellow fainted when he had received another *one hundred and fifty lashes*; but, the Surgeon deeming him still capable of a little more punishment, another thirty-three were inflicted. A second faint and convulsive action of the eyes put an end to his torture. He was removed to the guard-ship, and, having taken *three hundred and eighteen lashes*, the remaining *one hundred and seventeen* were remitted by order of the Admiral. The ship sailed for a cruise in the North Sea; and some months after we heard that poor Evan Evans had been sent to the prison of the Marshalsea, where he fell into a consumption and ended his days. This was just what I expected : for it was clear that the first flogging had given the death-blow to the unfortunate Welshman.''

* There are many records showing that the *second* flogging invariably tore a *considerable* amount of flesh from the back. See *The Soldier's Wife*, quoted on p. 176.

K

In another account it is remarked : —

"I think that any argument against the system of torturing our seamen would have little effect with those readers whose minds are not made up to condemn it after perusing the above account, which is not in the slightest degree exaggerated; and I have no observation to make to those who have, like myself, already determined that it is as offensive to humanity as it is contrary to good policy."

In 1845, ten years after the Royal Commission had published its findings, the punishment of flogging round the Fleet had not yet been abolished, nor had it fallen into disuse. A court martial was held on board Her Majesty's ship "Minden", at Hong Kong, on the 5th January, 1844, to try two seamen for desertion, Rear-Admiral Sir Thomas Cochrane, C.B., being President. They were both found guilty, and each was sentenced to receive one hundred lashes.

On the morning of the 9th January the yellow flag, the signal of punishment, was displayed from the "Agincourt", the gun was fired, and fourteen boats, manned and armed, assembled to attend the punishment, which was executed in the usual barbarous manner. Notwithstanding the cruel character of the local Chinese punishments, the oriental inhabitants witnessed the exhibition with astonishment.

*   *   *   *

We now describe the summary punishments inflicted at the discretion of a Captain or Commanding Officer, "according to the laws and customs in such cases used at sea".

Flogging at the Gangway.—"This punishment," says Mr. M'Arthur, "is not so severe in the Army as in the Navy." He thinks one dozen of lashes applied to the bare back, by a Boatswain's Mate, furnished with a naval cat-o'-nine-tails, was equivalent to at least fifty lashes laid on by a Drummer with a military cat. This resulted not so much from the expertness of one executioner over another in the mode of laying on his lashes, as from the comparative thickness, hardness, and greater dimensions of the one instrument over the other, aided, no doubt, by the superior strength of the average Boatswain's Mate, when compared with that of an average Drummer, who was very often an adolescent. (See p. 168.)

The cat-o'-nine-tails in the Navy, according to Dr. William Burney, editor of an edition of *Falconer's Marine Dictionary* (1816), was composed of nine pieces of line, or cord, about half-a-yard long, fixed upon a piece of thick rope for a handle, and having three knots on each, at small intervals, the first being near the end.

By the regulations or usage of the Navy, in 1840, the Captain or Commander of every ship or vessel was authorised to inflict corporal punishment on any seaman, marine, or boy, by warrant under his hand; but until only ten years previously, he could order a man to the gangway to be flogged, without the formula of a warrant, whenever he thought it necessary to do so; and it was the usage of the Service to direct corporal punishment to be inflicted immediately, sometimes even by torchlight, or within a very brief period after an offence had been committed.

As an example of what was done in the summary way in the Navy, and, by inference, of what might be done with comparative impunity, we quote : —

"The late Admiral Cornwallis, who was commonly known in the Navy by the soubriquet of 'Blue Peter', came upon deck one day after dinner, and having found fault with something which was going on, he ordered the Lieutenant, who was the officer of the watch, to be flogged at the gangway, which was accordingly executed forthwith. Having been informed next day of the circumstance, it was with difficulty that he would credit the statement; but the exhibition of the officer's back was proof irresistible. The Admiral then took a cane, or staff, and, presenting it to the officer, said, 'I have disgraced you, and, as the only reparation I can make, I have to beg that you will lay in on my shoulders'. The officer declined doing so. Through the interest of the Admiral, the Lieutenant was soon appointed a lucrative situation, namely, to be a Collector of Excise in Scotland."

Some very judicious measures were adopted by the Admiralty, at the time of the Royal Commission, to abolish cruelty and restrain severity. Even as early as 1811, each Captain was directed to forward a quarterly report of punishments inflicted by his order, specifying the nature of the offence and the number of lashes; and after 1830, a custom was pursued of demanding special explanations—in all cases where the punishment had exceeded four dozen lashes—the warrant which the Captain issued before a man was punished, details of the nature of the offence, together with the evidence, and all other circumstances that were necessary to form a judgment of the case.

Another very important rule or usage, for restraining severe or inconsiderate punishments, was also adopted, being never to punish a man the same day on which an offence had been committed.

"A Commander of a man-of-war," writes Sir Robert Steele (*The Marine Officer, or Sketches of Service*, 1840), "can flog any man under his pennon, without even the mockery of a trial. I never think of this without my blood running alternately hot and cold within me. Take an instance of the result of the practice. It was the custom of Captain ———— of the A———— frigate, to flog the last man who lay in from the yard after reefing or handing sails; and it happened in a fresh gale that the captain of the foretop, the smartest and best seaman in the ship, after close-reefing the topsail, saw that the weather-earing was not properly hauled out. He was compelled, therefore, to lay out again to complete his work—having accomplished which, and recollecting the ignominy that inevitably awaited him, he threw himself from the yard-arm into the sea, and perished. But Retribution in this case took the monster singly to herself—the tyrant of the A——— was shot by one of his own people in the midst of battle, and the ill-fought badly defended frigate fell into the hands of the enemy."

"Some Captains of ships," says Sir Robert Steele, "kept their cats steeped in brine, to make their horrid punishments still more cruel." But this was comparatively unusual, and always reprobated.

The punishment of flogging at the gangway usually took place at half-past eleven a.m. (seven bells), and the infliction was executed in the following manner :—

"The carpenters are ordered to 'rig the gratings', that is, to fasten two gratings to the gangway, in such a manner that the culprit stands upon one, to which his feet are fastened, and leans forward against the other, to which his hands are secured. The officers appear in their cocked-hats and side-arms, and the marines are 'under arms', the ship's company stand on the opposite side of the deck. Near the gratings the delinquent stands, and close to him the Master-at-Arms, with his sword drawn. The Boatswain and Boatswain's Mates complete the line round him. One of the Mates is commonly standing ready with a cat-o'-nine-tails, half concealed under his jacket. These arrangements being made, the First Lieutenant reports the same to the Captain, who usually comes upon deck forthwith. The Captain sometimes addresses the crew, together with the culprit, and concludes by ordering him to 'strip'. When he has stripped the Captain says, 'Seize him up', and he is instantly fastened to the gratings. An article of war, relative to the punishment, is then read by the Captain, who concludes by ordering the Boatswain's Mate to 'give him a dozen'. While the article of war is being read, the officers, including the midshipmen, stand uncovered. The punisher, who is usually a powerful man, applies the cat slowly, and apparently with all his strength. It would appear that in some ships a Serjeant of Marines was employed to reckon the lashes, and regulate the time of infliction, by means of a sand-glass of a quarter of a minute.

"At the conclusion of a dozen, another Boatswain's Mate is called, for the purpose of inflicting an equal number, and so on until the Captain suspends the punishment."

However severe flogging at the gangway obviously was, some delinquents were known to make a joke of it, apparently for the purpose of annoying the officer who ordered the infliction.

A seaman named Collins had received four dozen without a word, and the Captain nodded to the Master-at-Arms, saying, "Cast him off". Collins quietly turned his head towards his superior, and with an indescribable air of drollery said, "Thank ye, your Honour, thank ye; I was just a-dozing off to sleep". A suppressed laugh ran among the crew, and a look of rage from the Captain, was the effect of this sally; the latter ordering the Boatswain's Mate to give him two dozen more, "which, failing to move his stoicism, he was at length liberated".

An exception amongst seafaring officers was, as stated elsewhere, Captain Collingwood, who hated corporal punishment. He used to keep, in his own handwriting, a record of punishments he was *forced* to inflict by means of the lash. During five months his records show that he only had a dozen men bare their backs, and these received nominal sentences such as seven lashes "on Peter James for beating Stephen Shore, a poor, silly boy"; or nine lashes for John White, for stealing half-a-guinea; or twelve lashes to Joseph Ash for bringing liquor aboard; or six lashes for riotous behaviour.

In the story of his life, written not long after Collingwood's death, his biographer says that the punishments which he inflicted instead of the lash were "of many kinds, such as watering the grog, and other modes now happily general in the Navy. Among the rest was one which the men particularly dreaded; this was the ordering of any offender to be excluded from his mess, and be employed in every sort of extra duty; so that he was every moment liable to be ordered on deck for the meanest service, amid the laughter and jeers of the men and boys. Such an effect had this upon the sailors, that they have often declared that they would much prefer having three dozen lashes".

Nowadays, extra duty and the doing of mean little jobs are every-day punishments in H.M. Forces, and flogging is no more. Doubtless when "men were men" the idea of being sent round a ship or parade ground collecting little bits of paper and odd stones was looked on as a worse disgrace than flogging—which, indeed, it still is to many. Hundreds are deprived of their liberty for weeks and months at a time, and each week made to do silly jobs, unnecessary except for the purposes of humiliation, the more modern form of "psychological punishment", now that the whip is "obsolete". Unfortunately, such "humiliation" and degradation of human dignity is as much taken for granted as flogging was years ago.

OFFICIAL FORMS REGARDING CORPORAL PUNISHMENT
AND THE CARRYING OUT THEREOF

Below are samples of Orders and Correspondence giving a typical slant on official procedure, 1770-1830 (approx.) : —

Orders for carrying corporal punishment into execution.
"To the Captain of the Flag ship. By etc.

"A court martial, held the 23rd instant, having sentenced Robert Hobday to receive three hundred lashes on his bare back with a cat-o'-nine-tails, alongside of such of H.M.'s ships and vessels at this port, at such times, and in such proportions as shall be directed by the Commanding Officer of the said ships and vessels for the time being.

"You are hereby required and directed to hoist a

yellow flag at the foretop mast-head of H.M. ship under
your command, and fire a gun at nine o'clock to-morrow
morning, as a signal for the boats of the Fleet to assemble
alongside of H.M.'s ship 'Wilton', to attend the said
punishment."
*"To the Captains and Commanders of the other ships
and vessels. Memoranda* : —
    "When the signal for the punishment is made
to-morrow morning, you are to send a Lieutenant with
a boat manned and armed from the ship under your
command to H.M.'s ship, 'Wilton', in order to attend
the punishment of Robert Hobday, pursuant to the
sentence of a court martial.
To the respective Captains, etc. Spithead."
    "To the Commander of the ship to which the prisoner
belongs : A court martial held on the 12th inst. on
board His Majesty's ship 'Albion' for the trial of B. B.,
a seaman belonging to the ship you command, having
sentenced him to receive three hundred lashes on his
bare back, with a cat-o'-nine-tails, alongside such of
H.M.'s ships and vessels in the port, at such times and
in such proportions as shall be directed by the Commanding Officers of the said ships and vessels, for the
time being; you are hereby required and directed when
the signal is made for this purpose aboard the 'Albion'
to-morrow morning, or the first favourable day afterwards (Sundays excepted), to cause one of the Lieutenants of the ship you command to attend and see the said
sentence put in execution, by the said B. B. receiving
twenty lashes alongside such of H.M.'s ships named in
the margin. (The ship's name to which the prisoner
belongs is always to be put in the margin with the others;
but in case the number should not fall even, he is to
receive the odd lashes over on board his own ship and
the words in the order are as follows, 'and alongside the
ship you command', you are to cause him to receive
'twenty-five, or more, or less, lashes'.) And you will
receive herewith a copy of the sentence, to be publicly

read by the Provost Marshal alongside each ship respectively."

Right Hon. Capt. Barrington, "Albion".

Given, etc.

R. SPRY.

(*Section 2, to the above*) : —

"Whereas I have, by an order of this date directed you to cause one of the Lieutenants of H.M. ship under your command to see the sentence of a court martial, on B. B. belonging to the same ship, put in execution : But as I would not have more of the said punishment inflicted on him, at one time, than he is able to bear, and as the Lieutenant may not be a proper judge of the prisoner's case, you are hereby required and directed to cause the Surgeon of the said ship to attend in the boat with the Lieutenant for that purpose, as well as one of his mates, in the long-boat, with the prisoner and you are to give the Lieutenant directions to stop the punishment till further orders, when the Surgeon shall give it as his opinion, that he cannot bear any more with safety, and return on board with the prisoner."

Order to the Provost Marshal : —

"Having ordered the sentence of the court martial on William Evans, the prisoner in your charge, to be put in execution next Thursday morning, or the first favourable day afterwards (Sunday excepted) : you are hereby required and directed to attend with him on board H.M.'s ship 'Albion', for that purpose, whenever the signal shall be made aboard the 'Ocean'; and when the said prisoner shall have received the whole of the punishment adjudged him, you are to release and deliver him to the Commanding Officer of the 'Albion'."

Given, etc.

To Mr. J. G., Provost Marshal.

To remit punishment : —

Admiralty Office, 17th May, 1780.

"Sir, I have communicated to my Lords Commissioners of the Admiralty your letter of yesterday's date, informing them that as the two seamen, named in the margin, had been sentenced by a court martial to receive five hundred lashes for mutinous behaviour on board the 'Invincible', you had excused one-half of the punishment to be inflicted upon them, and recommending them, for the reasons therein mentioned, as objects deserving their Lordships' pardon; in return, I am commanded by their Lordships to signify their direction to you to remit the remainder of their punishment."

PHILIP STEPHENS.

To Admiral Sir Thomas Tye.

CHAPTER FIVE

THE ROYAL MARINES AND THE MERCHANT NAVY

I

The Marine Corps was raised as a Force under the Admiralty in 1755, and very soon started to acquire a tradition and history all its own.

As far as corporal punishment is concerned, the Marine Corps was, very naturally, under the discipline of the Royal Navy, subject to the same courts martial on board ship as were the sailors proper and subject to the same punishments and sentences.

In 1800 a Lieutenant-General of the Royal Marines, was accused on charges brought by an infamous informer. It appears in the trial that George Jewson, the accuser, was some-time Sergeant of Marines under the General's command at Chatham, and was employed by a Deputy-Paymaster as a Clerk in the squad office; where he worked till September, 1800, at which date he deserted, taking with him £800 of public money. However, he was overtaken at Liverpool at the point of embarking for America. He was tried at a General Court Martial and sentenced to receive eight hundred lashes, to be drummed out of the barracks, and through the town, with a halter round his neck. At first glance, it would seem that the Sergeant received one lash for every pound he had stolen, plus the other indignities for having falsely accused his General. It is to be noted that this was a crime committed by a member of the Marines while on land, tried and the punishment executed on land.

As late as 1867 Sergeant-Major Lowe, of the Royal Marines, talking of the 1830's, told in an interview how he had spent his life from boyhood in the barracks and had frequently seen twenty men in a morning receive five hundred lashes each by a drum-head court martial for slight offences while on active service. At sea, however, though probably the lashes were each laid on more heavily, the amount would have been never more than a quarter as much. Sergeant-Major Lowe also tells our informant that he had often witnessed the punishment of *Back-Boards*, and those offenders not cured of unsoldierly posture by this punishment were lashed to a ladder for many hours at a stretch, a similar punishment being often applied to "Radicals".

Since the Marines were part of the Navy, the reader can take it that their punishments followed a similar pattern up to the days of final abolition of corporal punishment by flogging.

II

Not very much has been written about the merchant navy of these isles with regard to corporal punishment. It is certain that most of the punishments inflicted in the Royal Navy were never used on the ships owned by such commercial undertakings as the East India Company.

In privately-owned ships trading between the countries of the world, the Captain was, as now, the supreme head, and his word alone was law.

Despite this, distressing events were continually taking place aboard merchant ships, putting the passengers in fear of their lives and possessions.

The Captains of such vessels had no legal power to whip the crew, and the crew, aware of this fact, often played havoc, with many an unhappy result.

Although this book deals primarily with the Forces under the Crown, the merchant navy has become so allied in most people's minds to the Royal Navy, largely due to the wars in which that service has so often played an indispensable and heroic part, that we think it necessary and of interest to outline the state of the merchant service as it used to be.

In 1830, Christopher Biden wrote a book which he called, *Subordination contrasted with Insubordination: or a view of the Necessity for passing a Law establishing an efficient naval discipline on board ships in the Merchant Service,* to which we are indebted for the following : —

Hardly a ship went to sea without imposters on board, some of whom had been discharged as incurable from hospitals, others with forged certificates. These stirred up mutiny aboard, *often with the carefully premeditated intention of claiming damages in civilian courts on their return to England, for having been "illegally punished" at sea.* Frequently, as in the case argued before Lord Stowell in the Admiralty Court, where Commanders of East Indiamen were charged with having illegally flogged their crew, the Commanders were acquitted.

Among the numerous attempts to extort money from Commanders, Captain Younghusband, of the "Lord Castlereagh", presents an example worth attention. On the passage from Bengal, a seaman named Campbell, attempted to rescue his shipmate, Wilson, about to be punished at the gangway, and urged others to follow his example. Captain Younghusband, with his officers, seized Campbell, who, with eleven others, were made an example at the gangway. Prompt action on this occasion stopped what might have developed into a nasty situation. On the return to England, Campbell prosecuted the Captain. Most of the Captain's witnesses were absent, and perjury was committed by the plaintiff's witnesses. The Captain was acquitted, but the case cost him £165 from his private purse.

A Captain Driver reported, "When I commanded the 'Clyde' in the free trade, one of the seamen stabbed my chief mate. I considered myself justified in flogging him; but one of the rascals attempted to rescue this bloodthirsty villain. To preserve anything like discipline I flogged him also, but only inflicted eight lashes.

However, on my arrival in England, I had one of those hornets after me, called proctors. I employed another who said, if I gained the suit, the expenses would be heavy; and by his advice, I gave the informer ten pounds : this I did, which, in reality, is paying a man for behaving ill, and rewarding a fellow for attempting to rescue an assassin".

An interesting item of international law at that time comes to light with the conclusion of the above story, for on arrival of the ship at Batavia, the Captain of the English ship had the worst characters brought aboard the Dutch guard-ship, where the Captain of the Dutchman had the ringleader stripped, tied up, and given three dozen lashes.

On another occasion, a mild and kind officer was driven to whipping a grossly disobedient seaman. The crew rushed to rescue him, whereupon the officer went amongst the crew with a loaded pistol. The crew calmed down, and the cat was brought into use. Before evening the crew were abusing their whipped shipmate for being ungrateful to a good officer.

At an Indian post the ship's company were indulged by an allowance of two pints of grog instead of the usual one. They shouted for more, and the chief mate went ashore and informed the Captain of the affair. The Captain went aboard with a military guard to take the ringleaders ashore. But the ringleaders said the ship was outside the limit for this procedure. The Captain dined later with the Marquis of Hastings, and asked him to go aboard to flog the worst characters. He clapped the eight ringleaders in irons and addressed the rest. Whilst speaking, the prisoners escaped and called upon their mates to stand by them. After a scuffle, the Captain and his officers seized five of the men, three jumped into a sloop alongside and deserted. They were captured and returned in time to see the other five receive their flogging.

These cases are interesting because they throw considerable light upon the tough characters who helped build up our modern merchant service. It is inconceivable that such conduct could happen in this day and age. With this belief we draw the attention of the reader to the merchantman which was held up by a pirate vessel. The men refused to fight and chance losing a leg, or arm, with no certainty of pension, or reward. The Captain called upon them, saying it would be better to lose a limb and fight, rather than face the certainty of having their throats cut. The end of the story is that the merchant ship turned away and did not attack. She, in turn, was not attacked, and we must presume that the affair ended there.

In 1823, aboard an East Indiaman, a Court of Inquiry was held upon Seaman Jones for answering back an officer in an insolent manner. He was found deserving of punishment. The chief mate went to the Captain's cabin to report that he believed there would be resistance. The Captain went on deck and ordered the men from one side of the ship to the other. They refused. The Captain went up to the ringleader and tried to drag him aft by the collar. A scuffle ensued, and the Captain drew his sword and cut the man down. One of the others received a cut wrist as he was about to knock down the Captain. The man, Jones, was seized up and given twenty-five lashes.

1787. The men refused to wash decks when told to do so by the boatswain. The previous day a seaman had been put in irons for mutinous behaviour. On repeating the order they did as they were told. But at 1 p.m. they rushed on deck with marline-spikes and a variety of weapons. They threatened to murder any man who stopped them rescuing the prisoner below. They released the prisoner and knocked down the third mate with a marline-spike. The officers armed themselves, and the men, seeing this, took possession of the gun-deck, secured the ports, knocked away the ladders, broke open the fore-scuttle, pointed the two bow guns aft, and had pokers and bolts in the fire to serve for matches. They threatened to blow up the ship rather than be taken prisoner. Finding the boats from different ships were approaching, officers, petty officers and mechanics were ordered to arm themselves. They cleared the upper deck in less than two minutes, and the mutineers were made prisoners. One week later nine of the mutineers were punished according to their sentences. Two were flogged round the Fleet, two received five dozen lashes each, three received three dozen lashes, and two were given two dozen.

Of the above story it is interesting to note that the men punished were sent to different ships to receive their floggings, the better to show an example to the other men. The senior officer concerned held a full Court of Inquiry, before awarding punishment. The Captain of the mutinous ship was sent to England for trial. He was quite properly acquitted, and additionally complimented on his handling of the situation. His law expenses were paid for by the Court of Directors.

In 1818, a mutiny broke out aboard a ship about to sail to the East.

In an evolution an accident took place to the sail; the second mate picked out the men who had been at fault and ordered them to be "started". This caused discontent amongst the other men, and some of them used insolent and threatening language to the chief and second mates. They were clapped in irons, which caused further discontent. The Captain came aboard at night and was informed of the events, and after a short investigation hands were turned out for punishment. The scene must have been very impressive. The lanterns were brought out, the crew on deck, and one of the prisoners brought up. His shirt was pulled from his back and he was tied by hands and ankles to the grating. The crew was murmuring as the Captain made a short speech to them and the boatswain drew the cat

COBBING

[Face page 146

through his fingers. He was ordered to lay on the first cut, the prisoner tensed the muscles of his back, the skin became taut . . . and a volley of belaying pins, iron bolts and bits of wood came flying amongst the officers. The men attempted to rush the officers, who quickly armed themselves. The petty officers took the side of the officers, and the man, already tied up, was flogged. He was cut down, and the second prisoner tied up. Immediately, from the other side of the ship came another volley of missiles . . . But the sight of the determined officers soon quietened them down and on this occasion one of the ringleaders was caught and seized up. Without further ado, he was given six dozen lashes across his back. Five more were punished the same way.

Another unusual incident in the merchant navy took place in 1825. On this occasion an ordinary seaman was given over to the ship's company for punishment. His crime : Open mutinous conduct to the chief mate. He was cobbed, which meant that he was held down by several men whilst volunteers beat him on the buttocks with a cane or a rope's end. In the Navy these cobbings were very severe, often as many as three hundred strokes being given whilst the cobbed man writhed in the strong grip of his shipmates. It has frequently been contended that corporal punishment on the fleshy part of the thighs is more painful than on the back, but in cobbing, the man was seldom stripped, though often made to wear a garment of extra thin material.

In the agitation of the 1820's for some kind of discipline in merchant ships, an argument was advanced in a pamphlet that, "ninety-nine out of an hundred professional men will agree that the terror and disgrace of flogging is the truest preventive to crime, and the best and safest alternative that can be resorted to, in order to preserve discipline". The author, an authority on matters maritime, and himself a sailor, goes on to say, "I declare I have never known one instance of a man's

L

spirit being broken, his health injured, or even his services lost for more than one day, and even that not above
twice, during the whole of my experience at sea; and the
horrible stories about flogging are intended to distort
truth and justice, and to mislead persons whose minds
are imbued with ready beliefs in all subjects, however
false or exaggerated".

Even American Congress is brought into the urgings
for the new law, as witness this paragraph : "The old
method of punishing offenders by flogging has been
abolished in the American army, by an act of Congress,
dated 16th May, 1812 . . . ever since, so far as I have been
able to learn, from inquiries in every part of the Union,
the discipline of the troops has been gradually declining
. . . the soldiers also appeared discontented with the
great variety of other punishments . . . it has not been
proposed by the Americans to tamper in the same
dangerous way with their Navy, and the consequent
difference between the two services is one of the most
striking things I ever saw".

There follows a telling argument which, slightly
altered, applies (because of the great improvement in
"creature comforts") to our prisons to-day even more
than it did in the early 1800's. "Solitary confinement
. . . is nothing at all . . . to a person accustomed to hard
labour. These men are so little accustomed to the
independent exercise of their own thoughts, that we
expect a great deal too much if we expect them to turn
their confinement to good account. He will brood over
his sentence, and become vindictive . . ."

In 1830, *The Times* newspaper printed portions of a
pamphlet about the shocking state of seamen in the
East India Company's service, and the result was a
flood of letters condemning that company's method of
paying, feeding, and generally treating (or mistreating)
its sailors. On October 30th *The Times* ended the
correspondence with the following : "We find from
communications that we have received from several

quarters, that some statements which have lately appeared in this paper respecting punishments in the navy, and particularly on board 'The Howe', when commanded twenty-five years ago, by a gallant admiral, now high in office, are the same as were made and refuted in the House of Commons in the year 1825. The number and respectability of those communications, as well as our own enquiries, have satisfied us; and we therefore feel in candour bound to state our conviction, that these charges, and the reproductions of them, of which our columns have inadvertently become the channel, are wholly unfounded, and, as we see reason to believe, arise from the malice of one individual, from whose pamphlets we quoted them".

EXTRACTS FROM SHIPS' LOGS

In the Naval Journals, between the years 1794 and 1812, the following are reproduced because of their unconventionality:—

Names of Persons Tried	Ships or Stations	Nature of Charges or Offences	Purport of Sentences
Harris, R.	H.M.S. "Bedford" (Seaman).	Disobedience of orders.	To be tied over a *bar* and there to be whipped 48 times over his breech.
Marriott, A. Lloyd, W.	H.M.S. "Couper" (Boy Seamen).	Coming on board late.	Each to be tied over a capstan bar and there each to receive 24 lashes of a cane whip upon their bared posteriors.
Hassall, W.	H.M.S. "Court" (Seaman).	Ignoring of Orders.	To be stripped and tied to a ladder and to receive five dozen lashes alternately on his legs and breech.
Anderson, A.	H.M.S. "Wilton" (Seaman).	For being part drunk.	To be tied flat to a bench and to receive 5 dozen lashes with a rope's end on his posterior.
Warburton, R.	H.M.S. "Vernon" (Seaman).	For not coming aboard.	He shall be tied with his arms above his head and shall receive 24 lashes wherever they shall fall.
Marshall, G.	H.M.S. "Glasgow" (Marine).	For insolence to his Officer.	To be tied over a gun and there to receive 4 dozen lashes with a cat-o'-nine-tails on his bare ———.
Stephens, B.	H.M.S. "Eagle" (Seaman).	Drunkenness on two occasions.	To be *cobbed* by 3 of the ship's crew after he has been secured over a *bar*, but not on his *bare* breech.
Whitford, J. Kelly, L.	Portsmouth. Chatham (Seamen).	Stealing tobacco and refusing orders.	They shall both be tied to two gratings and shall each receive 50 lashes on the bare breech with a cat-o'-nine-tails.

150

A chronological list of some Trials by Naval Courts Martial under the then existing Laws; specifying the Nature of Charges and Offences, and the Purport of Sentences. The whole exhibiting an authentic Scale of Military Crimes and Punishments Extracted from the Admiralty Records.

When Tried	Names of Persons Tried	Qualities	Ships	Nature of Charges or Offences	How Proved	Purport of Sentences
May 1, 1756.	Thomas Golden.	Seaman.	"Centurion".	Theft and desertion from the hospital.	Fully.	Three hundred and fifty lashes.
Sept. 9, 1756.	James Spencer.	Boatswain's Mate.	"Nottingham".	Sodomy.	Proved.	Twenty lashes alongside of each ship in Halifax harbour.
Oct. 10, 1756.	Thomas Fuller.	Midshipman.	"Chichester".	Great misbehaviour to the Lieutenant when in search of deserters.	Fully.	Degraded from the station of a midshipman, rendered incapable of receiving any preferment, and to be towed standing up in a boat, with his hands tied up to the sheers, and his sentence read alongside of each ship in Halifax harbour.
Feb. 21, 1757.	Francis French.	Midshipman.	"Defiance".	Sodomitical practices.	Uncleanliness and scandalous actions.	Three hundred lashes with a halter round his neck and rendered incapable of serving.
Feb. 26, 1757.	Wm. Burling.	Marine.	"Eagle".	Desertion.	Fully.	Two hundred lashes.
April 27, 1757.	William Ruffel.	Midshipman.	"Prince George".	Desertion.	Fully.	Turned before the mast and received 200 lashes with a halter round his neck.
May 14, 1757.	William Hobbs, Wm. Wifeman, Thomas Grey.	Seamen.	"Iris". "St. George".	Desertion.	Fully.	Five hundred lashes with a cat-o'-nine-tails, to be divided at three different times alongside of such ships, etc.

151

When Tried	Names of Persons Tried	Qualities	Ships	Nature of Charges or Offences	How Proved	Purport of Sentences
Sept. 14, 1757.	James Mansfield.	Seaman.	"Union".	Stealing £19 16s. from another seaman.	Proved.	Four hundred lashes with a cat-o'-nine-tails.
Jan. 21, 1758.	Fifteen Men.	Seamen.	"Namur".	Desertion.	Fully.	To suffer death.
	Hugh Jackson.	Seaman.		Suspected of having written an injurious letter respecting Capt. Arbuthnot, signed All Hands.	Proved.	Three hundred lashes.
Jan. 2, 1759.	Richard Bird.	Seaman.	"Norwich".	Attempting to desert by swimming on shore the 14th Nov., 1758.	Proved to have been attempted on 15th Nov.	Acquitted.
Jan. 22, 1759.	James Aldred.	Seaman.	"York".	Attempting to rescue a man belonging to the "Medway"; then in possession of Lieut. Martin by threats and knocking him down.	Fully.	Four hundred lashes.
May 26, 1759.	William Lewis.	Marine.	"Griffin".	Theft.	Fully.	Five hundred lashes.
Aug. 6, 1759.	John Curtis, John Murphy.	Seamen.	"Portland".	Desertion.	Fully.	To suffer death.
Aug. 14, 1759.	John Gazard.	Seaman.	"Magnamime".	Refusing to obey a midshipman's orders.	Fully.	Three hundred lashes at two distinct times.
June 13, 1760.	James Collins.	Seaman.	"Royal Ann".	Mutiny and drawing knife against the Master-at-Arms.	Fully.	Five hundred lashes.
Dec. 12, 1760.	Robert Hook.	Boatswain.	"Lyme."	Embezzlement of stores.	Proved.	Dismissed the Service.
June 19, 1761.	John Rookey.	Seaman.	"Unicorn".	Mutinous and riotous behaviour, and extremely disorderly during the ship's voyage.	Proved.	Thirty lashes alongside of each ship in commission at the port, and 12 months' confinement in the Marshalsea.

When Tried	Names of Persons Tried	Qualities	Ships	Nature of Charges or Offences	How Proved	Purport of Sentences
Nov. 8, 1761.	Joseph Stout.	Boatswain's Mate.	"Weazel".	Disobeying the master's mate's orders, and taking him by the collar.	Partly.	Twelve lashes alongside of each King's ship in Lisbon River.
Nov. 10, 1761.	John Woodward.	Seaman.	"Jason".	Mutiny and desertion.	Desertion proved, sedition partly.	Twelve lashes alongside of each ship in commission at the port, and 12 months' imprisonment in the Marshalsea.
Mar. 26, 1762.	Isaac Portion, Rob. Taylor.	Seamen.	"Terrible".	Theft and robberies in Portsmouth harbour.	Fully.	Each twenty lashes alongside of each ship in commission in Portsmouth harbour.
Mar. 31, 1762.	Mariot Arbuthnot.	Captain.	"Gaurland".	Twenty charges exhibited by the purser.	Frivolous and malicious except one, viz. carrying women to sea.	Reprimanded.
Aug. 27, 1762.	Alex Whitfield.	Lieut. Marines.	"Quebec".	Drunkenness and scandalous behaviour.	Fully.	Dismissed the Service, and rendered incapable of serving as an officer.
Oct. 12, 1762.	John Bryan, John Johnson, and John Brown.	Seamen.	"Ocean".	Feloniously stealing a purse of thirty-six guineas belonging to another man of the ship.	In part.	The first to run the gauntlet on board the said ship once, the second three times, and the last offender four times.
Oct. 23, 1762.	Robert Garbett.	Boatswain.	"Spy", Sloop.	For attempting to commit sodomitical practices.	In part.	Dismissed the Service, and to be publicly drummed on shore with general marks of ignominy.
Nov. 3, 1762.	Richard Chilton.	Seaman.	"Seahorse".	Guilty of indecent practices.	Fully.	To be hanged.

153

When Tried	Names of Persons Tried	Qualities	Ships	Nature of Charges or Offences	How Proved	Purport of Sentences
Oct. 29, 1755.	Tom Edwards.	Seaman.	"Phoenix".	Breaking into the State Room and robbing a box of a quantity of money.	Fully.	To suffer death.
Dec 4, 1765.	Samuel Boyd.	Gunner.	"Greyhound".	Behaving with contempt to his Captain.	Fully.	Mulcted of one year's pay and reprimanded.
May 25, 1767.	Walter Dees.	Gunner.	"Aeolus".	Getting drunk and beating the midshipman.	Fully.	Dismissed the Service.
Dec. 22, 1770.	Jeremiah Styles.	Seaman.	"Spy", Sloop.	Throwing a shot at Lieut. A. Pye Molloy, and striking him therewith.	Partly.	Eighty lashes.
July 5, 1771.	Richard Jones.	Purser.	"Resolution".	Scandalous and indecent behaviour, and fraudulent practices.	Fully.	Dismissed the Service, and mulcted of all the pay due to him.
Jan. 10, 1775.	William Malby.	Captain.	"Glasgow".	On a charge exhibited by the gunner for cruelty and oppression.	In part.	Dismissed from the command of His Majesty's ship "Glasgow".
Feb. 21, 1777.	Mr. John Brown, Officers and crew.	Lieut. and Commander.	"Tryal".	Having lost and burnt the "Tryal" Schooner.	Fully.	The Lieutenant and Commander dismissed from His Majesty's Service, and likewise Leonard Mosey, master of the said sloop.
Jan. 6, 1778.	W. A. Halsted.	Captain.	"Jersey".	Injustice, and not behaving as an officer and gentleman.	Partly.	Admonished by the court; and other parts of the charges found to be malicious, ill-founded, and unsupported by evidence.

154

When Tried	Names of Persons Tried	Qualities	Ships	Nature of Charges or Offences	How Proved	Purport of Sentences
April 27, 1778.	— Brown.	Boatswain.	"Launceston".	Indecent behaviour and disobedience of orders.	Proved.	Dismissed the ship.
Dec. 30, 1778.	Benj. Brots.	Serj. Marines.	"Shrewsbury".	Theft, and other infamous behaviour.	Fully.	Reduced to a private, and to receive two hundred lashes.
Dec. 30, 1780.	Twenty-three.	Seamen and Marines.	Different Ships.	Desertion.	Proved.	From fifty to five hundred lashes.
Jan. 18, 1781.	Wm. Brannon.	Seaman.	"Ajax".	For mutinous behaviour.	Fully proved.	Five hundred lashes.
July 25, 1781.	Sam. Wickham.	2nd Lieut.	"Lizard".	Contempt and disrespect to the Captain on the quarter-deck.	Proved.	Dismissed His Majesty's Service.
Dec. 24, 1782.	Thirty men.	Seamen.	Different Ships.	Desertion, drunkenness, etc.	Proved.	Fifty to five hundred lashes.
Aug. 18, 1783.	John Mitchell.	Seaman.	"Chaser".	Writing a mutinous and seditious letter.	Fully proved.	To be hanged.
Nov. 8, 1783.	John Burn and Arthur Rice.	Seamen.	"Adamant".	Mutiny.	Proved.	Six hundred lashes.
April 29, 1784.	John Cumming.	Seaman.	"Trusty".	Striking Daniel Ford, Boatswain of the said ship.	Proved.	To be hanged at the fore yard-arm.
July 30, 1792.	James Allen.	Clerk.	"Medusa".	Insolent and mutinous behaviour.	Proved.	Broke and rendered incapable of ever serving again, and to receive 100 lashes.
April 6, 1793.	Rob. Brown, John Gordon.	Pilots.	"Fox".	Running the said ship on the Gunfleet Sand.	Proved.	Both rendered disqualified from hereafter taking charge of any of His Majesty's ships, and to be imprisoned six calendar months in the Marshalsea.

Year	Names of Persons Tried	Qualities	Ships	Nature of Charges or Offences	Purport of Sentences
1829.	T. Lapham.	Marine.	"Magnificent".	Disobedience of orders and contempt to his superior officer.	100 lashes, to be mulcted of all pay due to him, and to forfeit and lose all claims of every description which he may be entitled to by reason of his previous servitude.
1829.	J. Bathie, J. Lada, W. Scott.	Seamen.	"Cruizer".	Desertion.	150 lashes each.
1830.	H. M'Vea.	Marine.	"Winchester".	Theft, and an attempt to desert.	100 lashes.
1830.	W. Mitchell.	Seaman.	"Champion".	Attempting to desert.	50 lashes.
1831.	J. Horsley.	Marine.	"Nimble".	For a breach of the 2nd, 19th, 22nd, 23rd, and 27th Articles of War.	100 lashes and lose three years time.
1831.	F. Thomas.	Seaman.	"Firefly".	Mutinous and insulting language towards Lieut. J. H. M'Donnell, commanding the "Firefly".	50 lashes, to be mulcted of all pay due to him, and discharged from the Service.
1835.	J. Pascoe. T. Barnett. W. Hawkes. J. Hilborn. C. Webber. G. Tarm, J. Lodge.	Seaman. Marine. Marine. Marine. Marine. Seamen.	"Caledonia".	For a breach of the 19th Article of War.	T. Barnett acquitted. J. Pascoe, 60 lashes. W. Hawkes and J. Hilborn, 100 lashes each, and to be discharged with disgrace from the Service; and C. Webber, 80 lashes.
1839.		Seamen.	"Castor".	Mutinous and contemptuous behaviour.	100 lashes each round the Fleet or alongside H.M.S. "Castor"; G. Tarm to be imprisoned one year and J. Lodge six months in the Marshalsea.
1841.	W. Ansfield.	Marine.	"Cambridge".	Disobedience of orders, making use of threatening and mutinous language.	48 lashes.
1842.	J. Bingham.	Marine.	"Pickle".	Leaving his post while in charge of prisoners.	60 lashes.

Year	Names of Persons Tried	Qualities	Ships	Nature of Charges or Offences	Purport of Sentences
1842.	W. Avery.	Marine.	—	For behaving in a mutinous manner to his Commanding Officer when on duty at the residence of the British Consul at Carthagena.	50 lashes.
1842.	S. Sheep, B. Bass.	Seamen.	"Calcutta".	Gross indecency.	48 lashes each, drummed round the squadron, imprisoned for twelve calendar months, and discharged from the Service with disgrace.
1842.	S. Cowker, E. Keys, J. Metham, N. Division. J. E. Ball.	Seamen.	"Curlew".	Signing a mutinous document called a "round robin", and from deserting from the cutter of the said ship while on duty at Rio de Janeiro.	S. Cowker and E. Keys, 48 lashes each. J. Metham, 72 lashes, *two weeks' solitary confinement*, and discharged from the Service with disgrace. J. Russell, 48 lashes, *and one week's solitary confinement.* N. Division and J. E. Ball, 36 lashes each.
1843.	The Honourable Elliott.	Boy 1st Class. Boy 2nd Class. Captain, C.G.S.B.	"Spartan".	Flogging a midshipman.	From the extraordinary and parental anxiety manifested by the prisoner on all occasions for the well-doing and general instruction of all the young gentlemen on board his ship, and looking at the circumstances under which the punishment was inflicted, only severely reprimanded.
1843.	N. Nedwick.	Marine.	"Ocean".	Desertion.	48 lashes and to be imprisoned six calendar months.
1844.	C. Meeking, H. Gardener.	Seamen.	"Minden".	Desertion.	100 lashes each.
1844.	H. Bartlett.	Seaman.	"Illustrious".	Striking Robert M'Clarty, captain of the forecastle of that ship.	50 lashes, to be imprisoned for the space of six months, and to be mulcted of all pay due to him for the period of his servitude on board the "Illustrious".

Year	Names of Persons Tried.	Qualities	Ships	Nature of Charges or Offences	Purport of Sentences
1844.	J. Randolph.	Seaman.	"Alecto".	Theft.	50 lashes, to be mulcted of six months' pay, and discharged, with disgrace, from the Service.
1845.	J. Hitchcock.	Marine.	"Alfred".	Insubordination.	36 lashes, and to be imprisoned.
1847.	T. K. Beatty.	Assistant Surgeon.	"Daphne".	Disrespectful language to the Surgeon.	80 lashes.
1847.	J. Savage.	Seaman.	"St. Vincent".	Desertion.	50 lashes, and to be imprisoned in Her Majesty's Gaol at Winchester for twelve months *and kept to hard labour*.
1847.	J. Smith.	Seaman.	"Recruit".	Desertion.	50 lashes, to forfeit all pay due to him, and to be imprisoned twelve months *and kept to hard labour*.
1848.	J. Warren.	Boatswain.	"Andromeda".	For refusing to inflict corporal punishment lawfully ordered on a seaman.	Dismissed the Service.

BOOK III

EXTRACTS FROM CERTAIN CONTEMPORARY ACCOUNTS

In order to paint as graphic a picture as possible of life in and out of the armed forces in the early nineteenth century we quote a number of excerpts from works which, we believe, will provide the reader with an accurate and realistic background to the subject of this work.

I

First, a few excerpts from *The Memoirs of John Shipp*, who entered the Army as a boy soldier of ten, in 1795, and who published his reminiscences in 1832 : —

"During the first eight years of my military career, it was my painful duty to inflict, some three times a week, the punishment which I so heartily deprecate.

"When I was orderly-officer of the main guard at Cawnpore, several men were condemned to be punished. Among the rest was a youth not more than twenty years of age. The morning on which the punishment was to be inflicted, I visited the prisoners early, and such was the change observable in this poor young fellow, from reflecting during the night on his approaching degradation, that he looked like one whose constitution had, in a few hours, undergone all the diseases incident to the country. His eyes were glassy and inexpressive, his cheeks sunk, and his deportment stooping and loose. Altogether he looked the very picture of woe, and his extreme dejection was so obvious, that I could not refrain from asking him if he was unwell. 'No,' replied he, 'but I am one of those who are to be flogged this morning,' and he wept bitterly. 'Come,

come,' said I (and it was as much as I dared say), 'Keep up your spirits; your extreme youth, and the fact that this is the first time you have been brought to a court martial, may probably obtain your pardon.' He shook his head, but said nothing in reply. I regret to be obliged to add that this poor fellow received a hundred and fifty lashes; and, from the day he was flogged until the period of his death, I can venture to assert that he was never two hours sober, and at last he died in the hospital from drunkenness . . .

"One wintry morn when the bleak wind whistled along the ranks of a regiment paraded to see corporal punishment inflicted, the Commanding Officer, with stentorian lungs pronounced the awful words, 'Strip, sir !' The morning was bitterly cold, the black clouds rolled along in quick succession and the weather altogether was such that the mere exposure of a man's naked body was of itself a severe punishment. The crime of this man was repeated drunkenness, of which he had undoubtedly been guilty.

"When the offender was tied, or rather hung up by the hands, his back from the intense cold and the effects of previous floggings exhibited a complete blue and black appearance. On the first lash the blood spurted out some yards. After he had received fifty his back from the neck to the waist was one continuous stream of blood. The sufferer flinched not a jot, neither did he utter a single murmur, but bore the whole of his punishment with a degree of indifference bordering upon insensibility, chewing all the while what I was afterwards informed was a piece of lead, or a bullet. When the poor fellow was taken down he staggered and fell to the ground. His legs and arms, owing to the intense cold and the long period they had remained in one position still continued distended and he was obliged to be conveyed to the hospital in a dooly, a kind of palanquin in which sick soldiers are carried. This unfortunate creature shortly afterwards shot himself in his barrack room in a sad state of intoxication and was borne to his solitary pit and hurled in like a dog. . .

"In the experimental corps in which I commenced my military career I recollect two boys being sentenced to be flogged for desertion. They were brothers and the elder was not more than thirteen years of age. They had deserted together and probably intended to go home, not much relishing their new mode of life. The elder boy was tied up first, and having received about *six dozen lashes* he was ordered down and it became the turn of his younger brother to occupy his place. Afflicted by the idea of what his little brother was about to suffer the senior boy begged in the most earnest manner that he might be permitted to take his brother's punishment, even though his own back was bruised and bleeding, protesting most solemnly that he was the sole cause of his desertion. When this was refused and the younger one was ordered to strip, the shrieks of the two rent the air. They flew into each other's arms and clung together in a sweet embrace of fraternal affection. And when they were torn asunder the tear of pity started to the eyes of all around. The little fellow received every lash to which he had been sentenced and in little more than a year after this there were not two greater reprobates or vagabonds in the whole corps. The elder boy soon died. Of the fate of the younger I cannot speak with certainty, but I think he was found drowned in Table Bay at the Cape of Good Hope."

Shipp describes a number of floggings he inflicted as a boy-Drummer, reported elsewhere in this history, and continues : —

"Have the advocates for the continuance of this barbarous system ever handled one of these savage instruments? *Have they ever poised the cat in their hands when clotted with a soldier's blood after punishment has been inflicted? If not, let me inform them that it has then almost weight enough to stun an ox, and requires the greatest exertion and dexterity in the*

Drummer to wield it. I have heard poor fellows declare that, in this state, it falls like a mass of lead upon their backs."

II

In the following digest of a novel published in 1850, the reader will find details of military corporal punishment which, because of its detailed realism, must have been drawn from eye-witness experience and accounts by the author. He had already published a dozen novels, and he was the founder of *Reynolds' News*, George W. M. Reynolds. (His paper was banned in the Army in 1850.)

"THE SOLDIER'S WIFE"

A digest of the novel by

GEORGE W. M. REYNOLDS

The scene is a typical village in the heart of the English countryside; down the cobbled street, at a steady jog-trot, rolls the carrier van which plies between different towns. From the van, on this lovely May night in 1828, steps a personage of impressive appearance, dressed in military uniform—a scarlet coat turned up with white on the tails, and blue on the cuffs and collar. He has a sword and a sash. The village baker insists he is a Sergeant, and that a Sergeant is higher than a General. But the cobbler assures the gathering crowd that a Sergeant is next to a Captain. But the baker, Mr. Bates, who knows everything, put them all to rights as to what a Sergeant really is. Then, stiff as a poker, and looking as if there were no elasticity in his body, the Sergeant walks into the local inn.

Now the village is owned almost in its entirety by the squire who lives in a mansion overlooking it, and the squire has a son—a weedy, spoiled individual who has lived a life of ease and debauchery at Oxford University and is, at present, doing little else than that at the family mansion.

Date		N. of Comp.	NAMES	Quality.	For what Offence.
Day and Month	Year.				
10ᵗʰ September	1827	48	Joseph Cole	Pre?	For irregular and unsoldierlike Conduct in being deficient of part of his Necessaries —
10 September	1827	47	Edward Hill – –	Pre?	For irregular and unsoldierlike Conduct in being deficient of part of his Necessaries
10ᵗʰ September	1827	47	Edward Price – – –	Pric	For irregular and unsoldierlike Conduct in being absent three Nights and 6 days and making a Practice of absenting himself. —
14 Sept – – –	1827	47	Wᵐ Duffell – – –	Pte	For irregular and unsoldierlike Conduct Whilst on the chain Guard on the 14ᵗʰ instant
14 September –	1827	35	Robert Smith – –	Pte	For irregular and unsoldierlike Conduct in being deficient of part of his Necessaries breaking his Barrack Confinement and making a Practice of it
14ᵗʰ September	1827	75	Edward Gidlow	Pte	For irregular and unsoldierlike Conduct in Breaking his Barrack Confinement and being deficient of part of his Necessaries

PAGES FROM A COURT MARTIAL BOOK.

How Tried, by General or Regimental	Sentence.	Punishment.	REMARKS.	When Conf[irmed]
Regimental	200 Lashes	Carried into Effect 11 Sept. 1827	And further to be put under stoppages not exceeding the half his pay until the deficiency in his Necessaries be made good. —	9 Sept.
Regimental	One Months Solitary Confinem.t on Bread & Water	Carried into Effect	And further to be put under stoppages not exceeding the half his pay until the deficiency in his Necessaries be made good	9 Sept.
Regimental	50 Lashes and 14 days Solitary Confinement on Bread and Water	Carried into Effect		9 Sept.
Regimental	100 Lashes	Carried into Effect		11 Sept.
Regimental	300 Lashes and Drummed out	Received 200 Lashes	And further to be put under stoppages not exceeding half his pay 'till the deficiency in his Necessaries are made good	18 S.
Regimental	Three weeks Solitary Confinement on Bread & Water	Carried into Effect	And further to be put under stoppages not exceeding half his pay 'till the deficiency in his Necessaries are made good	14 Sept.

ROYAL MARINES, PLYMOUTH, 1827

On the morning of the day about which we write, the squire's son, whose name is Gerald, has met and has had a row with our hero, Frederick Lonsdale, whom we will now introduce into the story. Fred is a believer in the Rights of Man, and has not grovelled at Gerald's feet, nor touched his cap to the son of the village squire. Fred is tall, handsome, dark, of high courage and has what is currently known as "sex appeal". When Gerald tells Father about Fred, Father causes Fred to lose his job. That evening Fred meets his beloved, a simple and honest girl, Lucy. "Frederick—dear Frederick, something has occurred, you are unhappy."

"I cannot conceal it from you, beloved Lucy," answers the young man. "I have been insulted—cruelly insulted—almost trampled upon by one whom the accident of birth has made what the world calls my superior."

"Who has done this?" inquires Lucy, suddenly becoming painfully excited; and the tears start out upon the long dark lashes which shade her deep blue eyes.

"Gerald Redburn," returns Frederick. "When I think of what took place I am surprised that I restrained my hand from tearing him off his horse and spurning him at my feet. I should have done so perhaps; but miserable, enfeebled stripling as he is, it would have been a coward's blow on my part. And yet I was bitterly provoked!"

"Yes, dear Frederick, you must have been—you must have been—to talk thus and to feel so deeply too. Oh!" exclaims the generous-hearted and devoted girl, "what can I say—what can I do to console you? Ah! methinks if I had ever been so much provoked, yet that in your society I should experience a soothing solace." Then, as if she had said too much for maiden modesty, she drops her eyes, blushing deeply.

All of which helps to show what Lucy and Fred thought of one another.

But now we return to the inn, and the Sergeant is

M

taking his ease and a glass of ale in the saloon. Around him are collected the admiring villagers. The Sergeant has now admitted that he is in the village for the purpose of obtaining recruits for His Majesty's Army, and this announcement puts fear into the hearts of those present. They try to ask questions, but the astute Sergeant wards them off and never stops talking. The barber sticks to his points, and the Sergeant flatters him and appoints him his perfumer and hairdresser.

"Ah, I know very well what thought strikes you now," says the Sergeant, "you know there is such a thing as flogging? Well, let me tell you gentlemen, strange though it may seem, that it's a very delightful process, it's an excitement, produces an agreeable change, gives a healthy action to the circulation, causes an issue for all humours that would otherwise corrode the whole vital system—and leaves behind it such a glow that one feels just as if one had come out of a vapour bath. But that is not all, gentlemen, it purifies the heart, it chastens the soul, it reminds the soldier that great though he is, he is but a mortal after all; and I am sure that you, gentlemen, as good citizens, as fathers of families, as husbands, and as moral men, will admit that these are truly beneficial effects. But let me tell you one thing, gentlemen, I never knew a man who, when he had been flogged once, didn't come back to the triangle to be flogged a dozen times again, and if that doesn't prove, gentlemen, that the men themselves, know it to be good for them, then I am done and won't say another word."

The Sergeant thereupon brings out a handful of silver and has all present drink the health of the King at his expense.

Meantime Lucy's father has discovered Frederick's clandestine meetings with her. He is furious because he has plans for a meeting between his beautiful daughter and the son of the squire, despite their difference in social standing.

At the mansion the vicar is having a chat with the squire. The squire is delighted to hear of the arrival of the recruiting Sergeant, "because it will take from the village the idle labourers for whom no work exists. It is time that scum did some work".

The reverend expresses the wish that the Government should bring in a bill for the impressment of all paupers and those in the workhouses, and the squire says what an excellent idea because the rates would be less. The reverend adds that he has rebuked poor Fred for his sinful ideas about the rich oppressing the poor, and that the impertinent scoundrel had left him without even taking off his cap.

But the Sergeant is after Fred, whose fine bearing and superior air have so impressed him, and by trickery and the fact that Fred is out of work and will not allow Lucy to lend him her savings, the Sergeant finally ensnares his signature for the Army, keeping two pounds ten shillings of the bounty money Fred is entitled to, and handing Fred only ten shillings. Fred tries desperately to escape, but fails, due to the bribe given Mr. Bates, the local tradesman.

By now Lucy's father has asked Gerald to drink a glass of cider at his cottage, and Gerald has, of course, fallen heavily for Lucy.

And it is now time for the Sergeant, Fred, and the other half-dozen recruits the Sergeant has obtained for the Army, to depart for the headquarters of the regiment.

We are informed, "There were two ensigns attached to the depot. One was a youth of twenty—the other of about seventeen, and had just got his commission from the Royal Military College at Sandhurst. The ensign of twenty was the Hon. Gustavus Ferdinand Richard Fitzmorris, the son of a nobleman who had a host of children to provide for, and had therefore foisted them all in the usual way upon the public service—sending one into the Navy, another into the Church, a third into the House of Commons (with instructions to vote always with the Ministers), a fourth as attaché to an Embassy, a fifth to some Colonial appointment, and a sixth into the Army". This last, "would have inspired disgust and contempt with all rational persons".

The book goes on . . . "there were many fine men . . . who had been deluded into the ranks by the misrepresentation of the recruiting-officers. The soldiers were accustomed to club together some portion of the pittance which remained to them out of their pay . . . to take a weekly newspaper. As this, however, was a democratic journal they were compelled to be particularly careful how they left it lying about . . . for fear of an explosion of anger against those who subscribed to it. They took in this particular paper for two reasons. First, it was the one which most fearfully advocated the private soldiers' cause, exposed the tyrannies to which he was subjected, and as mercilessly denounced the horrors of the lash as the lash itself fell mercilessly upon the soldier's back. Sometimes a soldier would write a letter explaining particular or general grievances to the editor of that newspaper;* and though he gave his real name and that of the regiment to which he belonged, as a guarantee of good faith on the part of the writer, yet he invariably appended a postscript beseeching that the editor would suppress those names in giving publicity to the document. For (in those days) a private could scarcely be guilty of a greater crime in the eyes of his officers than that of daring to let out the secrets of military despotism through the medium of the newspaper press. The martinets of the Army tremble at the power of that press; and they use all their endeavours to vilify and cast odium upon any liberal prints which expressed sympathy towards the private soldier. Captain Courtenay had issued a special order that the newspaper in question should not be admitted to barracks—

* *Reynolds' News.*

a monstrous assumption of power against which, however, there was no appeal . . . it is impossible to conceive any system more calculated to enslave, imbrute and mechanise the mind than the British routine of military discipline . . ."

The Recruiting-Sergeant then informs Frederick that he will not know his place until he has a taste of the cat, and he promises him this before he is much older.

Gerald, as the reader may have guessed, also joins the Army and is posted to Fred's regiment where he makes life for the boy from his village, the "true-love" of the girl who has spurned his own pathetic advances, "a hell on earth".

After much unhappiness, Fred decides to desert and meets Lucy by chance at Coventry whilst Lucy is being taken by her father to Portsmouth (where the regiment now is) to marry Gerald by force. They flee together to Carlisle, marry, and Fred finds work as a school-master and Lucy as a seamstress. Cruel fate! Bates, our shopkeeper from the village, has taken over the local post office, and has been sent to Carlisle to trace a missing £50 note. He runs into Fred, extorts money from him for his silence, and then betrays him for the £10 deserter's reward. Fred is arrested and taken to barracks and court martialled. All the officers are in ill-humour—the Colonel has just lost at the gaming tables the previous night, the others have been drinking. Fred is condemned to receive five hundred lashes. Lucy hears of the sentence and comes to Portsmouth to intervene and beg mercy. The Colonel makes love to her and intimates that Fred will not be whipped if she agrees to be seduced by him. She refuses, which, of course, makes things even worse for poor Fred. After which Gerald meets her and tries a similar manoeuvre and is also rebuffed.

In three days a communication is received from Horse Guards to the effect that the proceedings of the court martial are approved, and that the punishment is to take place. Very early in the morning of the fourth day, two young Drummer-boys might have been seen in an outhouse of the barracks, practising with a cat-o'-nine-tails on a sack of sawdust placed in a leaning position against the wall. These youths are to inflict the atrocious punishment—a task which they have never performed before; and as they know that they themselves will be punished if they do not accomplish their loathsome and revolting duty in what Sergeant-Major Langley terms "a scientific manner", they are thus practising the handling of the "accursed instrument of torture".

"I don't think I shall be able to do it," observes one, suddenly flinging down the murderous weapon.

"Don't you?" exclaims the other, likewise desisting from the experimental flogging of the sack. "Well, that's exactly my feeling. It already makes me heave at the heart."

"I feel all over so queer," resumes the first, "that it seems as if I am going to faint. I am sure I shall never get through it"—and then the Drummer-boy, who was not above sixteen, wipes the tears from his eyes.

Half-an-hour afterwards, the regiment is drawn up in the barrack-square, in the midst of which the triangle is erected. This consists of three poles, about twelve feet in length, fastened all together at the top, and the other three ends spread out in such a manner that the triangle becomes self-supporting. Several of "the accursed weapons" lie upon the ground near. We should observe that the cat consists of nine lashes fastened to a wooden handle; and each lash has *five* hard knots—those at the ends being tied round with pieces of twine or very strong pack-thread, so as to hold them secure and prevent the lashes from unravelling. Each lash is about twenty inches long; and "they are made of a cord knit with a peculiar compactness in order to render the blows they inflict more stinging, cutting, and mercilessly effective".

Near the triangle stands a pitcher of water and a
drinking cup, "so that the victim may be from time to
time refreshed, the better to endure the full amount, or
at all events as large an amount as possible, of the satanic
punishment".

The regiment is drawn up in a square, the triangle
being in the midst—"so that every eye can command a
view of the hideous ceremony". The Colonel, the
Major and the Staff-Officers are upon horseback; the
other officers are in their accustomed places. "Presently
the Drummers advance up to the immediate vicinity of
the triangle, so that by the rolling of their drums they
may as much as possible drown the cries of human
agony, should the victim send any forth." Then, everything being in readiness, Frederick Lonsdale is led out
from the black-hole, in his undress uniform, and
accompanied by a guard. He walks with a firm step; his
countenance is ashy pale—but in the strongly compressed lips, the sternly fixed eyes, and the rigidity of all
the muscles of his face, may be read the deeply taken
resolution to meet his punishment with as much
fortitude as possible. Upon reaching the triangle, his
jacket and shirt are stripped off him; and he thus appears
naked to the waist. "The flush of shame at being thus
exposed in semi-nudity to so many eyes, sweeps over his
countenance, which then again immediately relapses
into ghastly pallor." He is now commanded by
Sergeant Langley, who advances to the spot—his cane
in one hand, and a little memorandum-book in the other
—to stretch himself in such a manner against two poles
of the triangle, with his face inward, that one arm and
one leg might be attached to each. His arms are distended upward to their fullest stretch, so as to be high
above his head; and then the process of binding
immediately commences. With strong cords is he thus
fastened at the wrists, the elbows, the knees, and the
ankles, to the poles; so that being held tight in every
limb, and at the principal joints of those limbs, he is

powerless and immovable—"save and except for the writhings and convulsions of excruciating agonies". The regimental Surgeon now appears upon the scene; and the two Drummer-boys who have been selected to inflict the chastisement, likewise advance. Their countenances are very pale; and notwithstanding the brandy they have been given, they shiver visibly from head to foot. Langley bends upon them a stern and threatening glance; and again, as when he had appeared before them in the outhouse whilst they had been at practice upon the sawdust sacks, are they literally frightened into a plucking-up of their courage. Lonsdale is firm and resolute; and thus these poor youths have to exercise greater efforts to collect their own fortitude to inflict the chastisement, than he had to meet it.

"Now, then, first Drummer-boy!" says Langley : "take up the cat and do your duty"—and having thus spoken, he opens his memorandum-book and takes a pencil to write down the number of each lash as he counts them one after the other.

The Drummer takes the murderous weapon in his hand—makes the nine lashes swish twice round above his head—and at the same moment that the drums beat, the first blow is inflicted. Nine long distinct marks of a livid hue, appear upon Frederick's back; while the Sergeant-Major calls out "*One !*" in a loud voice. The victim feels a strong quiver of mortal agony thrill along every nerve, fibre, and muscle, from the crown of his head to the soles of his feet; but no sound escapes him. His lips are compressed firmly together, as if to keep down even the slightest murmur that might be passing behind.

The Drummer-boy draws the tails of the murderous weapon smartly through the fingers of the left hand, and then looks on the palm to see if any sanguinary stains are there; but blood had not been drawn by that first stroke. He has stepped back a pace or two after inflicting it—then he swings the instrument twice round his head again—advances—and deals the second blow. The Sergeant-Major calls out *"Two* !"—but amidst the rolling of the drums, not a murmur, much less a cry from the lips of Lonsdale, "mingle therewith". Yet it had seemed as if a quantity of red-hot cinders had been suddenly thrown upon his back. Of a livelier red were the traces which the accursed instrument has left behind; and a close observer might have seen that the precise spots which the knots touched were marked by a little larger space and with a brighter red. The third blow falls—and this time, as the Drummer-boy draws the lashes through his left hand, the stains of blood are left behind. Lonsdale has writhed with a quick spasmodic movement; but still no sound from his lips ! The fearful work goes on up to twenty-five strokes; and then Sergeant Langley cries out "Halt !".

Lonsdale's back is by this time a lump of raw flesh; the blood is trickling down upon his pantaloons—and clots fall upon the ground. Not a murmur has as yet escaped him, although at each successive blow the anguish has become more intense—so that it seems as if boiling oil or molten lead is being sprinkled upon all the nerves laid bare—"or as if vulture-talons were fixed upon every fibre and muscle, rending, tearing, and pulling them pitilessly". The Surgeon feels the victim's pulse; and water is given to him. He maintains a firm look while the medical man gazes upon his countenance; but he drinks the water with avidity—for his throat feels as dry and parched "as if he has been swallowing ashes".

The second Drummer-boy now takes a fresh cat; and prompted by a fierce and threatening look from Sergeant Langley, he commences his turn with a vigorous arm. Blow after blow falls, the Sergeant counting them in due order, and the drums rolling "but still not a sound—not a cry—not a murmur, from the lips of Lonsdale ! Yet at each fresh stroke it appears as if every fibre and muscle in his back, being completely laid bare, have knives scraping rapidly over them. Now pieces of skin and flesh come off with each successive blow; and the Drummer-boy sickens at the sight and the contact, as he draws the lashes of the weapon through his hand to clear them thereof. The second twenty-five strokes are given; and again the Sergeant cries, 'Halt !'.

"Meanwhile several private soldiers of the regiment have fallen out of the ranks in a fainting fit at the horrible spectacle; but as soon as recovered by their comrades, they are forced to stand up again. The Colonel gallops up to each who thus falls; and as they come back to consciousness, he levels the most brutal imprecations at their heads—threatening to have them served in the same manner 'if they show any more of their nonsense'. But while the men are thus succumbing beneath the influence of their horrified and sickened feelings, not one of the officers exhibit the slightest emotion."

The Surgeon having again felt Lonsdale's pulse, and more water having been administered to him, the first Drummer-boy resumes the cat, and the punishment progresses. "It must not be thought that a repetition of the blows render the flesh gradually insensible to pain; there is no numbness of the kind; but each fresh stroke produces a livelier and a keener sense of excruciation. Sometimes there is a horrible tingling—then it feels as if all the cords are furnished with razors that smite edgeways upon the flesh—then as if myriads of pins, propelled by some powerful force, have shot with their points deep into the raw palpitating flesh—then as if a bunch of brambles have suddenly been pressed hard upon the back—and then again the tearing of the vulture-talons at the fibres—the scraping of the nerves with knives—the dropping of boiling oil and molten lead : these are the excruciations—varied, intense, ineffable—which the victim has to endure !" Thus the punishment goes on, until he has received three hundred lashes; and during the whole time he has not uttered a sound. "But it is impossible even for that strong, resolute-minded young man to repress the awful writhings and convulsions which seize upon him !''

By this time the two Drummer-boys are all covered with blood from head to foot; and there are pieces of skin and flesh adhering to their garments. "Oh ! it is horrible, horrible, to think that they should thus be besmeared with the gore of a fellow-creature—horrible, most horrible that morsels from the living man should thus be cut away to affix themselves upon their clothes ! But still more horrible to look upon that back there the skin is all literally cut up and flayed off, and where the quivering muscles are laid bare amidst the raw, palpitating flesh ! Many of the soldiers continue to fall fainting from the ranks; but no emotion is exhibited by the officers."

Three hundred blows having been inflicted, there is a longer halt. The Surgeon feels Lonsdale's pulse for some minutes in the presence of Colonel Wyndham, who had stationed himself near the triangle.

"I can endure more," says Lonsdale, in a low, subdued voice, "and would rather receive at once all that it is intended to give me."

"Then d—n his eyes, let him have it !" vociferates the Colonel, resolved to avenge upon the husband the humiliating rebuff he has received at the hands of the wife. "Go on, Langley."

"I don't think, sir," returned the Sergeant-Major, carrying his hand to his cap, "that these two boys can do any more."

"Then let us have two fresh ones," says the Colonel; and forthwith the order is obeyed.

The punishment is resumed with strong and vigorous arms, and with fresh cats. "But that point has now at length been reached when the intensity of the pain begins to subside—and Lonsdale's head falling forward, he has no longer need to compress his lips or exercise any control over his feelings; for there is a sort of dull, heavy, dead numbness upon him. Yet his senses have not abandoned him; he knows what is going on—but he has not the same active power of thought as hitherto; while to the eyes of the beholders, it seems as if the Drummers are wielding their weapons against a lump of inanimate raw flesh. All traces of distinct weals have become merged into one general mass of rawness, from the nape of the neck to the waist-band of the trousers, and round upon the ribs. It is one tremendous laceration, as if the whole skin has been flayed away in one piece, and then the flesh has been cut up with myriads of sharp short hacking instruments like those used in the process of cupping. Thus doth the atrocious punishment progress until the end. The whole five hundred lashes are administered; and the two Drummer-boys who have succeeded the first set, retire from the scene as besmeared with blood as their predecessors."

It is done—"the satanic work is over"—and Lonsdale, now in a state of total unconsciousness, is born away to the hospital—to be cured, if possible—or to die, if beyond the reach of medical aid.

Our hero recovers in hospital and rejoins his comrades in the regiment. Fred's life in barracks continues to be made impossible by the officers and he and Lucy, in addition to a small boy which Lucy has borne him, flee to London. Three happy years pass, Fred again as schoolmaster and Lucy again as seamstress, when, of course, Mr. Bates again runs into Fred, again outside a post office where Bates is again making enquiries about a missing letter and Fred is again posting a letter. Bates again asks for money and this is again given to stop an immediate arrest of Fred. But Bates is trusted no longer, and Fred and Lucy and the small child flee to France where they found a school. Lucy hears that her father, who has disowned her for not marrying Gerald, is dying and wishes to see her. She writes that she is coming to the village, but, inevitably, Mr. Bates, in charge of the post office, intercepts the letter and informs the authorities who arrest Fred on landing at Dover.

But Bates is under suspicion and is searched at the local inn and opened letters and rifled monies are found upon him. He is tried and sentenced to fourteen years' transportation. And what of Frederick?

On being delivered up at the barracks where his regiment is stationed, Lonsdale is consigned to the black-hole. "It is not our purpose to linger upon this portion of our narrative; to do so, would be merely a repetition of what has been placed on record before. Suffice it to say, that a court martial being duly summoned, Frederick is condemned to receive five hundred lashes—and in addition thereto, to be branded as a deserter ! That he has rendered himself liable to this last mentioned horror, he all along too well knew : but never, when on the few occasions he and Lucy have, ere leaving England for France touched upon the eventualities which may arise from his detection, has he dropped a hint to her that there is a penalty provided by the remorseless tyranny of the military code in addition to the already sufficient atrocities of the lash. To be branded—Oh, it is indeed something frightful to contemplate !—and it is chiefly because he has apprehended this, that he counsels his wife to remain far away with their child until the measure of his punishment is accomplished. But now he learns, to his dismay, that he has to undergo the flogging first; and not till he is cured will he be subjected to the process of branding."

On the following morning Frederick Lonsdale undergoes the "lacerations of the scourge" in the presence of the entire regiment. Sergeant-Major Langley is in attendance, as on the former occasion; and under his directions there is no chance of the Drummer-boys being permitted to spare the full vigour of their arms or the satanic power of the lash. Without a murmur from his lips, "but with rage in the heart and frenzy in the brain, does the unhappy Lonsdale receive the merciless infliction". Though the wounds of the former flagellation have long since been healed and the skin grown over them, yet is the whole of the back and the space extending round upon the ribs most painfully tender; "and inasmuch as a field which has once been ploughed, is all the more easy to plough up again, so is it with the flesh of the unhappy Lonsdale". This time the very first blow fetches blood; "and ere many are inflicted, the thongs of the accursed scourge begin to tear away the skin, cut up the flesh, and hack out morsels with a merciless excruciation". Again many soldiers fall fainting from the ranks—and again the officers look on—stern—implacable—unmoved, at the flaying process. "But what words can convey even a tithe of all the mortal agonies that are endured by our unhappy hero beneath the ferocious lash? The sentence is that he receive five hundred blows; every blow might be multiplied by nine : and thus when the punishment is over, he has in reality received four thousand and five hundred stripes ! He bears it with a fortitude displaying the natural magnanimity of his soul; and by an almost incredible effort of his manly will, he suppresses the utterance of even a sign or a murmur indicative of the agonies he is suffering. Yes—the whole sum of five hundred lashes does he thus receive; and in a state of complete unconsciousness is he borne to the infirmary."

Two months elapse from the date of the flogging, before the Surgeon pronounces Frederick Lonsdale convalescent. The period is therefore now come when he is to undergo the remaining portion of his sentence. He has been advised by some of his humane comrades, whom he met in the infirmary, or who visited him there, to petition Colonel Wyndham for a reprieve in respect to the branding : but while thanking his advisers for the good feeling which prompts this counsel, our hero steadily and sternly refuses to seek a favour at the hands of "any one of those whom he can not regard otherwise than as his enemies". It is on the morning of the 15th of March, 1835, that the regiment is drawn up in a square on the parade ground—the same as if it were to witness

a scourging process; and Lonsdale is marched forth from
the infirmary to be branded as a deserter. He neither
walks so erect as is his wont, nor with the same firmness
of step; but it is not that his heart fails him—it is because
he is still weak and feeble from the effects of the awful
punishment he has received. Indeed, he is so emaciated
—his countenance is a ghastly white—that he looks but
a ghost of his former self. "Still there is a stern decision
in his eyes and in his compressed lips; and he exerts all
his energy to surmount as much as possible the sense of
enervation which bends his form somewhat and renders
his pace slow and languid. Is there any pity felt for that
unfortunate man as he thus painfully drags himself
towards the centre of the square? Yes : an illimitable
compassion on the part of the private soldiers—but none
on that of the officers.

"When stationed in the midst of the regiment, Lonsdale has again to submit to the degradation of being
stripped naked to the waist. The Surgeon is present to
superintend the branding process—not so much, however in his medical character, as merely to instruct the
Drum-Major, whose duty it is to operate, how to
accomplish his task : for there is in reality no danger
attending the process, and comparatively little pain—at
least for one who had gone through the hideous excruciations of the lash. But then the infamy—Oh ! it is *this*—
it is *this*, that constituted the pain—the agony !

"Our hero being stripped to the waist, as above
stated, the Drum-Major dips a camel's hair brush into a
small bottle which has been furnished him, and which
contains a thick black liquid. He then traces with this
brush the letter 'D' on Lonsdale's left side, two inches
below the arm-pit, and upon a part which the scourge
had cut up two months back and which has only just
skinned over. The letter itself is about an inch in length.
The Drum-Major then takes a small bundle of saddlers'
needles, three-sided and serrated : with these he pierces
the skin all over the tracing of the letter, so as to draw

blood—which heaven knows is easily done on that sore spot, which has so lately been flayed, ploughed, furrowed, hewed, and hacked, by the remorseless scourge ! Lonsdale remains motionless as a statue—save perhaps in respect to a slight quivering of the lips and the eye-lids : for he feels that, even as in the lowest depth there is a deeper still, so that beyond the degradation of the cat-o'-nine-tails there is the greater infamy of the brand. When the puncturing process is over, the Drum-Major takes some gunpowder between his finger and thumb, and rubs it in upon the wound for the purpose of rendering the mark indelible. The explanation of the process is this : that the charcoal of the gunpowder is forced into the small orifices punctured by the needles, and remains in the skin without festering after the wound has healed up : so that as a matter of course the black colour of the charcoal renders the letter 'D' not merely visible, but likewise indelible.

"And there stands Lonsdale, enduring this crowning infamy—half-naked in the presence of his comrades— his back showing the deep red marks of the scourge which had lacerated it two months back !—there he stands, this unfortunate man—in a civilised country—in a land of Bibles and Missionary Societies—to have the mark of Cain affixed upon him ! When the process is over, he is conducted back to the infirmary—there to remain until the wound should be completely healed, when he may resume his military duties."

On the sixth day after the marking process Frederick is discharged from the infirmary. Before he returns to his quarters, he is summoned to the presence of Colonel Wyndham.

Frederick is then told that, as his desertion counted as nothing, he has still nearly five years to serve. But these blows are having their effect on him. He is drinking and his behaviour towards Lucy has become offhand and thoughtless.

Bates has escaped his transportation order and is

BRANDING A DESERTER WITH THE LETTER D

[*Face page* 178

down—but not quite out. In Portsmouth, on the knowledge he has gleaned, he arranges for Gerald to visit Lucy in a house of ill fame, having found Lucy and told her he had arranged a meeting with Fred at a certain house. He then tells Fred in barracks that his wife has been kidnapped and leads him to the house. Fred confronts Gerald and knocks him to the ground. The Colonel wants to hush-up the whole unpleasant affair, but Frederick will have none of it. He is therefore court martialled for striking an officer, and is sentenced to be shot to death. In his condemned cell he resorts to the last terrible evil of the bottomless pit—all brought on by flogging, of course—*he begins to smoke*! Lucy has another child. Later she visits him in his condemned cell and he goes on his knees to her and begs her forgiveness for all his unkindness to her, including the destruction of her work basket with which she earned a living!

And now the squire finds his son is worthless, and mostly for private reasons offers the Colonel a bribe of one thousand guineas to ask for a reprieve for Fred.

We complete this story by reprinting the details of our hero's end from the time at which the Adjutant in charge of the execution is talking with the Colonel. The Colonel is speaking : —

"It appears that Sir Archibald has been using all his interest—and that is not a little—with the Horse Guards to get this fellow off."

"And you sent a recommendation to mercy, did you not?" inquires the Adjutant.

"Oh ! of course," answers the Colonel. "Redburn told me that his father had known Lonsdale ever since he was a child—that he had been brought up at Oakleigh, which is on the family estate—and that the Baronet did not like the idea of one of *his people*, as he calls them, dying in such a way. So he sent Redburn to ask me to interfere."

"It's all right and proper enough," observes the

N

Adjutant. "One does these kind of things to oblige persons of Sir Archibald Redburn's rank and standing."

"Precisely so," says Wyndham; but he does not think it at all necessary to add that he had not signed the recommendation to mercy before Captain Redburn promised him another loan of a thousand guineas.

"I presume, Colonel," says the Adjutant, "that I am to issue the necessary orders just as if no reprieve were expected?"

"Unquestionably," replies Wyndham : "and if we hear nothing by ten o'clock the sentence must, of course, be carried out. Under the circumstances we can stretch half-an-hour so as to give the fellow a last chance."

"Then I will counter-order it from ten o'clock, and specify half-past," says the Adjutant : and the Colonel having nodded approvingly as he wiped his razor on the shaving cloth, Mr. Scott issued from the room.

Two hours pass; and a little after nine o'clock, as Colonel Wyndham is enjoying his muffins and chocolate, with other delicacies, at the breakfast table, his letters are brought in and placed by his side. He takes them up—turns them over one after another—"but perceives amongst them no despatch bearing above the address the formulary of 'On His Majesty's Service' ".

"Any intelligence yet?" inquires Scott, once more making his appearance.

"None," responds Wyndham, but to make perfectly sure he opens the letters—glances at the signatures—and repeats the word, "None".

Another hour elapses : it is now half-past ten o'clock —and no intelligence has been received. Captain Redburn comes not; neither letter nor message reaches the Colonel in respect to the sentence pronounced on Frederick Lonsdale. He looks forth from his window; the regiment is drawn up in the spacious barrack-yard; and his presence is now alone awaited in order that the awful ceremony may be proceeded with. He accordingly descends into the yard; and the Adjutant accosts him with the wonted salute, to receive his final orders.

"I have heard nothing, Scott," says Colonel Wyndham. "We must go on. Have you picked out the firing-party?"

"Yes, sir," replies the Adjutant : "fourteen in all."

"Some from each company, I suppose?" says Wyndham, inquiringly.

"Yes, sir. I left it to Langley's discretion—and he has chosen eight of the oldest hands and six youngsters. They have all received their instructions."

"To keep themselves steady and take good aim?" remarks the Colonel. "But the signals—are they agreed upon?"

"The Drum-Major, sir, whose duty it is to give them, has made all arrangements with the firing-party. Everything will be properly understood between them."

"Then let the Major proceed, Scott," says the Colonel : and the Adjutant hastens to convey his instructions to the officer alluded to.

The regiment, when taking its station on the parade ground, is drawn up in companies; the command is now given by the Major for them to wheel into line; and the firing-party is marched to the front. The aspect of the soldiery is at that moment deeply and solemnly interesting. Every countenance is pale, with an expression of mingled anxiety and awe upon it; every one who glances at his comrade, beholds in his features the reflection of his own feelings. The sentiment of commiseration for Frederick Lonsdale, and of horror at the punishment about to be inflicted, is all but universal —some of the officers and non-commissioned officers constituting the only exceptions. Though the full measure of the wrongs and persecutions which our hero has endured is not known—yet a sufficiency has come to the knowledge of his fellow-soldiers to make them regard him as the victim of a long series of cruel misfortunes and bitter tyrannies, rather than as a wilful and wicked offender against the laws of military discipline. They therefore feel that it is as a martyr, and not as a culprit, he is about to undergo the sentence that has been pronounced upon him.

Immediately after the firing-party has been moved to the front of the line, Frederick Lonsdale is brought out, under a small escort, from the guard-house. He is dressed in his uniform, but without his shako, his cross-belts, and side-arms. His countenance is pale as death —that death which he is advancing to meet . . . "but he walks with head erect, with a firm step, and with a resolute expression of countenance. Those who have seen him twice flogged and once branded, feel assured that he will not flinch now; and they are right. The moment he appears upon the parade ground, his eyes sweep over the scene that meets them; it is awful and imposing to a degree. All that pomp of military parade —that force of eight hundred men, marshalled for the purpose of beholding one humble individual done to death ! He beholds compassionate sympathy and harrowing suspense depicted upon almost every countenance. For a moment he feels touched by those evidences of sympathy on the part of his comrades; the next instant he nerves himself with an iron fortitude— for the *other* was a feeling to which he dare not give way.

"With looks as firm as his steps, does he advance towards the centre of the yard; and there he stops short. He knows that it is his privilege—the *last* he can claim on earth—to address a few words to the parade; and he proposes to avail himself of it. This is a moment of even a more profound suspense and a more awful anxiety for the assembled soldiery than they have before experienced : it seems to them as if they were about to listen to the words of a dead man ! There is a silence as deep and as solemn as if some spell has suddenly alighted upon all who have gathered there—turning them into statues. A pin might have been heard to drop on the hard frozen ground where the troops were drawn up. The breath is suspended; the very pulses themselves seem to have ceased to beat. All is still and silent : but yet there is a .terrible amount of keenly active and acutely felt vitality expressed on the countenances along whose pale array Lonsdale's eyes slowly travel. At length that solemn pause—that dread silence—is broken.

" 'Friends and comrades,' says the doomed man, 'you see before you one whose eyes in a few swift brief minutes will be closed in death—whose heart will have ceased to beat—whose form will be reduced to a mere lump of clay. I am about to appear in the presence of a higher tribunal than that whose sentence has placed me here to die; and if I tremble at the thought of so soon standing before the sublime judgment-seat, it is not on account of that deed for which the earthly one of the other day has condemned me. No : it is because I feel that whatever faults I may have committed, have been offences against those who provoked them not—who merited them not. I allude to the best of wives—to the dearest of children.'

"Here his voice falters for a few moments, and tears dim his eyes. Tears, too, are trickling down the pale cheeks of those in the serried rank; and the sob which rises up into the throat of many a soldier there, finds a similarly half-stifled echo in that of a comrade standing next. But Lonsdale, hastily dashes away his own tears, draws himself suddenly up, as if to show that having resolved to be firm, he would be; and then his speech is continued thus : —

" 'And yet I scarcely tremble at the thought of appearing before that celestial judgment-seat; for the Almighty who sitteth there, can attest that the only errors of my life have been those to which I ere now alluded, and which rebounded upon my wife and child. That angel-wife of mine has forgiven me in her own name and in that of our son. Yes—by *them* I am forgiven : and my Maker will not show me less mercy than I have experienced at their hands. I stand not here to admit

the justice of my sentence : I proclaim it to be unjust !
Imagine not, therefore, my heart will fail me now that
in a few short minutes I shall meet Death face to face !'

"Lonsdale ceases : but there is not altogether a dead
silence now—for the sobs of many of the soldiers are
plainly audible. The doomed man, turning round,
walks slowly—but with head erect and firm footsteps—
to a greater distance from the line; and he halts about
twenty feet in front of a coffin which has been silently
and stealthily borne on the ground and placed there
while he is in the midst of his speech. His looks do not
quail when, on turning round, he catches sight of that
sinister object : he knew that it would be there—he was
prepared to behold it; and even if it were otherwise, his
fortitude is nerved to a degree well calculated to shield
him against a sudden shock. Taking off his red coat, he
throws it upon the ground—and then sinks on to his
knees, his hands clasped in silent prayer. A soldier,
especially appointed for the purpose, approaches him as
noiselessly as if treading in the chamber of death and
advancing up to the couch of death itself; and proceeds
to fasten a bandage over his eyes. At the same time he
whispers, 'Lonsdale, forgive me for having any share in
these proceedings : but I cannot help it !'

" 'I forgive you, my poor friend,' is the low and
solemnly uttered response of the doomed man. 'You
are but an automaton, as every one is who enters the
ranks of the Army. Farewell ! God bless you !'

" 'God bless you,' murmurs the weeping soldier, as
he presses the hand which Lonsdale stretches out. He
then withdraws : and our hero, again joining his hands,
abandons himself altogether to his devotions—praying
for heaven to have mercy upon his own soul, and not to
desert the wife and the children whom he is leaving
behind.

"Immediately Lonsdale has knelt down, the Drum-
Major of the regiment, who has stationed himself near
the firing-party, gives a peculiar flourish of his cane; and

the fourteen soldiers who are selected to perform the hideous part of executioners, advance to a stack of muskets immediately in front of them—and each takes a piece. There are fourteen of these weapons—as many muskets as there are men in the firing-party : and it is known that but thirteen were loaded with ball, and one with powder only. The firing-party has been as profoundly touched as any of the rest by Lonsdale's speech : each and all of those fourteen soldiers would fling down the weapons of death if they dare, and vow that though they would fight their enemies in battle, it was an outrage to their feelings to ask them to murder a friend in cold blood. But, no : they dare not !—these living automatons have no power of volition : it is their's only to *obey* !

"When the fourteen men of the firing-party have taken their fourteen muskets, and have promptly formed themselves into a rank again—all this taking place in the deepest silence—there is a pause more dreadful than can be described. But it is a pause of only a few moments. The Drum-Major again fixing his eyes earnestly and expressively upon them—and satisfied that the looks of them all were riveted upon him—gives the second signal, namely, another flourish of his cane. It is likewise the last ! The fourteen muskets are raised and levelled; another pause, but only of three moments—and then the loud report of the fire-arms strike quick and sharp upon every ear. Lonsdale's hands are thrown upward—and he falls heavily upon his back. The spasmodic shudder which simultaneously quivers along the whole line, is something not merely to be *seen*—but likewise to be *heard* !

"The victim is not dead. Though pierced by several balls, life yet lingers in him; his hands wave like the fins of a fish when taken out of the water and in the last agonies of death. The Drum-Major has four more loaded muskets at hand : these he promptly orders the four oldest and steadiest of the firing-party to take.

They obey him—obey also the few rapidly whispered instructions he gives : and hastening towards the prostrate form of their comrade, they place the muzzles to his head and pour in the last volley, crashing his skull and scattering his brains upon the ground where he lies. If the former acts of the tragedy were hideous and horrible, this last one is satanic, hellish, and damnable !

"Promptly is the word of command given for the line to break by falling back into companies; and the next order is to 'march past in slow time'. As each company comes in a line with the body, the word is given to 'mark time'—which is a process of lifting the feet but bringing them back to the spot whence they were raised, so that the *corps* while thus engaged makes no advance. The order, 'Eyes Left', is then issued, for the purpose of compelling the company thus marking time to fix their looks upon the corpse which lies brained and skull-shattered there; it is to produce a mechanised and slavish obedience under the terrorism of a frightful example.

"While the regiment is thus marching past in slow time, each company being successively compelled to pause and gaze in the manner described on the slaughtered victim, the quick galloping of a horse's hoofs is heard, from the outside of the barrack wall—approaching the gates, which have been closed during the execution.

"A fearful sensation seizes upon all present : the troops come to a dead halt without any word of command to that effect. Everyone understands what it is. A reprieve has arrived—but it has come too late !"

III

We now come to an aspect of naval life which, we believe, has hitherto remained unrecorded in histories of the nineteenth century.

In August, 1821, a privately printed statement of one hundred and fifty copies was published and addressed to the Lords Commissioners of the Admiralty. This has proved too long to quote in full, but we reproduce all the most relevant disclosures and arguments presented by the authors in their effort to improve the conditions of life at sea, and to expose the immorality habitually condoned at that date (and for many years later !) on board His Majesty's ships.

We cannot trace the official reaction to this statement and so cannot comment on the effects—if any—it had upon naval discipline, but the reader can be assured that there was no immediate or noticeable change in the Navy as a result of its disclosures. We feel, therefore, that when taken as a background to the punishments and discipline already detailed in Book II, this unique statement has great value.

STATEMENT RESPECTING THE PREVALENCE OF CERTAIN IMMORAL PRACTICES IN HIS MAJESTY'S NAVY
AUGUST, 1821

"It has become an established practice in the British Navy to admit, and even to invite, on board our ships of war, immediately on their arrival in port, as many prostitutes as the men, and, in many cases, the officers may choose to entertain, to the number, in the larger ships, of several hundred at a time; all of whom remain on board, domesticated with the ship's company, men and boys, until they again put to sea. The tendency of this practice is to render a ship of war, while in port, a continual scene of riot and disorder, of obscenity and blasphemy, of drunkenness, lewdness, and debauchery. During this time, the married seamen are frequently joined by their wives and families (sometimes comprising daughters from ten to fifteen years of age), who are forced to submit to the alternative of mixing with these abandoned women, whose language and behaviour are usually of the most polluting description; or of foregoing altogether the society of their husbands and parents. These all inhabit the same deck, where, whatever be

their age or sex or character, they are huddled promis-
cuously together, eating, drinking, and sleeping, without
any adequate means of separation or privacy, for the
most part even without the slightest screen between their
berths; and where, in the sight and hearing of all around
them, they live in the unrestrained indulgence of every
licentious propensity which may be supposed to actuate
inmates of this description . . .

"One naval officer of large experience asserts, that
from the time he entered the Navy, about twenty-eight
years ago, he had served in no ship in which, while in
port, the custom of permitting women of the very worst
description to come and remain on board was not
tolerated, and even encouraged, by the Commanding
Officer. The Lieutenants and grown Midshipmen were
allowed to have women in their respective mess-rooms;
where the younger Midshipmen were obliged to sit at
table and associate with them, and to be witnesses of the
debauchery and indecency which took place, not only
there, but among the men also. It was even common
for the women to employ all their arts to debauch these
youths, who generally were caught in their snares, and
became their prey.

" 'It is well known,' he goes on to observe, 'that
immediately upon the arrival of a ship of war in port,
crowds of boats flock off with cargoes of prostitutes.
Having no money to pay for their conveyance, the
waterman takes as many as his boat will hold, upon
speculation, and hovers round the ship until she is
secured at her anchors and the necessary work done;
when he, with others, is permitted to come alongside.
The men then go into the boats, and pick out each a
woman (as one would choose cattle), paying a shilling
or two to the boatman for her passage off. These
women are examined at the gangway for liquor, which
they are constantly in the habit of smuggling on board.
They then descend to the lower deck with their husbands, as they call them. Hundreds come off to a large

ship. The whole of the shocking, disgraceful transactions of the lower deck it is impossible to describe—
the dirt, filth, and stench; the disgusting conversation;
the indecent, beastly conduct, and horrible scenes; the
blasphemy and swearing; the riots, quarrels, and fightings, which often take place, where hundreds of men and
women are huddled together in one room, as it were;
and where, in bed (each man being allowed only sixteen
inches breadth for his hammock), they are squeezed
between the next hammocks, and must be witnesses of
each other's actions; can only be imagined by those who
have seen all this. A ship in this state is often, and justly,
termed by the more decent seamen, "a hell afloat". Let
those who have never seen a ship of war, picture to themselves a very large and low room (hardly capable of
holding the men) with five hundred men, and probably
three or four hundred women of the vilest description,
shut up in it, and giving way to every excess of
debauchery that the grossest passions of human nature
can lead them to; and they see the deck of a seventy-four
gun ship upon the night of her arrival in port. Add to
this, that many of these poor wretches have dreadful
diseases, which they communicate to the men. Let it
also be imagined what must be the situation of the
decent married women, who are either forced to come
into the midst of such brutality, or remain still separated
from their husbands, after probably a long absence.'

"Another officer thus states his own experience with
respect to the above practice. After detailing many of
the same facts which are contained in the foregoing
communication, he thus proceeds : —

" 'The next step which, in many ships, is insisted
upon, before the seaman is allowed to take his prostitute
on the lower deck, is to get her examined by the assistant
surgeon, to ascertain whether she is infected with the
venereal disease, in which case she is sent out of the ship.
It must, however, be mentioned, to the honour of the
assistant surgeons in the Navy, that some of them have

resisted this order of the Captains, and have rather chosen to brave all consequences, than to submit to actions so degrading . . .

" 'It is frequently the case that men take two prostitutes on board at a time; so that it sometimes happens that there are more women than men on board. And if it be kept in mind that a frigate's lower deck (I speak only of frigates) is already much crowded by her own company, you may figure to yourself its state when an addition of as many more women as there are already men, is made to this crowd, all of the most abandoned and infamous description, giving way to every species of debauchery and abomination . . .' "

Another officer states his own experience in the following detail : —

" 'In 1807 I joined the ————, Captain ————. The men had their prostitutes on board; the midshipmen had too, who messed in the berth with the young gentlemen, and generally sat with them during the day. The conversation at times was blasphemous, and their conduct indecent in the extreme. They remained in the ship until we sailed for ————, and on our return they were again admitted.

" 'In 1808 Captain ———— joined us. He granted the same indulgence, *and even allowed about nine women to go to sea in the ship.* They were mustered on the forecastle on Sundays, and inspected by the Captain and First Lieutenant. Their conduct was so infamous, that after our arrival in the ———— two or three were turned out of the ship into a brig, for a passage to England; *and most of those that remained were common to the ship's company. Of one, I recollect its being stated that she admitted nineteen men to her embraces in one night.* The matter was regarded with the utmost indifference, or made the occasion of obscene jests. It was common for the midshipmen to have these women. Indeed, the Captain himself did not hesitate to take a foreign girl to live with him for some time, while we

remained in those seas; and during that time the ship
was in a continual state of discord, from their blasphemy
and drunkenness. On our return to England she was
filled as before.

" 'I then joined another vessel. There also the midshipmen had their women on board. The men had their
women also. Some of them went to sea in the ship,
and behaved in their accustomed manner, being almost
continually drunk, spirits being given them by the
officers, mates, and midshipmen, in payment for their
occasional visits.

" 'At ——— the scene was truly horrible, *there being
more women than men on board*; the boys having free
course among them likewise; and the midshipmen
having four or five girls on board, who lived in the mess,
and who, I have reason to believe, enticed the younger
midshipmen on shore to their haunts."

"Again : 'In the ships of war which are not of the
line these awful iniquities take place on the same deck
which the midshipmen occupy, the hammocks of those
youths being hung up close to those of the men, in
general without any intervening partitions or curtains
to prevent their witnessing the abominations that take
place. The effect may easily be conceived . . .'

" 'When the ——— was lately preparing to sail for
——— she was so crowded with women that the con-
fusion and filth were intolerable. No business could be
done, and the men were deserting daily. At length the
First Lieutenant from mere necessity turned them all
out of the ship, and sent them on shore. The Captain
met them there as they landed. They addressed him,
saying, they were sure he was too much of a gentleman
not to allow them their privileges; and he ordered them
on board again. The Lieutenant, of course, received
them. The next day, however, nothing could be
effected towards putting the ship in order. On the
following morning she was paid off. The Jews and other
shop-dealers came on board to sell their wares. Their

boxes were broken open and pillaged. The women, on this, were sent on shore a second time and the ship ordered to drop down to ———.'

"For our own part, we can perceive no difference, in point of principle, between the practice which prevails in our Navy, of receiving and even inviting, on board His Majesty's ships, the number of prostitutes required for the use of the seamen, and that which we have supposed, of admitting into the palaces of His Majesty, or into the houses of our noblemen—of the First Lord of the Admiralty for instance—the number of prostitutes required for the use of the male servants. The same pleas of indulgence, of convenience, of economy, or whatever else may be the plea, may be urged in the one case as in the other. And if in the one case we should regard such a house as no better than a brothel, and its owner as degraded to the moral level of the keeper of a brothel, why should we judge differently in the case of a ship of war? There is, indeed, this material difference in the two cases, that in the latter the practice, as we have seen, is attended with such brutalities, such outrageous violations of the decencies of life, as to sink His Majesty's ships even below the level of the lowest brothels . . .

"One of the reasons most frequently given for tolerating prostitutes aboard His Majesty's ships is : If the licence complained of herein be not given, we must lay our account with the growth of unnatural crimes.

"But to this we boldly and confidently reply, that if there really exists a danger of this kind in the Navy, it arises more from the very practice which we have been reprobating than from any other cause. What can be more *unnatural*, more contrary to all the feelings of our common nature, than the open, undisguised, unblushing, promiscuous concubinage, which now takes place on board His Majesty's ships of war? Is not the person who has been tutored in this school of impurity and licentiousness, and who must there have bid adieu to those feelings which operate the most powerfully as a restraint on new modes of criminal indulgence, less likely than others to shrink from any other abomination which may be suggested to his mind? Suppose a ship, fixed for months on a blockading station, or sent on a tedious cruise, who are the men who would be most likely to be guilty of unnatural practices—those who had for weeks inhabited the lower deck of a man of war, and had been witnesses and actors in the brutalising scenes we have described; who had had their imaginations contaminated by all sorts of obscenity, and their consciences scared by the sight and participation of all sorts of polluting exhibitions; or the men who, whatever may be supposed the force of their natural passions, had never passed through so debasing and demoralising an ordeal? It is either when the appetite is palled or sated with enjoyment; or when a familiarity with gross pollution has prepared the mind for further grossnesses, that such enormities are to be apprehended. Indeed, all crimes are progressive; they are proved to be so by individual observation and experience, as well as by the whole course of history and the whole tenor of Scripture. And it may further be observed, that all nations, whether ancient or modern, in which the apprehended crimes have prevailed have been remarkable for the immorality of their women and the shameless licentiousness of both sexes.

"If the practice we complain of has the effect of preventing unnatural crimes, it can only be while it is allowed; and it ought to be especially allowed, therefore, where there is no other opportunity of vicious indulgence. It is wholly inconsistent with this principle, to withhold the indulgence while a ship is at sea, or on a blockading station, and the seamen are shut out from all intercourse with women; and yet to permit it in port, where there is less necessity for it. Unless, therefore, our ships continue to be brothels at sea, as well as in port, the danger of unnatural crimes, which is made the plea for this licence, will be increased instead of diminished; for, by occasional indulgence, passion only acquires strength. Such, also, is the social character of vice, that it is vain to expect that by permitting one mode of vicious indulgence we can exclude others; on the contrary, we only prepare the way for the admission of other vices of the same stock and family. Nay, it has been ascertained—and some unhappy instances of recent occurrence, if accurately examined, will prove it —that, as far as unnatural practices have existed in our Navy, they have been introduced into it by those abandoned wretches, the very women who were vainly and impiously employed to prevent them.

"But the alternative in this case is by no means fairly given by those with whom we are arguing : for we are here called to choose between a vice which is licensed, established, regulated, and even enforced; and one which is proscribed, detested, and punished. We are also called upon to choose between a certain and a very uncertain evil. To prevent the possibility of one vice in a few individuals (and we believe that, without the schooling now administered in a man of war, the risk of that vice would be exceedingly small), we expose the whole crews of every ship of the whole Navy of England to almost inevitable and overwhelming depravity.

"Sailors, before they enter the Navy, and even while occupied in the merchant service, must be pretty much like the rest of that community from which they have been drawn; with the same natural propensities to evil, but kept in check by those various restraints which, even where religious motives have little or no influence, contribute to preserve decency and good order in society. On entering a ship of war, however, all these restrictions are removed, and the corrupt propensities of our nature are permitted, nay, encouraged, to expand into a full and fearful magnitude. When a man is introduced into this Circean den, the brutalising process commences. He is tempted to throw off the reserve and modesty

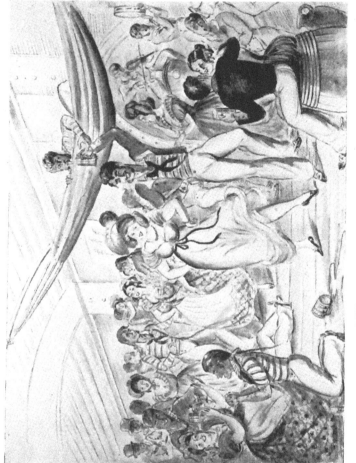

SCENE ON BOARD A WARSHIP
c. 1820

which may have accompanied him thither, and to revel in unrestrained and undisguised licentiousness. Let the sailor once be fairly plunged into this life of beastly indulgence, and the desire of forming domestic ties, or of maintaining those already formed, begins to cease; his connection through these with his country, begins to be dissolved, he becomes less capable of enjoying the quiet comforts of home, and pants for the criminal indulgence to which he has been habituated; he has no inducement to economise; but, on the contrary, every temptation to wanton and profuse expense is presented to him, on the part of those with whom, by a mistaken and cruel policy, he is brought into temporary alliance.

"Nor is the extent of this evil to be estimated merely by the number of men who may at any one time be employed in our Navy. The whole of our merchant seamen may be considered as having already passed some period of their lives in the king's Service, or at least as being liable so to do. And even at the present moment, there is a constant and considerable interchange of men between our ships of war and our merchantmen. The contagious influence, therefore, of the immoralities practised in our Navy, may be regarded as extending itself to the whole body of our mariners.

"But the evil, it is obvious, is by no means confined to seamen; it flows back on the community at large, through a variety of channels. Is it possible, after reading the foregoing statement, to contemplate, without dismay, the tide of impurity which must have visited every corner of the land, and penetrated the domestic circle in every rank of life, when, on the termination of the war, thousands, who had been engaged in the scenes and practices that have been described, returned to their native homes, to poison their moral atmosphere, and to spread the deadly contagion of vice and profligacy in many a hitherto uncontaminated vicinity? . . ."

o

BOOK IV

THE MOVEMENT AGAINST CORPORAL PUNISHMENT

During the early years of the nineteenth century a growing opposition to corporal punishment had been recorded, until by the 1830's the burning question of flogging was on everybody's lips.

Pamphlets and books were published, advocating the abolition of corporal punishment. One of the most widely read, authoritative and best-documented was by Major-General Charles Napier, published in 1837, and entitled *Remarks on Military Law and the Punishment of Flogging*. In it Napier commences, "Men are governed by punishments and rewards; and the necessity of the first is very much increased by the neglect of the last; yet the English government appears to forget that men are quite as much influenced by the one, as by the other. Indeed, the human mind seems to be more bent upon punishing delinquency, than upon rewarding merit. Nevertheless, such expressions as 'the painful necessity of punishment', 'I am forced to punish against my will', and the like, are eternally in the mouths of those who possess power. Then they express 'the highest gratification in rewarding such merit', and 'it is most pleasing as well as just to reward such good conduct', yet their hearts seem resolutely bent upon executing the painful duty, while the pretended pleasurable one is often neglected. Our statesmen seem to rush forward with ardour towards the infliction of punishment; while (exclaiming against extravagance) they refuse those rewards to private soldiers which they admit he has justly earned".

Napier then goes on to write about the rewards that

are given to "Classes" in England, and gives, for example, the Order of the Bath and the Order of the Garter, Orders which no soldier of non-commissioned rank has an earthly chance to obtain. He quotes the Legion of Honour in France, which, when founded by Napoleon, was arranged in four grades to cover every type of person who might merit it. Thus *all* Frenchmen had the chance of the *same* reward. We give this example of General Napier's to show his clear and democratic thinking.

An admirable order by Wellington, followed by one from Lord Hill, put a stop to the more irresponsible and sadistic amusements of officers and N.C.O.'s. "It is to be observed," says Napier, "that when men are charged with the infliction of any punishment (no matter how revolting it may be in its nature), they generally become desirous of adding to its severity : their minds grow hardened by seeing such punishments inflicted, and they erroneously believe that the bodies of their fellows grow equally indurated." The story of the old woman, who, when seeing some sentimental gormandizer of eels express his horror at seeing them flayed alive, said, "Lor' bless you, Sir, they be so used to it they don't mind it," is a much more bitter satire on human nature than at first appears. Napier argues that to condemn a man to be flogged is putting various numbers of lashes into a bag and drawing out one, for all men feel pain differently.

In the final chapters of his book, Napier asks, "can flogging be done away with entirely in the Army?" And he answers that it can be, but by a gradual process, and his great ally in this view, Sir John Moore, is quoted. To the question, "Can it be done away with in time of Peace?" Napier answers, "Yes, and at once".

In his suggestions for substitutes for flogging, Napier would like to see death, transportation, imprisonment, the treadmill, forfeiture of pay, and of pensions, blistering the back, and several minor punishments to be inflicted by Commanding Officers without court martial. The Major-General is a firm believer in *blistering*.

At the same time efforts were constantly being made in the House of Commons to bring to the public notice —and to express the widespread public disapproval—this question of "To flog, or not to flog".

In 1808, Sir Francis Burdett had renewed a demand in the House that regimental returns of corporal punishment should be presented, but there were only four votes in favour.

In 1811, an order from the Admiralty demanded the returns from each ship and all Admiralty Establishments of the number of men flogged, their crimes, and other details.

On the third reading of the Mutiny Act, 1812, six voted for the abolition of flogging and seventy-nine were against. Again in 1812, a motion was rejected, seventeen for and forty-nine against, that returns of corporal punishments and the crimes for which they were inflicted should be presented to the House.

All in the House agreed that flogging was disgraceful to the soldier and put him on a par with ruffians who had committed crimes of violence in civil life. The difference of opinion was as to whether discipline could be maintained without whipping.

In a committee on the Mutiny Bill, 1813, Sir Samuel Romilly in vain attempted to obtain a declaration from the Judge-Advocate against the practice of bringing out a man to receive the balance of his punishment. The Judge-Advocate, however, expressed his opinion of the impropriety, injustice, and even the illegality of inflicting the second part of a sentence, or by threat of inflicting them to make the convicted soldier sign a declaration to serve abroad. (In 1824, Mr. Leycester submitted a similar motion, which was lost.)

On the 8th March, 1815, when the report of the Military Bill was brought up, Sir Samuel Romilly moved that a clause should be added to it in these words : "And it be further enacted, that it shall not be lawful for any court martial by its sentence to inflict on any offender a greater number of lashes than one hundred". Mr. Manners Sutton, the Judge-Advocate, said that he wished to have time to consider the proposition, and to consult military men upon it, and requested Sir Samuel to withdraw his motion for the present, which he did; this Bill being to continue for only four months.

When the Mutiny Bill was brought into the House, on the 21st June, Mr. Bennet gave notice by a motion for leave to bring in another Bill, to limit the number of lashes which courts martial may, by their sentence, inflict; he made the motion on the same day, and it was lost.

A great point was, however, gained by this motion, Mr. Manners Sutton, the Judge-Advocate, having declared, in the course of the debate, that in his opinion, *"when a criminal had been brought out, and had suffered some portion of the lashes to which he was sentenced it was ILLEGAL to inflict any more of them on him at any future time or by the threat of inflicting them, to compel him to enter into any other regiment"*. In the military phrase, to *"keep the lashes hanging over him"*.

Not a word of commiseration seems, however, to have been expressed in regard to the hundreds of thousands, who, prior to this date, had been illegally punished by the infliction of second, third, or fourth punishments. On the other hand, the inhumanity and injustice of the measure, appears to have been long obvious to medical officers. Dr. Hamilton had observed almost thirty years before : "If a delinquent be taken down, cured of his wounds, and then tied up again, he suffers a punishment equal to the whole each time, should he be tied up ever so often; surely this is what the court martial never intended".

1828 (10th March). House of Commons. Lord

Nugent moved a clause to be inserted in the Mutiny Bill for the purpose of abolishing :—

"The punishment of flogging or any other such bodily chastisement to be inflicted on any offender, save and except for drunkenness on actual military duty, theft, fraud, or for assault with intent to commit a felony", which was thrown out without a division. Lord Nugent remarked, "that the continuance of this system of corporal punishment is a national disgrace and reproach to us in the minds of foreigners. We are in the habit of censuring the barbarous customs of other times and other countries, and taking credit to ourselves for pre-eminence in the freedom of our institutions, yet we are the only country in the world who inflict the punishment of a slave on the soldiers of our free state".

In 1829, Mr. Hume moved that a court martial should not be authorised to award a sentence of more than five hundred lashes. This was negatived.

In 1832, Mr. Hunt moved for a return of the number of courts martial held upon private soldiers, between the first day of January, 1831, and the first day of January, 1832, stating the charges upon individuals and the numbers of lashes inflicted. The motion was lost by sixty-one to twenty-eight.

In 1832, Mr. Hunt moved that corporal punishment in the Army should be suspended for one year, which was negatived, Sir John Byng observing that he had been thirty years in the Service and that "the punishment as now inflicted is not one fiftieth part of what it used to be". "God knows," said Mr. Hume, "what the state of the British Army must have been then."

In June of the same year, Mr. Hunt moved that returns of punishments for seven years should be made. The Secretary of War agreed to this and returns were published 1831-1838.

In 1833, Mr. Hume, who seems to have been very busy on behalf of abolition, moved that it shall not be lawful to inflict corporal punishment on soldiers in the

British Isles except for certain crimes, which motion he lost.

During 1833, the following order was issued by the General Commanding-in-Chief : *"Sir, His Majesty's Government having signified to the General Command-ing-in-Chief the King's command that, until further orders, corporal punishment. may be applied to the following offences only, I have the honour to express Lord Hill's desire that you guide yourself accordingly, taking care that, except in the instances herein specified, the said punishment shall on no account be inflicted. First : for mutinous insubordination, and violence, or using or offering violence to superior officers. Secondly : Drunkenness on duty. Thirdly : Sale of, or making away with, arms, ammunition, accoutrements, or necessaries, stealing from comrades, or other disgrace-ful conduct. It will doubtless occur to you that the object of these instructions is not to render the infliction of punishment for the future more frequent, or more certain than it is at present, even in the cases to which it is now to be restricted, but, on the contrary, that the intention is to restrain it as much as possible to do with safety to the discipline of the Army".*

Horse Guards, 24th August, 1833.

More motions were proposed during the year for the abolition, and interesting and often heated debates and discussions took place.

On the 21st July, 1834, the Secretary of War, Mr. Ellice, announced his intention to submit the whole burning question to a military commission. "It is my intention," said Mr. Ellice, "to ask His Majesty to issue a commission . . . to inquire into the state of our military code and into the state of codes in other countries, and to collect a body of information on which the whole system may be revised."

The specific object of this commission was to examine : *"Whether after a careful reference to all the circumstances and conditions under which the British*

Army is constituted and governed, and all the services which it is called upon to perform, it may be practicable to dispense with the power of inflicting corporal punishment, or to make any other changes or modifications in the punishments now applicable to offences committed by the soldier, without detriment or danger to the paramount consideration of maintaining strict discipline and effectually repressing crime, in the ranks of the British Army throughout all the various contingencies of military service to which our troops are necessarily liable".

*   *   *   *

With a metaphorical roll of drums and an imaginary fanfare of trumpets, we have reached the climax of this history of excesses. We have arrived at 1835, the year of the Royal Commission on Corporal Punishments.

CHAPTER TWO

THE ROYAL COMMISSION, 1835-1836

COMMISSION

"William IV, by the Grace of God, of the United Kingdom of Great Britain and Ireland, King, Defender of the Faith. TO Our right trusty and well beloved Councillors James Archibald Lord Wharncliffe, and Sir James Kempt, Knight Grand Cross of the Most Honourable Order of the Bath, and Lieutenant-General in our Army, Our trusty and well beloved Dudley Ryder, Esquire (commonly called Viscount Sandon), Our right trusty and well beloved Councillors Sir Edward Hyde East, Baronet, and Robert Cutlar Fergusson, and Our trusty and well beloved Sir Edward Barnes, Knight Grand Cross of the Most Honourable Military Order of the Bath, and Lieutenant-General in our Army, and Sir Thomas Reynell, Baronet, Knight Commander of the Most Honourable Military Order of the Bath, and Major-General in Our Army, Greeting : WHEREAS We have thought it expedient for divers good causes and considerations, that a Commission should forthwith issue for the purpose of inquiring into the several modes of Punishment now authorized and in use for the maintenance of discipline and the prevention of crime in our Land Forces; NOW KNOW YE, That We, reposing great trust and confidence in your zeal, discretion and ability, have authorized and appointed, and do by these presents authorize and appoint you, the said (all the names again, without orders) or any Three or more of you to be Our Commissioners for making the inquiry aforesaid : And We do hereby authorize and empower you Our said Commissioners, or any Three or more of you, to obtain information thereupon by the

*examination of all persons most competent, by reason of
their knowledge, habits or experience to afford it; and
also by calling for all Documents, Papers and Records
which may appear to you, or any Three or more of you,
calculated to assist your researches and to promote the
formation of a sound judgment on the subject : And
We do also hereby give and grant unto you, or any
Three or more of you, full power and authority when
the same shall appear to be requisite, to administer an
Oath or Oaths to any person or persons whatsoever to
be examined before you, or any Three or more of you,
touching or concerning the premises : And We do
hereby require and command you, or any Three or more
of you, to report to Us, under your hands and seals, with
all convenient speed, your opinions whether, after a
careful reference to all the circumstances and conditions
under which the British Army is constituted and
governed, and all the services which it is called upon to
perform, it may be practicable to dispense with the
power of inflicting Corporal Punishment, or to make
any other changes or modifications in the punishments
now applicable to offences committed by the Soldier
without detriment or danger to the paramount consideration of maintaining strict discipline, and
effectually repressing Crime in the Ranks of the British
Army throughout all the various contingencies of
Military Service to which our Troops are necessarily
liable : And We will and command, and by these
Presents ordain, that this Our Commission shall continue in full force and virtue, and that you Our said
Commissioners, or any Three or more of you, may from
time to time proceed in the execution thereof, although
the same be not continued from time to time by adjournment : And We do hereby command all and singular
Our Justices of the Peace, Sheriffs, Mayors, Bailiffs,
Constables, Officers, Ministers, and all other Our loving
subjects whatsoever, as well within liberties as without,
that they be assistant to you and each of you in the*

execution of these Presents : And for your assistance in the due execution of these Presents, We have made choice of our trusty and well beloved George Collin, Esquire, to be Secretary to this Our Commission, and to attend you, whose service and assistance We require you to use from time to time as occasion shall require.

In witness whereof, We have caused these Our Letters to be made Patent.

Witness Ourself at Westminster the Fourth day of March, in the Fifth year of Our Reign.

By Writ of Privy Seal.

Signed : EDMUNDS."

Thus was put into motion the momentous Royal Commission. The first question to its first witness was on the 12th March, 1835, and the last on the 20th February, 1836. In the period between these dates five thousand nine hundred and twenty-eight questions were put to seventy-one witnesses; witnesses varying from Field Marshal the Duke of Wellington down to privates and recruits of the Army. Papers were laid before the Commission, French officers were questioned about disciplinary punishments in the French Army and the Commission examined extracts of General Orders concerning soldier's libraries in India, extracts from General Orders from various Presidencies in India, the number of persons tried by courts martial, the number sentenced to various punishment other than corporal punishment, and the number on whom corporal punishment was inflicted.

In addition to the French officers, a pamphlet on the organisation of the Army of Prussia was carefully con-·sidered; in fact, the Commissioners assiduously did their duty in every way possible to prepare for His Majesty, Parliament, and the country an unbiased and factual report and examination of this subject : a subject that was by this date a matter of heated controversy up and down the realm, in every town and hamlet of the British Isles, debated at length in the Press, passionately at the bar of every inn, a subject, in fact, that concerned the whole nation and every strata of society in that year.

It would not be possible to give a history, such as we attempt here, of corporal punishment under the Crown, without dealing at length with the Royal Commission, its discoveries, findings and its final report.

A large and encyclopaedic volume, voluminous and in fine print, published in 1836, was presented to both Houses of Parliament by Command of His Majesty and runs to well over a quarter of a million words. We have done our best to extract from it items of exceptional interest, but in so doing have of necessity had to omit the vast majority of the reports, statistics, findings and opinions, the evidence for and against corporal punishment presented eventually to the public.

To give a factual picture of the method of enquiry we reprint some of the more pertinent questions asked by the Commission.

To the Adjutant-General of the British Army, the Commission put this question, Number 13, in their report : —

"Will you state the limitation at this date on regimental courts martial in respect to a sentence of corporal punishment?"

The answer was : "In the year 1812 . . . limited the award to three hundred lashes. It so remained until the Mutiny Act of 1832, this restricted the sentence to two hundred lashes; and so it remains now. In 1812, general regimental courts martial was introduced and were restricted to an award of five hundred lashes".

In replying to Question 41, the Adjutant also stated that in 1835 while on the march, a man refused to obey orders. The Company Officer ordered him to be tied up and the offender received fifty lashes. "The prompt application of punishment," the Adjutant maintained, "is a great means to supporting the discipline of the Army".

In his response to Question 103, he also adds "there is no disgrace in the eyes of the other soldiers", to flogging.

In Question 164, the Adjutant was asked how long it took to cure the wounds and wheals resulting from a flogging and the reply was that recovery depended upon the man flogged, the climate and circumstances, *etcetera*, but that the average recovery was effected in ten to fourteen days.

The answer to Question 270, addressed to a Major, resulted in evidence that one man chose, when offered the alternative, three hundred lashes to three weeks solitary confinement !

Question 472, investigating the same possible alternative to flogging, addressed to a General, elicited the information that with reference to the Dragoons, at any rate, confinement in prison as an alternative to corporal punishment was inclined to punish other men in the regiment because they had to tend the punished man's horses and undergo many extra duties on his behalf and in his absence.

Question 495, addressed to a Colonel in the same regiment of Dragoons, received a reply that showed the French Army had abolished corporal punishment, but that there were many more crimes punishable by death in that Army than in the British Army.

Replying to Question 503, the same officer when asked if it was his opinion that flogging improved men, said, "I've known it to result in a definite improvement, even (of some men that were flogged) to be made N.C.O.'s".

A Major-General, in Question 564, was asked : "If merited, do soldiers look upon it (flogging) as too severe a punishment?" And he replied that the greatest care was taken to inflict the cat only when merited—but he did not actually answer the question as put. His other replies to following questions showed that this officer was "all in favour" of corporal punishment and further believed that the solemnity of a drum-head court martial had a salutary effect upon the minds of young soldiers.

Question 774, to a Major and M.P., referring to his younger days in the Army, brought this reply : —

"There was not a morning while I was there [Halifax] that I was not turned out at six o'clock to witness three or four floggings. In that garrison there were two or three deaths while I was there; there were foreigners who committed suicide rather than be flogged. I recollect a Grenadier, a fine young man, who shot himself rather than be punished".

Questions 935 and 936, addressed to a Lt. Colonel, regarding the comparative discipline in foreign armies and the British, established that drunkenness was far greater in the armed forces under the Crown, but as a result of corporal punishment discipline itself was far higher.

A Sergeant of the Guards was questioned and in his replies to numbers 961 to 965, with reference to solitary confinement as being more or less effectual than the lash, gave it as his firm opinion that flogging was the more effective upholder of discipline; he also considered that drunkenness, petty theft, and insubordination had increased in those regiments where confinement had replaced corporal punishment for those offences. Further questioned, the Sergeant said that in his opinion corporal punishment made men better soldiers and he personally knew of definite improvements in individuals after a flogging.

Question 971 : "Does corporal punishment harden rather than soften a man?"

Answer : "No, I do not think it has ever hardened a man, more the other way."

The next five questions concerned the effect upon the regiment watching a punishment parade : some men fainted, some were quite unaffected by the bloody sight, some were noticed to faint more easily over one individual being flogged than another, by the youth or popularity of the man being punished, *etcetera*.

Question : "Fainting is caused by the sight of the back?"

Answer : "Yes, and by his cries. His cries are as disturbing as the sight."

Question : "It has a great effect upon the minds of those watching?"

Answer : "Yes, most seriously so."

Question : "Disgust or fear?"

Answer : "Fear."

Question : "Does flogging deter soldiers from committing crime?"

Answer : "I believe it does."

The above Sergeant further points out that very little effect is produced by the reading of a solitary confinement sentence before a regiment.

Question 1079, addressed to a private, received the answer that he could neither read nor write and had never attempted to learn and that he was quite happy to remain a private.

This man was examined at some considerable length, and Question 1131, "Have you any company court martial where you sit over each other?" received the reply : "We have such things".

"How do you punish in those instances?"

"By what we term in the regiment sling-belting them."

"What is that?"

"By giving them so many dozen with the sling of a fire lock."

"Upon the bare back, is it?"

"No, with a shirt on."

"Where abouts is it?"

"On the bottom."

"With his trousers on, do you mean?"

"Yes."

"He is held by his comrades?"

"Yes."

"He is laid down on a bench, is he not?"

"Yes."

The private pointed out that the disgrace of a man being punished by his comrades was greater than that of being flogged by a drum-head court martial.

Question 1523, was addressed to another private, one in the Guards. He told the Commission that stoppage of pay was the greatest deterrent and punishment known to a soldier and that the loss for misbehaviour of a medal received for gallantry, and hard-earned, would hurt him far more than corporal punishment or imprisonment.

Question 1533, received the answer that some men will not be deterred from crime no matter what punishments are levied.

Question 1626, was addressed to a Lt. Colonel. He said a better class would come into the Army if corporal punishment were abolished, and he thought that some men may have heard such bad reports of the brutal floggings in the Army that they might for that reason be deterred from enlisting.

In replying to Question 1994, a Colonel thought that if military prisons had hard labour and solitary confinement there would be little need for corporal punishment except in exceptional cases of violence.

A Sergeant in the Coldstream Guards, replying to Question 2041, when asked what men say among themselves about flogging, said : "I never heard them name it or speak of it with any dislike of it".

The Sergeant also said that two months on the treadmill made prisoners swear they would prefer two hundred lashes, and that the lash was definitely the most effective punishment he knew of.

In replying to Question 2095, a Corporal in the Coldstream Guards said that flogging had *increased* considerably since his enlistment and was due to an increase of drunkenness, and that soldiers sent to prison (instead of

Date		N.º of Company	Soldiers.	Quality.	For what Offence.
Day and Month	Year				
24. February —	1827	67	William Shrickland	pte	For irregular and unsoldierlike Conduct in Absenting himself from Head Quarters and leave on a about the 6.th inshant; and being deficient of part of his Necessaries
2.th February	1827	91	William Handford	pte	For the Crime of Desertion, on or about the 31.st of March last —

N.B. — This Man taken in to the Captivity Hulk at this port by Serj.t White of the Boat) the 2.d April 1827)³ Company Order 31.st Mar 1827 — on which is the time for his Baby — also See Adj.t letter same date

| 15.th March — | 1827 | | Emanuel Grace — | g.º | For irregular and unsoldierlike Conduct in Absenting himself from Head Quarters on the Evening of 11.th And not returning till 14.th — he making a frequent of practice of being absent without leave — |

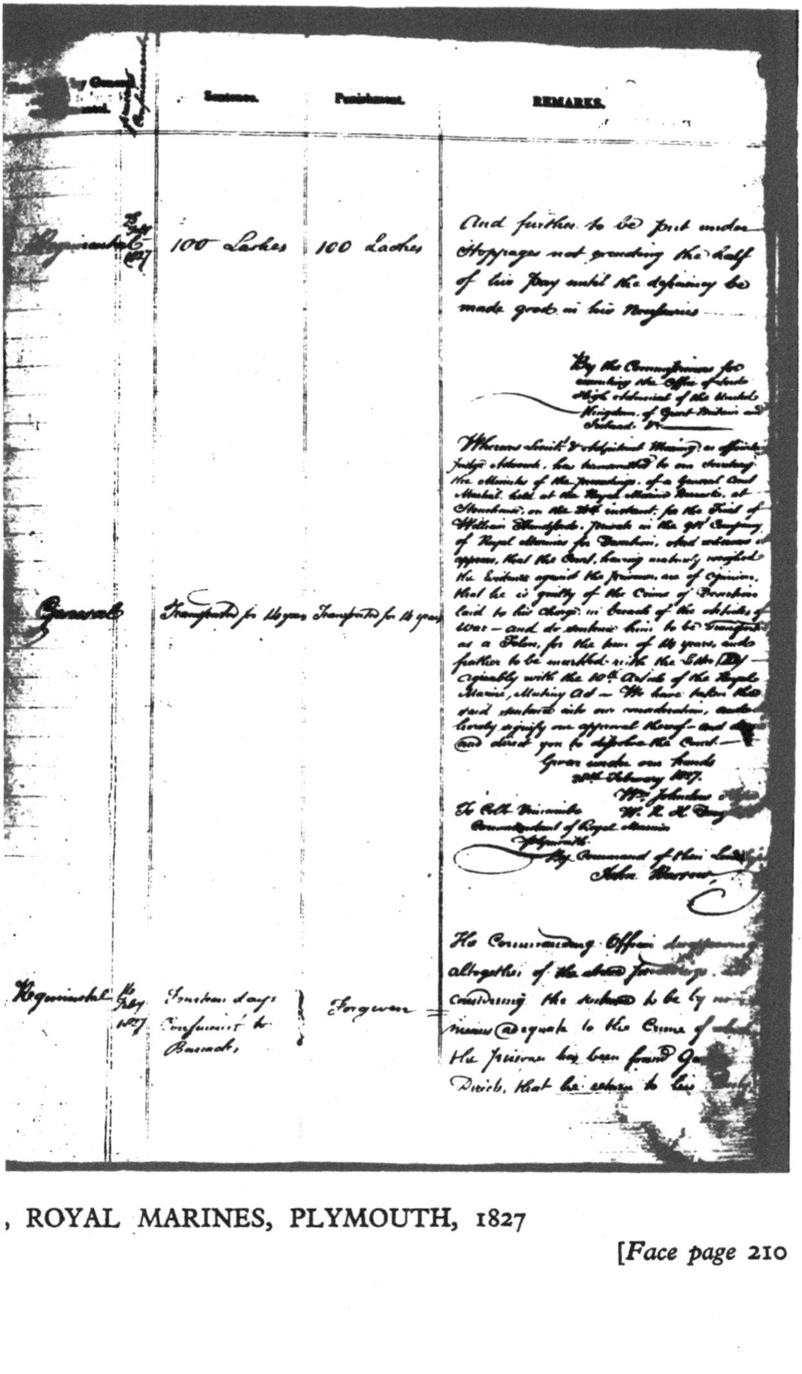

... by General ...		Sentence.	Punishment.	REMARKS.
Regimental	... 1827	100 Lashes	100 Lashes	And further to be put under Stoppages not exceeding the half of his Pay until the deficiency be made good in his Necessaries
General		Transported for 14 years	Transported for 14 years	By the Commissioners for executing the Office of Lord High Admiral of the United Kingdom of Great Britain and Ireland. &c. Whereas Lieut. & Adjutant ... as officiating Judge Advocate, has transmitted to our Secretary the Minutes of the proceedings of a General Court Martial, held at the Royal Marine Barracks, at Stonehouse, on the 20th instant, for the Trial of William ..., Private in the 91st Company of Royal Marines ..., and whereas it appears, that the Court, having maturely weighed the Evidence against the prisoner, are of Opinion, that he is guilty of the Crime of Desertion laid to his charge, in breach of the Articles of War — and do sentence him to be Transported as a Felon, for the term of 14 years, and further to be marked with the Letter (D) agreeably with the 10th Article of the Royal Marine Mutiny Act — We have taken the said sentence into our consideration, and hereby signify our approval thereof — and ... and direct you to dissolve the Court — Given under our hands ... February 1827. Wm. Johnstone ... W. R. H. ... To Col. ... Commandant of Royal Marines Plymouth. By Command of their Lordships John Barrow
Regimental	16 Feby 1827	Fourteen days Confinement to Barrack,	Forgiven	The Commanding Officer ... altogether of the above proceedings ... considering the sentence to be by no means adequate to the Crime of which the prisoner has been found Guilty ... Directs that he return to his ...

, ROYAL MARINES, PLYMOUTH, 1827

[*Face page* 210

being flogged) came out " a good deal worse" than when they went in. "We should not know them to be the same men," he said.

Question 2176, established that now that corporal punishment was less frequent the men were more satisfied and that men were now only flogged in deserving cases, and also that their respect to N.C.O.'s was now greater; but that were there no power of inflicting corporal punishment "the soldiers would not behave so cheerfully as they do now".

Questions 2203-2204, were addressed to a Colonel. He considered confining men to jail had no effect of deterring others from crime, but he states : —

"On the occasion of the last court martial there were a great number of recruits present and twenty-five or thirty fell out and some actually fainted—though the punishment was extremely slight, only one hundred lashes".

The Colonel goes on : —

"No disgust was caused by the punishment (itself) but the formal ceremony had the effect it did".

A Prison Chief, in reply to Question 2369, said that "hard labour" was always the treadmill. He also stated that the treadmill was much disliked, and sometimes he resorted—on order of the magistrates—to flogging soldiers in prison; sentences of two dozen lashes being in his opinion laid on more severely than when executed in the Army. Such punishment with a civilian cat "had great effect. The soldiers have been very well behaved ever since".

Question 2387, asked if the effect of the cat was such as to make it evident to the Prison Chief that the infliction of corporal punishment had a much greater effect over the men (both those punished and other inmates), than confinement in solitary cells. The reply that there was no doubt but that such was the case and that the effect was immediate.

This Prison Officer, further questioned, was of the

P

firm opinion that corporal punishment hardened the victim rather than reformed him, that some men would and did desert rather than be flogged, have deserted often in consequence of a flogging, and that to most soldiers "the horror of suffering was very great"; but that no doubt flogging deterred many who would otherwise commit crimes and that he had, in fact, during his experience known many flogged soldiers become "good and orderly". "But it is not a very common thing," he adds, realistically.

A Sergeant-Major was questioned considerably, and his replies to Questions 2438 to 2486, established that flogging sentences had once been much more severe than they were in 1835. "I have known cases of six, seven and eight hundred lashes given to a man at a time." "The cats were much larger than they are at present." He thought that corporal punishment was carried to an excess at one time, but that now it was too seldom used, that it had a *good* effect on the witnesses and, finally, that if flogging were done away with it would be quite impossible to maintain discipline in the Army.

2487 : "Are you aware of any great feeling among the men of your regiment against the practice of corporal punishment?" "No, I cannot say that I am, and I do not think there is."

The Sergeant-Major was firm in his opinion that "with the class of men we have, it is impossible to do without corporal punishment", and that "really bad characters" number "from thirty to forty in the regiment".

A private of the Foot was examined at great length and some of his replies, namely to the Question 2702, and ones following, are worth noting : —

"Have you heard your comrades talk of flogging?"

"I often hear some of them who have been put in gaol on account of the hard labour say they would sooner receive three hundred lashes than get three months' hard labour in gaol."

"If a man gets three hundred lashes, or two hundred lashes, it is all done at once; but he is starving to death, lingering there and breaking his heart."

"There are some men that do not care for three hundred lashes, and others that are nearly killed by it."

A Major-General was next examined and to Question 2799, he answers : "We seldom dismiss men with ignominy unless they are marked. A flogging gives them a mark that they never get the better of; then, if they are deserters, they are marked with the letter D."

And to the next question the same witness included the following remark in his reply : "In former times you tied a man up and flogged him, and the example was immediate and good; now, a man knows exactly how far he may go (before he is liable to be tried by court martial) . . . he will keep within the extent, knowing he will have only a few days of confinement for that . . ."

A Major was given the following Question 3054 : —

"Supposing those offences to have been punished by a tying up at the halberds, that would have had more effect or less, as an example, in deterring the rest from committing such offences?"

"It might have had more effect in the way of example, but I have an objection to sending out these young men with such short service (aged eighteen to twenty-two), with the marks of infamy on their backs to the regiment."

"It exposes him afterwards to his comrades for ever, to be pointed out as a man who has been sent out to the regiment with the 'record of his having been so punished . . .'"

A Sergeant-Major of the Royal Artillery, answering Question 3566, said : "I have seen two hundred lashes given as bad as four hundred; in other cases, some, when they receive their corporal punishment, make a great noise, and appear to be much affected by it, others will hang just like a stone, so that it causes no impression on the young soldiers (watching); those who make a noise and do not appear to like it, cause the greater impression."

The answer to the following Question, No. 3893, is interesting in that it sums up perfectly the majority opinion amongst officers, even the most "progressive" and humanitarian : —

"Are we then to understand that your opinion is that corporal punishment should be resorted to in cases of necessity only, but that the power of inflicting it should be retained?"

"Most decidedly," replied the Colonel. "I conceive that, if you were not to retain the power of punishing men by flogging, the officers might as well pull off their hats to the regiment, and wish them goodbye."

Another Colonel, when asked by the Commission if he thought it a good idea for there to be present on the board of the court martial one man of the same rank as the man being tried—as they sometimes did in European armies—replied that this system had, in fact, been tried in England but had not proved very successful; and that in many such cases and especially in the instances of company courts martial formed by the men themselves, "they used to flog the men most severely; in fact, they used to flog their comrades a great deal more than they would have been flogged had they been tried by the officers for the same offence".

The Rev. Harry Stuart reported many case-histories of soldiers to the Commission, some of great length and detail—others were very brief and poignant, as this : —

"P. H., who had got four months in Aberdeen Bridewell, writing to a comrade soon after says, 'I am now in hospital after three hundred, and I could take three hundred more rather than get another four months of Aberdeen Bridewell' ".

"D. L. said he would rather take five hundred than two months solitary," a sentiment that is echoed time and again !

"Sergeant M., thirty-six years in the Service, thinks flogging breaks the constitution; observed that men during the war, died more frequently from fatigue and disease, if they had been flogged. Company punishments bad; men are more afraid of a company punishment than of a legal one : company often like a punishment to get fun." The Sergeant is here referring to the extra-legal courts martial permitted the men among themselves.

While examining a Colonel, the Commission pointed out in its 5305th Question that "In the year 1835, it appears that the number of lashes awarded considerably exceeded the number awarded in any other year since 1826".

This was one of a long series of questions with reference to the death by lock-jaw of a soldier who had been flogged before the regiment, who had received one hundred and thirty-four lashes of the one hundred and fifty sentenced, but who—on the advice of the Surgeon —had been remitted the full punishment, though he was well enough to be *marched* to hospital. He died a fortnight later and there was considerable public agitation locally as to his death : "With respect to the division— was there any great sensation produced by it [the man's death] in the division itself?"

"Not at all; none whatever."

The same Colonel, replying to Question 5329, said : —

"I have had a man thank me for flogging him, he has been so much better for it".

A Surgeon who had tended punished men both in the Army and Navy was asked by the Commission in Question 5448, if the punishment in the Naval Service was more severe than that in the Army. "Much more severe. The cat is heavier, the blow is heavier, but the stripes are fewer."

"Each stripe is a more severe punishment?" "Yes."

Surgeon Parkin, in his memorandum to the Commission, gave his opinions on corporal punishment at considerable length, dealing with the conditions of service, the type of man recruited, and the best punishment suitable to his character, background, and sensitivity. He says that in his opinion no moral degradation is experienced by the men flogged, and indeed, as will be seen, it would be difficult *morally* to degrade most of the men who commit the type of crime punished by flogging. To support this opinion the Surgeon gives the following illustration : —

"The man who is picked up drunk from the kennel, kicked out of a bagnio, bleeding from wounds in the head and face, and brought almost insensible into the barracks and hospital; or has been *one of five*, three of his own comrades and two prostitutes, wallowing in the same bed together for a night, cannot suffer a *moral degradation* from the lash".

When debating the question of corporal punishment as administered in the early nineteenth century, it is imperative and essential that the period and social "types" of the majority of those men who enlisted be borne in mind : or else the life they led and the punishments they endured—when thought of in twentieth-century terms—become impossible to visualise and the floggings themselves inhumanly brutal acts of legalised sadism, which they were not—except perhaps in a few cases.

The most difficult problem set the Royal Commission was not that of discovering whether or not corporal punishment should be abolished, for they very soon established that even in the majority of officers' minds the *punishment* was degrading, demoralising, harmful, cruel, and dangerous to the soldier's body, mind, usefulness, and future discipline; the problem that faced the Royal Commission was rather that of finding and recommending some other alternative punishment that would be an as effectual *deterrent,* especially when flogging was administered *before* the regiments and crews. Flogging, no one claimed, cured a criminal; but it prevented many from being rash and undisciplined. It was *feared* by those who would otherwise have taken a chance of some other form of punishment, though to the majority of those on whom it was inflicted it made very little or no good effect, rather the opposite. And, while willing to try any experiment, no alternative punishment could be conceived that was as practicable— apart from the obvious and Continental punishment for similar crimes : *death!*

"In the year 1832, there were, in England and Wales, one thousand nine hundred and eighty-one men flogged, and persons privately flogged one hundred and one, making in that year over two thousand persons flogged by order of the civil authorities. In the same year, the number of soldiers flogged in Great Britain and Ireland was four hundred and eighty-five. I mention these facts to show that whilst individuals in the House of Commons are so intensely anxious to abolish corporal punishment in the Army, it is inflicted by the civil law of the land to a great(er) extent, and, when abolished, is recommended to be revived by a committee of the most benevolent persons in the country." So said Major-General Sir H. Hardinge to the Royal Commission of 1835, and his last sentence echoes across time to be as true and up-to-date to-day as it was one hundred odd years ago. It seems that though the man-in-the-street of to-day, or the soldier in the ranks, might no longer be so physically constituted that he could so stoically take three hundred lashes of the cat-o'-nine-tails on the bare back and then march erect to hospital, "the most benevolent persons in the country" have not changed to an *equal* degree—though we recognise that in this age and country no one has yet voiced the opinion that *hundreds* of cuts of the lash should be inflicted. It may well be that a lesser number of lashes would to-day be an equal punishment to the hundreds of strokes administered just over a hundred years ago . . .

*   *   *   *

Among other methods of obtaining information, the Royal Commission circularised Commanding Officers of regiments and barracks, asking replies in the strictest confidence to certain pertinent questions. Upon the replies received they made a special report and, in addition, used their information in their final report to the King.

Here is the letter sent out : —

Horse Guards,

(Secret and confidential.)   15th October, 1834.

Sir,

In transmitting to you the enclosed list of queries, I have it in command to acquaint you, that the General Commanding-in-Chief expects your candid and unreserved sentiments on the several points referred to you, without bias or leaning to any pre-conceived theory, or any supposed opinions of superiors, it being Lord Hill's sole object to ascertain the authentic results of practical experience.

You will readily perceive the propriety of this communication being considered strictly private and confidential, and you will, of course, deal with it in every respect accordingly.

I have the honour to be,

Sir,

Your very obedient humble servant,

JOHN MACDONALD, A.G.

Officer Commanding.

P.S.   You will be pleased to write your answers to the enclosed queries on the number of blank spaces left for that purpose, and return the whole to me.

Below we give the most relevant questions and an analysis of the replies received by the Commission : —

Question Four. "What is the result of your experience as to the effects of these punishments (corporal), imprisonment with hard labour, and solitary confinement, on the discipline of the corps? Have the men returned to their duty with better dispositions, and have they subsequently conducted themselves in an orderly, soldierlike manner, or the contrary?"

Two hundred and six officers replied to this question, and from companies on active service in such places as Ceylon, Van Diemen's Land, Bombay, Bengal, the Mediterranean, Nova Scotia, Gibraltar, Malta, the West Indies, Jamaica, New South Wales, Canada, Demerara, Madras, the Cape of Good Hope, Mauritius, and, of course, from all over the British Isles.

A bare majority of the above opinion was that hard labour was most efficacious, though a few preferred solitary confinement rigidly carried into effect. There were many officers, however, who felt that imprisonment with hard labour did very little good and often did harm to men and discipline—very few men have "reformed" as a result of hard labour or "solitary", and a notable number of officers replied that "these punishments have had the very worst effect", "the men returning infinitely worse in disposition, and frequently committing crimes of a more henious nature . . . proving a total indifference to future punishment", . . . "these punishments have no very considerable effect", "these punishments are insufficient", "imprisonment had no effect", "offenders mostly habitual drunkards . . . no improvement in them after hard labour", "the dispositions of the men (so punished) have not improved . . . on the contrary, many instances have occurred of men getting drunk and committing fresh offences on the very day of their release", and so on.

So much for imprisonment, with hard labour—the terrible treadmill which men hated so much that they would barter three hundred lashes for three months in prison (see p. 207)—and the loneliness of solitary confinement.

Question Five. "In what light (as far as you know) have they appeared to view the punishments they had undergone, and in what terms have they represented these punishments to their comrades?"

The same two hundred and six officers replied to the general effect that the majority of men "made light of it", "treated it with indifference", "never spoken of as an excessive punishment", but there were many who replied that imprisonment was dreaded, especially the treadmill. Most soldiers seemed to fear "hard labour" far more than "solitary", but Major Gordon, on the other hand, "Has reason to believe they make a joke of the treadmill". As to how the soldiers spoke of such punishments *among themselves* none of the officers are very informative : and understandably so . . .

Question Six was concerned with the health and habits of men released from prison, and to this question the officers all replied briefly, mostly that habits and health had seldom altered, many that the soldiers deteriorated, and a very few claimed an improvement among the soldiers due to imprisonment.

Question Nine asked : "Always bearing in mind the efficiency of the culprit, as a soldier, what, in your opinion, is the maximum of imprisonment, with hard labour, that could be safely and beneficially inflicted?"

To this question the two hundred and six officers answered variously. The majority swayed between three, four, and six months, but many said nine months or a year. Lt. Colonel Bartley, consistently and conspicuously humane in all his replies, says thirty days. No officer recommended more than twelve months.

Question Ten. "And what the maximum of solitary confinement?" To which the officers in the majority said between six weeks and two months, many said thirty days, about fifteen per cent. of the replies were in favour of three months maximum, less than ten replied that ten

to fourteen days was a severe punishment, and
Lt. Colonel Bartley said, "Thirty days, or six weeks at
most".

One of the big problems at the beginning of the
nineteenth century, was that of accommodation for
punishment—as it is to-day. Military prisoners were
too often put among civilian felons in civilian gaols and
suffered rapid deterioration of character thereby, or
were put under conditions of overpopulation and as a
consequence made light of the imprisonment : for any
condition is easier to bear if shared, and if shared by
many is again—in direct proportion—easier to endure.

Consequently the officers recommended solitary
cells, strict bread-and-water diets, the minimum use of
civilian prisons, and in answering *Question Thirteen*
were unanimously in favour of Military Prisons, for the
reception of soldiers exclusively.

Question Fourteen asked : "Has any other mode of
punishment than those now in use occurred to you, as
likely to be advantageously employed, in maintaining
discipline and good order in the Army?"

The replies to this question were varied and con-
flicting. The principal alternatives to imprisonment
suggested by the two hundred and six officers were :
Stocks erected in the barracks yard; stoppage of pay;
cobbing (beating the buttocks with a stick); a dress of
disgrace for minor offences; discharge from the Army
after branding; remonstrance and advice (the "psychological approach"); "a drunken squad" to do menial
work only; transportation; foreign service (for varied
periods to "life"); reduction of pension; eight days'
solitary confinement; the log (a log tied to the ankle,
which has to be dragged around); forfeit of pay; longer
terms of imprisonment; confinement in a black hole;
distinguishing marks or clothing at parades to disgrace
offenders before the regiment; prevention of communication between prisoners; confinement to dark cells for
seventy-two hours; special "condemned corps for the

worst characters", and every punishment made as severe
as possible after first offence; confinement for days in a
"dry room" as a punishment for crimes committed
during drunkenness; servile corps placed for duty on the
most inhospitable stations to receive "but a bare sub-
sistence and restricted to menial work"; drills in heavy
marching order; discharge with ignominy; extra guards;
for three consecutive desertions one officer recommends
the penalty of death; drunkards should be segregated and
alcoholics forfeited and they excluded from the canteen;
a system of rewards for good behaviour (only two officers
suggested this alternative); a wheel or treadmill to be
established at all principal military posts; branding with
"B" for certain offences other than desertion; absolute
silence for one to seven days (or for six, seven, and eight
hours a day); keeping the prisoner within sight of his
comrades while being punished and not removing him
from the regiment—so that his punishment is witnessed;
and one officer suggests medals as a reward for good
conduct and a good-conduct book.

Twenty per cent. of the officers could not make any
suggestions for improving the punishments in the Army,
and a very considerable proportion in favour of flogging
more severely as an alternative to imprisonment. Our
friend Lt. Colonel Bartley advises stoppage of pay for
all minor offences, but makes no other recommendation.

It must be borne in mind that the main "parent" of
all crime in the Army was recognised as drunkenness,
and that the Commission knew this fact—even asking
the officers to make suggestions for controlling this vice.

Question Eighteen very closely approached the
whole point of the enquiry, asking: "Incidental
remarks on corporal punishment".

To this invitation the two hundred and six officers
did not unanimously respond; in fact, only sixty-four
replied, but the majority of those did so at length.

Firstly, the principal observation put forward was
that "corporal punishment would become less necessary

if the character of the Army could be improved by better recruits, but . . . with safety to the discipline of the Army, the *power* of inflicting it can never be given up".

Many of the officers who replied advised that if it were retained, corporal punishment should be reserved for only the most serious crimes, be very much restrained in use during peace time, and preserved for foreign service only in times of war.

On the other hand, many officers gave the opinion that "Abstaining from corporal punishment has produced insubordination, and its further abolition, without an efficient substitute, would surely endanger the discipline of the Army".

That "good men do not object to it" was another view frequently offered, and other officers claimed reformation and outstanding improvement in the discipline of men punished once by the cat-o'-nine-tails, even instancing cases of men who had been so lashed and afterwards risen from the ranks to become non-commissioned officers. Also, the fact that many men in each regiment approved corporal punishment and felt it a fitting chastisement to crimes that had thrown a bad light on the regiment as a whole, disgraced the corps, and embarrassed his comrades, was, in the considered opinion of many officers, strong evidence in favour of retaining the lash.

Another piece of evidence strongly in favour of the retention of corporal punishment, was that the men themselves organised troop courts martial among themselves, and that their sentences and the punishment inflicted on the offenders were in fact more severe and brutal than the official drum-head courts martial in the barrack-square. Men, on these unofficial punishment parades, were whipped and flogged with a course canteen strap or sling belt upon the bare buttocks, sometimes so cruelly that the system was frowned upon by Commanding Officers and in some cases prohibited. In addition, the punishments adopted by the successful

Naval mutineers (1798) were far more severe than those ever inflicted upon them by their lawful officers—and these facts, claims Lt. General Sir Hussey Vivian, "speak for the feelings of soldiers and sailors on the question of corporal punishment".

The *dread* of corporal punishment as a deterrent to crime, especially crimes of violence, was—claimed many officers—indispensable to the maintenance of proper discipline. Other officers stated flatly that flogging was a "revolting" punishment and recommended the stocks or other less violent disgraces. Some claimed "a soldier would rather undergo a flogging than have his pay stopped for any length of time", and yet, for the crime of drunkenness, the root and source of a soldier's misery, nothing appears so effectual as corporal punishment.

The fact that a flogging could be *promptly* inflicted on the spot, immediately after the court martial had found the soldier guilty of the offence charged, was to many of the officers the best argument in favour of its retention. Of the sixty officers who replied to this invitation to express their confidential views and "incidental remarks", over fifty per cent. were strongly in favour of retaining corporal punishment, with few changes in mode, procedure, acts of crime for which it could be awarded, or any limitation whatsoever.

Our humanitarian, Lt. Colonel Bartley, does not respond to the invitation by so much as one word, probably feeling that his replies to the other questions had shown him to be so consistently opposed to corporal punishment that any "incidental remarks" of his would have been superfluous.

It is noticeable, however, that quite a few of the officers opine that the soldier would rather undergo a flogging than endure prolonged solitary confinement—though we need to remember that the physical conditions of imprisonment in the early nineteenth century were "more than somewhat" grim, to use the most expressive yet factual expression we can command.

Under the heading "General Observations" most of the officers asked for their confidential opinions became of great use to the Commission, "letting themselves go" with literary detail and at a length that shows that they each of them had given the questions much thought, and under this final heading summarised their views—or very often elaborated them.

Major-General Sir T. M'Mahon was the most succinct : "No recruit should be enlisted in peace without a character". (Reference, we presume.)

The next officer suggested a system of rewards for exemplary behaviour, the following reiterates his opinion that extra punishments such as *cobbing* and *logging* should be introduced for minor offences, and from Van Diemen's Land, Colonel Arthur writes an almost impassioned essay of over a thousand words. He begins by stating that the officers themselves should do their best by example to raise the standard of behaviour and discipline (the first suggestion we hear in this investigation that the officers were or could be less than angels !), and he explores this aspect of his thesis for three hundred words—demanding from officers and Commanding Officers the highest intelligence, humanity, and integrity; by implication suggesting that the Army had within it many men who fell far short of his requirements of the officer he portrays. He considers that flogging, unless it can be shown that every other proper measure for the prevention of crime has been tried, is unjustifiable. He is very firm in his contention that punishment is mainly a deterring measure to show an example to others than the offender, not merely a vengeance. He again returns to the duty of officers to set an example of good behaviour, suggests more solicitous and comfortable attention to the housing of ordinary ranks, and ends by saying that the lash is a degrading punishment, and that rule by fear dooms itself and invites eventual rebellion.

A Major Champian claims "The frequency of courts martial has destroyed their effect, and young men do not dread them so much when they see good soldiers subjected to them for occasional irregularities", and Lieut. Colonel Freer agrees that "The frequency of courts martial has taken from the minds of the men generally the disgrace that should attach to appearing before such tribunals".

Another officer suggests "the establishment of a code of indulgences, amusements, and relief", and the next officer suggests that more games be organised among the men, that they "should be encouraged to play cricket, and other manly games".

Colonel Nicol anticipates this century by recommending "fives-courts, racket-courts, and a place for quoits or other manly amusements; and separate apartments for messing, which rooms the soldiers might occupy in the evenings for reading".

Many officers recommend medals and other such signs and rewards for good conduct, some the establishment of a savings bank in each regiment to stop the habitual expenditure of pay on drink, "from which rises every evil in a soldier's life", and one officer suggests that the men be divided into five classes of character, resultant upon the length of their service and the number of offences committed in that time.

Another officer is very much in favour of transportation for repeated misbehaviour, while another claims that soldiers thought so little of the transportation punishments then in force that some conspired to be brought before a general court martial in the hope of being sent to Bermuda, to which sunny island most transportees were sent at that date.

Another officer draws the Commission's attention to the evils he claims resulted upon the marriage of British soldiers with foreign women, especially in India, and the practice of volunteering for service in India (which country, it seems, had a licentious and pleasant reputa-

BRASS INSTRUMENT FOR BRANDING DESERTERS WITH THE LETTER D

(In the possession of the Author)

This device came into use throughout the Army about 1840, replacing the employment of a bunch of sewing-needles. Gunpowder was rubbed into the punctures to render the tattoo indelible.

[*Face page* 226

tion among the soldiers in England) should be discouraged.

From this mass of differing opinion the Royal Commission formed their own opinions on each aspect of the matter they were commanded to report upon.

* * * *

The General Commanding-in-Chief, Lord Hill, was as much opposed to the use of the lash for the maintenance of military discipline as Wellington was in favour of its retention and indispensability. Lord Hill, as a farsighted, cultured, and humanitarian politician, did his best in replying to the questions put by the Royal Commission, to present a damning argument against flogging as a corporal punishment. His examination was long and detailed; his answers including all the arguments for abolition to be found elsewhere in this history, coupled to and given weight by his name, rank, and the respect the country and Crown bore him, were of profound importance.

* * * *

By the time that the Royal Commission had reached Question 5796, they were asking Field Marshal the Duke of Wellington his opinion on the abolition of corporal punishment. The Iron Duke had resigned the command of the British Army in 1828, but he had, very naturally, kept in close touch with military matters and was continually intimate with the higher heirarchy of the Army, a friend to Royal circles, a friend of the King, and an associate of many of his most important ministers.

In answering his fifth question, Wellington established his firm belief in the necessity to inflict, *and to retain the power to inflict,* corporal punishment. He told the Commissioners of how, even in 1828, he was "on the other side of the fence" to many of the officers under his command with regard to the use of the cat and the

Q

lash, and that, rather than disagree with them openly and cause disaffection within his command, he had let those so inclined practise "humanitarian" experiments and to try as many substitutes to the use of corporal punishment as were available. Further, "knowing that the opinion of the public is that these corporal punishments ought to be discontinued as much as possible, I have considered it my duty to refrain from even giving an opinion upon the subject".

As a result of the efforts made to lower the frequency in the last ten years, the Duke says : "I am inclined to believe that there is less corporal punishment now, but, then, on the other hand, I am inclined to believe that there is now a great deal more crime".

And : "A great variety of other punishments had been invented, and I certainly thought that that system had not been very successful", when speaking of the alternatives, such as hard labour, solitary confinement, *etcetera.*

When asked if he made every effort, while in command of the Army, to diminish the frequency of drumhead courts martial and flogging in general, Wellington replied : "As much as possible . . . There is one very remarkable circumstance, which I beg the Board will never lose sight of, that is, that this punishment is always inflicted in public; that, supposing the Commanding Officer himself had no feeling in respect to the punishment which is inflicted on the individual, he must know that there are many present who do feel it in a very extraordinary degree; officers and soldiers both, who are excessively annoyed at this punishment. It is done in public, and there is security that it will not go to excess".

Replying to the next question, Wellington gave a very firm reply : "I don't think that it produced any effect", meaning the substitution of imprisonment and solitary confinement to corporal punishment.

Question 5804 and the three that followed concerned the Duke's opinions on drunkenness in the British Army, and he agreed that it was "Invariably the great parent to all crime in the Service". He further gave it as his opinion that "the British soldiers are taken entirely from the lowest orders of society". Consequently, he thought, only the severest discipline was sufficient to maintain an efficient Army.

The Duke did not think, in replying to the next question, that if corporal punishment were abolished and certain privileges were given to the ranks, it might have the effect of producing a better class of soldier.

"I do not see how you can have an Army at all unless you preserve it in a state of discipline, nor how you can have a state of discipline unless you have some punishment . . . There is no punishment which makes an impression upon any body except corporal punishment . . . The real meaning of punishment, if it means anything, is example—it is to prevent others, by example of what they see the criminal suffer, from committing the same or a similar offence. If that is not the intention of punishment—if the intention is to punish, or even to improve the conduct of the individual only—you may find other punishments; but you will have hundreds of others guilty of the offence, and you will have the whole regiment, by degrees, in a state of punishment" . . . "I say that it is a positive breach of faith with the good man if discipline should not be enforced" . . . "By not enforcing your discipline, and not enforcing your own orders, and not punishing when those orders are not obeyed, you are doing the grossest injustice to those who do obey your orders. That is a view of the case which is not generally taken; but it is a true view, and ought to be brought before the public."

The next questions are all concerned with the substitution of imprisonment for corporal punishment, and the Duke throughout is adamant in his long and detailed replies, in upholding his view that imprisonment as an alternative is impracticable and would by its very nature and manner of enforcement, never be as effectual a deterrent to crime in the Army, as was the example afforded on the barrack-square of a flogging at the halberds, before the assembled regiment.

A sojourn in prison, Wellington points out, no matter how strict and severe a punishment to the prisoner, is still an individual and unshared experience, a *secret*, inner suffering for the greater part. It is a punishment that lacks example, and the battalion not only lose sight of the man being so punished, but by its very nature cannot have acquaintance with that punishment. "I have no doubt of that whatever," replies the Duke, when asked by the Commissioners if he thinks that a certain number of lashes inflicted, after the reading of a court martial, in front of a regiment, would have more effect as an example, than any representation of the punished man's sufferings in prison. And, of course, we must all agree with Wellington, no matter how humanitarian we may think ourselves—to-day, as in 1835.

The next question, asking if His Grace had known of cases of corporal punishment having an immediate effect, of putting a stop to the prevalence of such crimes for which the man received the cat-o'-nine-tails, receives his most succinct reply to all the questions addressed him : "Certainly".

"I have no idea of any great effect being produced by anything but the fear of immediate corporal punishment. I must say, that in hundreds of instances, the very threat of the lash has prevented very serious crimes. It is well known that I have hundreds of times prevented the most serious offences by . . . fear of the lash."

"Having this subject in contemplation for six or seven years, I have turned it over in my mind in every possible way; and I declare that I have not an idea what can be substituted for it," says Wellington in reply to Question 5821.

Discipline in the French Army is discussed and questions put to the Iron Duke upon his experiences and

opinions upon matters concerning the comparison of
discipline and punishments in that army and in the
British Army. But the modes of conscription and the
human material available to the officers is once again
the stumbling-block that prevents a true comparison of
discipline and relative punishments. But Wellington is
firm in his contention that discipline is superior in the
British Army to that of the French—and who should
know better than he?

Question 5834 to His Grace was : "Was it ever presented to you, or did you ever observe, that a soldier
who had been corporally punished was a worse or
better soldier in the field from having received that
punishment?" "I never heard of it," answered
Wellington.

And, moreover, he did not think soldiers were
degraded by punishment at the halberds, or that their
comrades thought less of them after this public punishment. Nor had Wellington "ever heard" of a soldier
being made unfit from cowing of the spirit after infliction
of corporal punishment, for service in the field.

With reference to the proposed building of special
military detention barracks and prisons, the Duke was
again succinctly firm in giving his opinion on whether
they might produce a system as effectual as that of
corporal punishment for the preservation of discipline
in the Army : "Certainly not", said His Grace.

Wellington was further questioned, even cross-
examined, on his opinions regarding the abolition of
corporal punishment, to the extent of a further forty
questions, taking a considerable time to answer, and
upon subjects as diversely relative as the partial abolition
of flogging, the granting of special honours to the well-
disciplined soldier and the infliction of distinguishing
forms of dress on the misbehaved, the expense of erect-
ing special military prisons, the class of men most
suitable for recruitment to the officer-class, the recommending of commissions, the feelings of men from the

ranks elevated to commissioned officers, modes of procedure of every nature in foreign armies, systems which might be usefully imported from them into the British Army, the instigation of orders of merit, pensions, his varied experiences with the British Army in European campaigns, army service in India, and other subjects; and continually, the Duke of Wellington made it clear that he could see no alternative to corporal punishment as a means of upholding discipline in the British Army.

* * * *

"TO THE KING'S MOST EXCELLENT MAJESTY"

"WE, Your Majesty's Commissioners, appointed by Your Majesty's Commission, bearing date the Fourth day of March, in the Fifth Year of Your Majesty's Reign, whose Hands and Seals are here-unto set do humbly certify to Your Majesty—That,

"In prosecuting the Inquiry intrusted to us by Your Majesty's Commission, we have called before us and examined a great number of witnesses, including persons of all ranks in the Army, from the recruit and private soldier to the most experienced general officers in the Service, and to the General Commanding-in-Chief.

"We have also thought it our duty to examine several of those persons, who have publicly advocated the entire and immediate abolition of corporal punishment in the Army, or its gradual abolition by the substitution of other punishments. A further object of our enquiry has been the practice in the other armies of Europe, with regard to their discipline, and the means adopted for its maintenance . . .*

"We are, therefore, now prepared to lay our

---

* All cuts in this actual report have been most carefully considered and limited only to the eradication of repetitions, verbosity common to such an official communication, and to such cuts that make the report more easily readable and understood.

opinions upon the matters referred to us before Your Majesty, and have agreed to the following Report : —

"The object, for we have humbly conceived Your Majesty had pleased to direct this Commission to issue, appears to us to have been a minute and searching Inquiry into the means at present used to maintain the discipline of the Army, with a view to ascertain how far the resort to corporal punishment might be dispensed with, either immediately and entirely, or prospectively and gradually.

"We have, therefore, directed our attention to the following points : —

"1. The regulations which have been adopted of late years in order to render the infliction of that punishment more rare than at former periods, and to diminish the extent to which it may be carried by the sentences of courts martial.

"2. Whether some alteration in regard to the minor punishments now inflicted by the authority of the Commanding Officers of regiments, both as respects the summary and effectual application of those punishments . . . might not tend to diminish the supposed necessity of recurring to corporal punishment in many instances, without endangering the maintenance of proper discipline.

"3. Whether the punishments that are now resorted to as substitutes for corporal punishment appear to have been effectual and whether their substitution is likely to render an immediate and entire abolition of that punishment practicable and safe, or to hold out hope that by more stringent application of them, the necessity of its continuance may be gradually removed.

"4. Whether the infliction of corporal punishment may not be confined within still narrower limits than at present, both as to the number of lashes in the power of courts martial to award, and as to the offences to which they may be applied; . . .

"5. Whether some system of rewards to the good and well-behaved soldier while in the Service, either by promotion to commissions, by honorary distinctions, or otherwise, or by the prospect of some civil advantages combined with pension, or all of these might not have the effect . . . . of improving the moral character of the Army as to render the use of corporal punishment unnecessary."

(The Commission then give opinions and facts regarding the distinction between the British Army and other European Armies at that date; they summarise enlistment procedures, discipline, recruitment, conscription—which was the principal mode of building up most Continental armies—times of service required by the different countries, average educational background of men in the ranks abroad compared with the average soldier in the British Army, etc. They show that the mode of filling the ranks of the British Army differed in every way from that of every other European Army, and the fact that none of those countries, except France, had colonies to which it was necessary to send armies, also made a considerable difference in the reactions of the troops serving in them, and to the type of men recruited to them. All in all, the Commission decide that the British Army has in its necessary duties and in its traditional form of recruitment many serious disadvantages to overcome with respect to the proper maintenance of effectual discipline. Mainly perhaps, that the thousands of good, middle-class and socially educated civilians conscripted *out of duty to country* by European armies, setting a high moral example of self-sacrifice and good character, was absent in the formation of the British Army which, by its nature of voluntary enlistment attracted to its ranks only the lowest and most unsuccessful and often the most anarchistic, and undisciplined of characters; drunkards, thieves, gaol-birds and "social-trash" who had failed miserably in civilian life, all these made up far too large a proportion of the ranks, and had therefore to be kept amenable to proper and effectual military discipline.)

"The great body of our recruits consists of the inhabitants of the large towns and manufacturing districts, and of agricultural labourers, which last appear, generally to enter the Army, in consequence of some family difficulty, some scrape in which they are involved, or from some temporary difficulty of obtaining work, and become the best and most trustworthy soldiers, when they have undergone the necessary preparation of the drill.   Those, who come from manufacturing districts and large towns, are too frequently the most idle and dissolute, and require all the means in the power of their officers, to correct the intemperate and vicious habits, in which they have indulged, and to teach them, that subordination is the first duty, in the profession into which they have entered.

"In an Army thus composed, it is scarcely necessary to point out the evils of a relaxed state of discipline."

(An Army recruited by conscription from every class, it is pointed out, must inevitably have a much higher moral standard, and by advice and the example of its more educated conscripts, set a level for the recruits who are unfortunately less so.   The British Army has proved in the face of the enemy, to have a co-ordination of discipline equal to any contingency or enterprise, but without the discipline *forced* upon our soldiers by their officers, their *"character and habits are such as to lead them into great excesses, and frequently to render them unfit for any useful purpose"*.   Englishmen, the Commission think, are jealous of both their Army *and* their liberty, and the conflict of these two traditional prides makes it difficult for them to recommend conscription or severe corporal punishment even though a high standard of military discipline is the aim behind both alternatives.)

"In considering therefore the subject of the punish⸱ments, by which the discipline of the British Army has been created and maintained up to this time, it is well to see how far they have answered their purpose. To the superior discipline of the British Army, when on service in foreign countries, and even in the enemy's country, strong testimony will be found in the evidence, and more especially that of the Duke of Wellington, Sir Henry Fane, and Sir Henry Hardinge . . .

"The infliction of some sort of corporal punishment has been in use in the British Army from the earliest period.

"The antiquity of any practice, however, cannot be set up as a defence of it, . . .

"It appears from the evidence of the Adjutant-General, Sir John Macdonald, that in 1795, when he entered the Army, there was no limitation whatever of the power of regimental or other courts martial, of awarding corporal punishment, and that a great decrease in the number of those punishments has taken place of late years, in consequence of a more frequent use of the minor punishments in the power of Commanding Officers, and of the substitution of solitary confinement, imprisonment with hard labour, and transportation, in cases where corporal punishment used to be constantly awarded by the sentences of courts martial . . . in the year 1812 (corporal punishment was) limited to three hundred lashes. This limitation was in force till the Mutiny Act in 1832, when the award was further limited to two hundred lashes, and it so continues. In 1829 the award of a district or garrison court martial was confined to three hundred lashes, and it so remains. In consequence of the vigilance of the Commanders-in-Chief in watching these punishments, and checking the application of them with undue severity, has been the decrease before alluded to . . . Under this system it is stated, in

the evidence of several of the officers who have been
examined that, except in cases which require a prompt
example, or where minor punishments under the
authority of the Commanding Officer, as well as those
which have been substituted for corporal punishment
under sentence of a regimental court martial, have been
tried without effect, corporal punishment is rarely
awarded . . ."

(Corporal punishment at this date could be
inflicted for : Mutiny, insubordination—a term
admitting of wide interpretation !—and violence, or
using or offering to use violence to superior officers,
drunkenness on duty, sale of or making away
with arms, ammunition, accoutrements, or necessaries, stealing from comrades, other disgraceful
conduct.)

"Previously to the issuing of the circular, there was
scarcely an offence committed by a soldier which did not
subject him to corporal punishment at the discretion of
the court martial before which he was tried . . ."

The Commission said then that they found throughout the evidence taken by them that the prevailing
general opinion was "that the power of Commanding
Officers, with regard to the extent to which they may
inflict minor punishments, and the discretion by which
they are to be guided in bringing offenders before a
regimental court martial, as well as the range of offences
now cognisable by such a court, is too limited.

"We cannot help thinking that it would be desirable
to vest a greater discretion than is present permitted,
in these respects, in the Commanding Officers of regiments, and that the effect of such a relaxation would be
to diminish the number of courts martial, both regimental and district, and the consequent corporal
punishments.

"We come now to the main questions : —

"1. Have the punishments resorted to as substitutes
for corporal punishment, been effectual, and can they

be relied upon, so as to make an immediate and entire abolition of that punishment safe and practicable?

"2. Does our experience hold out a hope that, by an improved application of these substitutes, corporal punishment may be gradually abolished?

"Upon the answer to these questions must depend the whole case, for the retention or abolition of that punishment, and we proceed to consider them with a due sense of their importance, not merely to the soldier who is subjected to it, but to the country which he serves.

"The objections to the continuance of this punishment as at present employed, or altogether, will be found in the evidence given by [six highly experienced military officers who were also at this time Members of Parliament] . . . who nevertheless are decidedly of opinion, that the power of inflicting it should be retained, and an earnest desire expressed to avoid it as much as possible, and to have recourse to substitutes, if such can be found, as will be effectual.

"Undoubtedly the only ground upon which the continuance . . . of any punishment inflicting severe pain . . . must consist in its efficacy as an example, and although its effect in the way of reformation of the person undergoing it, should not be, by any means overlooked, that must be considered a secondary object.

"The objections to this punishment, as detailed in the evidence, may thus be stated.

"It is said to be inefficient for its object : To degrade the character, and to tend to harden rather than reform the individual. Its effect upon those who witness it, is said, to be that of disgust, and sympathy for the offender. It is said to fail before the enemy. It is also said to be contrary to the feelings of this country, in its present state of civilisation, and that the public mind is irritated against it, and that that circumstance alone calls for its abolition.

"With regard to the inefficiency of corporal punishment for its object, there can indeed be no doubt that if the entire prevention of all crime and offence, has been expected from it, it may be predicted of this, as of every sort of punishment hitherto thought of, that it has not attained its object. But if the object is taken to be the repression of crime, by means of example, it appears, from the evidence, that, in many cases, where every other punishment has failed, it has had that effect, and even by those who speak of its infliction inspiring disgust in the bystanders witnessing it, it is admitted to have great effect in deterring other soldiers, and especially the younger, from committing offences which will subject them to it.

"To the second of these objections we observe that, throughout the evidence, including even that of the non-commissioned officers and soldiers, who have been examined, great doubt is thrown upon the fact of its being considered by the soldiers, at all events, a degrading punishment, if applied in the case of a military offence only. Almost the universal answer to the question of whether a man who has been punished at the halberds, is considered, by his comrades, as degraded by that punishment and consequently shunned by them, has been in the negative, and that the nature of the crime led to degradation, and not the punishment. And with regard to its effect as hardening and not reforming the individual, it will be found, upon looking at the evidence, that such is by no means the universal consequence. Many instances are given of men, who have undergone this punishment, having become good soldiers and having reached the rank of non-commissioned officers, and even of officers in some instances. When indeed it is inflicted upon men of confirmed bad habits, and, generally speaking, those are the persons who now subject themselves to it, it has failed in effecting their reform. But it may be asked whether any description of punishment, would in such cases, be likely to succeed, and we need only to have recourse to the records of our civil prisons and our courts of law, to be satisfied how rarely the reform of a man who has contracted habits of vice and intemperance, has been effected.

"It must be remembered also that it is frequently thought necessary to inflict this punishment, in a military body, when the moral reformation of the individual is, in no degree, its object; instances of insubordination which cannot be passed over, may and often do, occur where the offender is anything but an immoral or vicious person. The prompt infliction of corporal punishment may be necessary in such a case, for the sake of example and to prevent the spreading of a disorderly or mutinous spirit; but it cannot be said that its object is the moral reform of the individual; and we cannot help thinking that this constitutes a great difference between offenders against the military and civil law . . .

"The next objection is, that it excites disgust and sympathy in favour of the sufferer.

"It will undoubtedly be found by the evidence, that the sight of corporal punishment has a great effect upon those present, and that with the young soldier, that effect is sometimes so powerful, as to produce physical weakness and fainting. It is difficult to say whether this is disgust or terror, but we must observe, that such circumstances cannot arise without a very strong impression having been made upon the mind, and that, from that impression, must be derived a confident hope of the efficacy of the example presented to the eyes. But with regard to the sympathy of the bystanders, we can collect nothing from the evidence to show that such a feeling is aroused by this punishment, in the minds of the comrades of the culprit; on the contrary, the feeling seems to be almost universal among them that no man is punished in that manner, in these days, who has not deserved it; . . .

"The last objection to corporal punishment is undoubtedly one which calls for the most anxious inquiry into the grounds upon which it rests. Nothing can be more certain than, in this country, and with the ample means afforded to every man in it, for the free discussion in Parliament, in courts of law, in public meetings, and through the Press, no practice can be long maintained which is contrary to the well-considered judgment and settled feelings of the country . . . But in order to be sure of what we are doing, we must, before we give to a feeling, such as is supposed to exist upon this subject, ascertain to the utmost of our power, in the first place, its real extent, and also whether it is founded upon reasons necessarily conclusive of the whole question at issue. In a country possessing such free institutions as ours, this caution is the only security we have against charges, which, upon their first being presented to us, bear the most tempting appearances. Upon the first of these points, namely, the extent of this feeling, it is difficult to form any very correct judgment, and persons, who are themselves impressed with any strong opinion upon any subject, are apt to overrate what they consider symptoms of a general concurrence with that opinion . . .

"It is said that it cannot be necessary to retain the power of punishing the soldiers of the British Army by the lash, when we have, before us, the example of some of the armies of Europe, and more especially that of France, in which no corporal punishment whatever is permitted . . .

"The history of those times . . . (the long wars of the French Revolution and Empire) . . . affords instances of a licence, in the French Army, when in hostile countries, which scarcely any attempt was made to repress. In our Army, on the contrary, even in hostile France itself, the disposition to that licence was so effectually subdued as to acquire the confidence of the inhabitants of the districts, which it occupied, in the protection afforded by its discipline."

(The Royal Commission then consider the views of Sir Henry Hardinge and the Duke of Wellington,

regarding the difference in the class of persons in
general in an Army raised by conscription and one
raised by voluntary enlistment. They point out
that, in fact, corporal punishment *was* used in the
French Army while it comprised a volunteer Army
and was only completely abolished when the Army
became a conscripted one and drew upon all classes
of the community for its soldiers.)

"Whatever objections there may be to this punishment, when inflicted upon persons of the description
and habits of those that are likely voluntarily to enter
on an indefinite term of military service in a free country, there can be no doubt that those objections have
immeasurably greater force, when persons of all classes
and habits, are torn, by an overruling power from their
homes, their families, and from the profession of their
choice, to perform a paramount duty to the state. A
conscription, such as exists in France, would be intolerable in this country; but if such were the law, it might
perhaps be unnecessary, and, if so, would certainly be
unjustifiable, to retain this power of corporal punishment . . .

"Still confining ourselves to the French Army (for
in most of the other armies of Europe some sort of
corporal punishment is in use) . . . It will be seen that
no less than forty-five offences, are, by that code, punishable by death; and, although that extreme punishment
is very frequently, in time of peace, commuted for long
terms of detention in the galleys or in prison, we are
led to believe a remission of it on service in time of war,
to be far from common. In our Mutiny Act and Articles
of War, authority to pass a sentence of death is always
coupled with the words, 'or such other punishment as a
general court martial may award'. In fact, an execution
of such a sentence in time of peace in the British Army
may be said to be unknown in these islands. On active
service although sometimes resorted to, it is by many
degrees less common than in the French Army, in which,

DATE			Name	Quality	For what Offence
Day & Month	Year				
Jany 20	1814		John Norton	Gunr	Desertion
Sepr 28	1814		John Morton	Gunr	Desertion
Augt 30	1722		James Nugent	Serjt	[illegible]
Novr 4	1817		Samuel [illegible]	Gunner	Desertion
Jany 5	1818		John [illegible]	Gunner	Desertion
July 23	1818		[illegible]	Gunner	Desertion
March 23	1818		James [illegible]	Gunner	Desertion
April 13	1818		[illegible] Teall	Serjt	Desertion
Augt	1846		Joseph Conner	Privt	For [illegible] himself without leave [illegible]
Augt 14	1818		Thomas [illegible]	Gunner	Desertion
Augt 25	1818		Gilbert Langdon	[illegible]	On the charge of having been seen amongst [illegible] [illegible] in a state of intoxication between the [illegible] [illegible] May 1818
Sepr 22	1818		James J Moore	[illegible]	On charges contained in [illegible] [illegible]

PAGES FROM A COURT MARTIAL BOOK, ROYA
The two officers

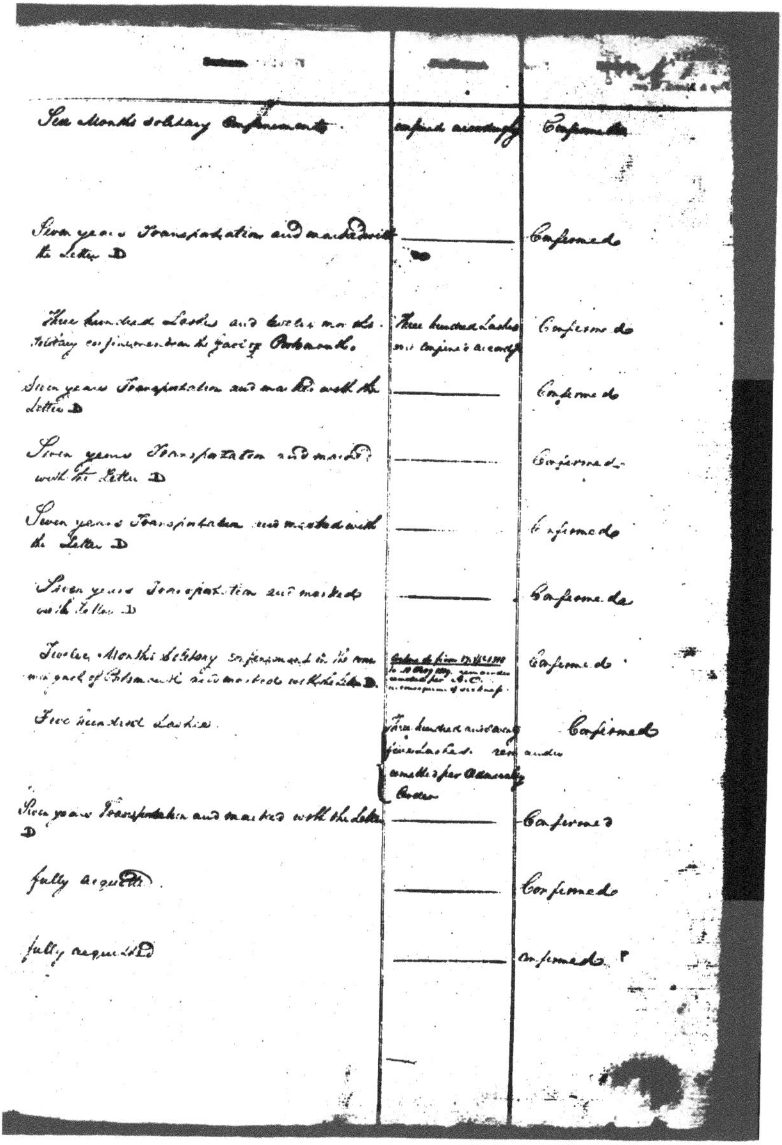

Six Months solitary Confinement	confined accordingly	Confirmed
Seven years Transportation and marked with the Letter D	————	Confirmed
Three hundred Lashes and twelve months solitary confinement in the Gaol of Portsmouth	Three hundred Lashes and confined accordingly	Confirmed
Seven years Transportation and marked with the Letter D	————	Confirmed
Seven years Transportation and marked with the Letter D	————	Confirmed
Seven years Transportation and marked with the Letter D	————	Confirmed
Seven years Transportation and marked with the Letter D	————	Confirmed
Twelve Months Solitary confinement in the common gaol of Portsmouth and marked with the Letter D	[illegible] remainder remitted per A.O. [illegible]	Confirmed
Five hundred Lashes	Three hundred and seventy five Lashes. remainder remitted per Admiralty Order	Confirmed
Seven years Transportation and marked with the Letter D	————	Confirmed
fully acquitted	————	Confirmed
fully acquitted	————	Confirmed

, MARINE ARTILLERY, PORTSMOUTH, 1816-18
were acquitted

under such circumstances, death by shooting is the
hinge upon which the whole system of discipline turns.
Twenty-six other military offences are punishable by
periods from five to twelve years, with or without what
is called the *boulet,* which is a cannon ball attached to
the ankle, leg, or body. Nineteen are punishable by
periods of imprisonment, or the galleys, of from one to
three years; and there are among other offences,
enumerated in these categories, many which, in our
Service, would subject the offender at most, to be tried
by a district court martial, the limit of whose power of
sentence in respect to corporal punishment is three
hundred lashes; . . .

"We cannot help thinking that it is a matter of doubt,
whether, if the option was given to the British soldier,
between the two codes, he would not infinitely prefer
that of our Service, even taking into consideration the
degree of degradation which is said to follow from the
punishment at the halberds. But, after all, it would
appear from the evidence, that the French code does
not produce, even in time of peace, a discipline, in any
degree equal to that which is enforced in the British
Army."

(The Commission next compare, note, and
analyse the difference in duties between the French
and British Armies, in their circumstances of service,
in the matter of embarkation for foreign service,
the plentiful supply in France of fortresses which
lend themselves readily for use as prisons [of which
the English had few], the matter of service and discipline in colonies, etc.)

The report continues : "Of late years, recourse has
been had by the military authorities (under alterations
in the Mutiny Act) to several punishments, by way of
substitutes, and in the hope of rendering the use of the
lash, to a great degree, unnecessary. In the sentences of
general courts martial, transportation of a felon for life,
or years, has taken place of those severe awards of

R

corporal punishment so usual in former times, where the ultimate punishment of death was not applied, which punishment, although retained in our military code, seems to be practically applied to cases, which only occur upon actual service, or under very peculiar circumstances . . . It appears to us to have been a wise course to endeavour to get rid of these extreme corporal punishments, which, after all, were generally inflicted, in time of peace, upon men not worth keeping in the Service.

"The other punishments which have been resorted to, as substitutes, are imprisonment, with or without hard labour, and solitary confinement; and we regret to say that the general predominant result of our Inquiry, is, to satisfy us, that, as hitherto inflicted, they have not so operated as to be depended upon as efficient substitutes."

(One great reason, the Commission point out, for failure in this respect, is the uncertainty with regard to the degree of severity with which these substitute punishments are enforced. The punishment, though called by the same name, varies considerably from one prison to another, being almost a joke to the culprit at some, in others the same punishment is very real—frequently far worse than was intended by the judges, sometimes so demoralising, hell, that the man never fully recovers from the experience.

Therefore, argues the Inquiry, some attempt needs to be made at standardisation of imprisonment, even going so far as to recommend the building of special detention barracks for military personnel only, in order to keep military offenders from the moral contamination with which, at that date, they could not but fail to be infected in a civilian gaol. But, argues the Commission, however improved become these substitute punishments to that of corporal punishment "they will still be deficient in one important requisite in military punishments upon certain occasions—a striking and prompt example".)

"A man, sentenced to corporal punishment, is brought out before the whole regiment; the preparations for his punishment are made; the sentence is read, he is stripped, and receives his punishment. All this passes before the eyes of his comrades. In the other case, the offender is equally brought out before the whole regiment, but there are no preparations for punishment to be seen; his sentence is read, he returns to his confinement, and is entirely lost sight of, by his comrades, until that period of confinement had expired. If this punishment have any effect upon his comrades, it must be by recital of his sufferings in prison, which can only be communicated by him to a few. They, in the mean time, have to perform his share of duty. We think it impossible to say that, under these circumstances, corporal punishment does not afford the more effectual example . . ."

(Moreover, the Commissioners imply that the punished man, fresh from prison, may make light of his experience, make himself out to be a hero while away, garble and distort the truth of his confinement to his own glory, whereas the flogging they have all witnessed is a direct and irrefutable event that they have all seen, each in some degree suffering as the cruel lash descends upon the culprit's back, each hearing his cries and seeing his blood flow, watching the wheals rise, and each counting the days of his sojourn in hospital, so that nothing he can say to belittle the experience will have any effect or impression whatsoever upon the hundreds of men who *saw* the cat-o'-nine-tails cut into the flesh, while the drums beat their tattoo.

The Commissioners then consider the use of corporal punishment in India and upon native troops and go on to the question of the formation of special punishment corps, composed of oft-offending soldiers.

The difficulty is recognised and considered, of how to punish men so "thick-skinned" and of such insensibility to physical pain, that they have no fear of corporal punishment, and that these irreclaimable types of offenders are of no use to the Army.)

"Frequent reference is made by the officers . . . to the difficulty of getting rid of such men, and they have even suggested that it would be very desirable that Commanding Officers should have the power of discharging them, if it were not for the fear of its leading to the committal of offences, for the very purpose of being discharged. The punishments in every regiment are very much confined to this description of men." Special gangs or companies of "tough" characters, supervised, but possible only if sufficient of the right type of officers for this work could be found, are next discussed.

"As a military corps . . ." opine the Commissioners, "and for the purpose of military service, we doubt whether a corps, consisting of the most hardened and unmanageable description of men, collected from different regiments, can be useful, or to be depended upon under any circumstances. Such a corps, would require the most careful selection, both of commissioned and non-commissioned officers, to serve in it, and the real efficient part of the Army would be deprived of their services. It would be dangerous to leave these corps, without the presence of some other troops, to watch and restrain them, if necessary; and, after all, these inconveniences would be encountered and all the consequent expense occurred, for the purposes of retaining in the Service, men who have previously been found not to be trustworthy, and to be incapable of being made useful soldiers. If the object be their reformation we beg to refer to the evidence of the officers of the French Army, who state that the regiments of discipline, which were established in that army for that object, have entirely failed in producing any such result, and in consequence they are about to be broken up. We have already said that the great excuse for the use of corporal punishment, consists in the prompt example it affords, which is presented to the eyes of those who witness that punishment. What advantage can there be in retaining the use of it, in corps, in which its infliction can have little or no effect?"

(However, continues the Inquiry, these gangs might "under proper restrictions, greatly tend to diminish the frequency of corporal punishment. In case this suggestion should be acted upon, these men should receive no pay, and be in every respect upon the footing of convicts, and not be allowed to return to service.)

"After a careful examination into the result of the several substitutes for corporal punishment now in use, we regret to say that none of them, as at present enforced, appear to have answered or to be likely to answer the purpose of rendering that punishment entirely unnecessary, nor have others been suggested to us which appear to promise to effect that purpose."

As to the popular suggestion that corporal punishment should be confined to the Army when actually on service and in addition entirely abolished as a punishment to be used in regiments quartered upon islands and in colonies, the Commission say : —

"We cannot recommend the adoption of this suggestion. If this power be taken away at all, the rule must be universal, and applied to all circumstances, equally" . . .

To place the soldiers under such an arbitrary law "would be both inconsistent and unjust, and cannot be defended".

"Hitherto," continues the Inquiry's Report, "our remarks have been applied to the entire and immediate abolition of corporal punishment; we now proceed to consider it, with a view to its restriction within narrower limits than at present, both as respects its severity and frequency.

"We assure Your Majesty, that we have looked at every part of the important question, which has been submitted to our Inquiry, with the most earnest hope, that its result might be, to satisfy our own minds, that it is possible, safely, to gratify the feeling, which has called for that abolition.

"In proportion, therefore, as the evidence, we have received, has weakened that hope, our anxiety has increased, to discover the means, by which, reserving the power, its infliction may, without endangering the discipline of the Army, be rendered still more rare than at present, and less obnoxious to those, who are impressed with the feeling to which we have alluded."

The Commissioners dismiss on the evidence obtained, the suggestion—one of the most common arguments for total abolition—that the officers in the Army will not do their best to use the lash as little as possible if corporal punishment is only curtailed and not completely outlawed.

"Officers of all ranks speak of it as an evil, rendered necessary by the description and prevailing habits of our soldiers, and more especially the vice of drunkenness, which is, we fear, far from being confined to the ranks of the Army, but pervades the population of the country to a great extent. It is over and over again repeated, that the propensity to that vice is, in fact, the occasion of almost all the faults, that are committed by British soldiers, and that, if it could be subdued, punishment of any sort would rarely be necessary."

(The Report then deals with the definition of offences liable to corporal punishment, and suggests that they be more clearly defined than at present.

Also, they ask, do they make the most of minor punishments, to obviate the use of the cat?

Next, they repeat their observation that there is a prevalence of opinion among all ranks of officers, that the powers available to the Commanding

Officers are too limited, and the Commissioners recommend a reconsideration on this point.

Returning to drunkenness, the *bête noire* of all Army discipline, the Commissioners again cover all the pro's and con's resulting from this vice and methods used to punish it; they discuss the interference with the soldier's pay, how any physical punishment also punishes the innocent, in that they have to do the culprit's work for him while he is being chastised, the fact that the punished man returns to his regiment from prison with arrears of pay to spend on further drunkenness upon receipt of his freedom; a vicious circle of cause and effect !)

"We are now arrived at the last point, to which our attention has been directed, namely, whether the effect of increased rewards and advantages to the soldier might not be such as to bring into the ranks, a better description of persons, and by so doing, render the retention of corporal punishment unnecessary. It is possible that a great increase of pay and advantages to the military, might have this effect, but that increase must go to an extent which we cannot contemplate, and which would make the expense of the Army so burdensome as would not be borne by this country.

"If the Army were not recruited as it is now, and a rigorous conscription was resorted to, forcing all classes of the inhabitants of this country into the ranks of the Army, it might, as we before observed, render corporal punishment unnecessary; but a conscription to answer such an object must be far more rigorous in its conscription than that of France, and be more analogous to that of Prussia."

(And were we to institute conscription to the Armed Forces in England, the Inquiry points out, that in France there is at this date, a system of *remplacans*, men who will for a fee of about £50, take the place of the conscript able to afford his services, in the French Army, when called up. That this system, legally or illegally, would soon be adopted in England, the Commissioners have little doubt, and of this they cannot approve. They also point out, that in time of war, these *remplacans* charged as much as £500 as substitute conscripts, which figure, in those days, was a considerable sum : *about £3,000 to-day!*)

"It is objected to our mode of recruiting, that those, who are employed upon that service, are not so strict as they ought to be, as to the previous character of the persons whom they enlist, and that this leads to the admission of men into the Army whose character and dispositions render the maintenance of discipline so difficult as to require the continuance of severe punishments.

"Upon this point, we have, in the evidence of Colonel Mackinnon, of the Coldstream Guards, the instructions under which that regiment is recruited, and it will be seen, that an enquiry into character, is directed by those instructions. Inquiry is, in fact, generally made as to the character of recruits in time of peace, and we are inclined to believe that men, who can be fairly said to be of confirmed bad character, if known, are not taken. But still there can be no doubt that men of habits, very difficult to reform, are enlisted . . . in time of war, or when any number of recruits are wanted upon an emergency, great nicety as to character is evidently impracticable, and therefore no very great alteration in the description of men who fill the ranks, can be expected to follow, from greater strictness in this respect.

"There will be found, in the evidence, suggestions with regard to increased attention and encouragement to regimental schools for the men, and to the providing libraries and a reading room in every barrack, to enable them usefully to occupy their idle hours, which in this country, and more especially in the warm climates of some of our foreign stations, hang heavily upon them . . .

"We think, too, that every facility should be given in barrack yards, for the enjoyment of manly games by the soldiers, such as fives courts, and rackets, and by providing additional spaces of ground, where necessary, for cricket and football . . . The public exercise of these and similar amusements, might also give additional attraction to the Service."

Religion and religious instruction and influence is next considered by the Inquiry, in relation to soldiers, their discipline and punishment. But the Commissioners have not a great deal to say on this side of Army life, except to observe : "That the arrangements . . . seem to be utterly inadequate to ensure the attendance of a respectable clergyman".

"The evidence of almost all the witnesses, we have examined, tends to encourage a hope, that the establishment of an order of merit, with a medal or some distinction of dress, bestowed in front of the assembled regiment, would have a considerable effect upon the discipline of the Army, and that the taking from the soldier of that distinction with the same ceremony, under sentence of a court martial, would operate as a heavy punishment . . . we cannot help earnestly recommending its adoption, with sufficient securities against its being bestowed indiscriminately or too frequently, and with different decorations for gallant conduct in the field, and upon other occasions, from that which is given for mere good behaviour."

(The Commissioners then consider the punishments as alternative to corporal, of endangering, lowering, or even making a man forfeit his pension as a penance for committing certain offences.

They then consider the best ways of recruiting to the Army, "the educated sons of individuals in comfortable situations in life", and all the matters pertaining to an ordinary man of humble origins, entering the Army in the ranks, and the circumstances of his working his way up to becoming a non-commissioned officer, and later even a commissioned officer. "Gentlemanly conduct" and general cultural education, table-manners, and the usual social graces were almost as important to the officer in the British Army of 1835, as a capacity for efficient military accomplishment, and the Commission confess themselves seriously worried by the obvious fact that those men who had, by hard work and application to the Service, "risen from the ranks", might well find themselves—indeed, too frequently did!— seriously embarrassed in their new-found glory, by their lack of social graces, education, and capacity to mix on an equal footing with their brother officers at mess. It is pointed out that the British Army could not tolerate the free-and-easy familiar intercourse between the officers and ranks so prevalent and remarkable in the French Army, and that consequently, an officer who had been created from a man who had spent most of the years of his service in the ranks, would never become socially fitted for an officer's life, or happy in it. Therefore, the Inquiry says, they cannot recommend that a greater facility of regulations to enable men to rise from the ranks into the officer-class, as a reward for good conduct and to promote better discipline, would be successful.

The Commission conclude their remarks in this Inquiry, by referring to a much suggested means of obviating corporal punishment—a means and argument that on first glance seems to have great force—by "what may be called moral discipline".)

"We have no doubt that rare instances have occurred of that sort, but it is too much to assume that, in fact, this moral discipline would have been so effectual, if there had not been the knowledge, on the part of the men, that, if driven to it, corporal punishment was within reach of their officers."

(And they finish their remarks by quoting the case of a distinguished Scottish officer who was able to

control his regiment, while in England, entirely by
moral discipline, having never to recourse to other
punishments, this regiment being almost wholly
manned by members of one clan. But later, in the
course of their duties, the regiment moved to the
West Indies, and losing many on active service, had
to be re-manned by men from towns and cities, Scots-
men still, but "foreigners" to the clan who had
originally formed the backbone of the corps. Discipline deteriorated so rapidly that the Commanding
Officer had to, much against his disposition and
feelings, punish crimes with severe corporal punishment before proper discipline was restored.)

"We have here an instance . . . in which the Commanding Officer, if he had been asked some years ago,
would have readily answered that he could, in his regiment, dispense with corporal punishment, and now says
that he again looks forward to being enabled to manage
that regiment without it, and yet, in the interval, in consequence of the climate to which they were sent in the
course of service, and the necessity of recruiting in a
manner more analogous to that of the rest of the Army,
occasioned by loss of men, corporal punishment became
necessary in spite of the feeling of the Commanding
Officer against its use.

"There now only remains for us to submit to Your
Majesty the conclusions which, in our judgment, are
the results of the whole evidence : —

"1. That the opinion of almost every witness, whom
we have examined, is that the substitution of other
punishments for corporal punishment in Your Majesty's
Army, upon actual service and in the field, is impracticable, and, if practicable, would be insufficient for the
maintenance of proper discipline.

"2. That the abolition of the power of awarding
corporal punishment, by sentence of court martial in
the British Isles and the Colonies, during peace, and the
retention of the power of inflicting that punishment

when the Army is on service and in the field, appears to us, for the reasons we have stated, manifestly unjust.

"3. That it does not appear to us, that the punishments that have been resorted to, as substitutes have hitherto had such an effect as to render it safe to abolish altogether that power in Great Britain or the Colonies, nor have any other punishments been suggested to us that appear to promise a more favourable result.

"4. That it appears to us, that, even supposing that some effectual substitutes for corporal punishment might be devised, or that those now in use might be made more effectual, so as to render corporal punishment ultimately unnecessary, it would be unsafe to proceed at once to abolish it entirely, and that, even in that case, its abolition should be gradual.

"5. That in order to give full effect to the punishments used as substitutes to corporal punishment, considerable alterations must be made in the means of rendering solitary confinement in the several barracks more effective, and that a certain number of prisons exclusively for military offenders should be provided as soon as possible.*

"6. That, although we have been unwillingly convinced of the necessity of still retaining the power of corporal punishment, and in proportion to our conviction of that necessity, we earnestly recommend, that no pains be spared to make its infliction less frequent.

"7. That, with a view to diminishing the frequency of this punishment, the offences to which it is limited, and the occasions upon which it should be resorted to, should be more clearly defined.

"8. That, with the same view, more discretion should be vested in Commanding Officers as to the power of making use of minor punishments, and in determining on the offences which shall, under their orders, be tried by regimental court martial.

* The inception of the modern detention barracks, or "Glass-house".

"9. That it appears to us that the extent of the sentences in the power of the several descriptions of courts martial to award, may, without danger, be more limited than at present.

"10. That encouragement should be given in the way of honorary reward and distinction, both to the gallant, and to the well-conducted soldier.

"11. That no consideration of expense, within reasonable bounds, should be allowed to stand in the way of attending to the comforts of the soldier while in the Service, and of a sufficient pension for the good and deserving man, after that service has been performed.

"We cannot close our Report, without assuring Your Majesty, that we find ample evidence of the earnest desire, and the most strenuous efforts upon the part, not only of the superior officers, but of officers of all ranks, so to conduct the discipline of the Army, as to render corporal punishment as rare as possible; and more especially, we observe that the Commanding Officers are fully aware of Your Majesty's gracious wishes in that respect, and we are satisfied that they will persevere in giving the fullest effect, by the strictest attention to the moral discipline of their regiment, to those wishes.

"How far the result of the Inquiry in which we have, by Your Majesty's Command, been so long engaged, will tend to remove or mitigate the feeling that now prevails against the use of corporal punishment in the Army, we know not; but we can assure Your Majesty that we have endeavoured to sift the questions, submitted to our Inquiry, fully and fairly, and without prejudice, and that we have formed our opinions upon the result of the very best evidence, that could be obtained upon the question."

(Finally, the Commission give it as their considered opinion that any form of rigorous conscription, such as is used to recruit the French Army, allowing a different form of discipline based upon example and a higher "moral" tone—and as a result,

allowing many more men to rise from the ranks to officers—would require "a change in the whole tone of the country, as to military service, such as we have no expectation of seeing effected".)

"We humbly submit this, our unanimous Report, to Your Majesty's Royal consideration.

Signed: Wharncliffe, James Kempt, Sandon, Edward Hyde East, R. Cutlar Fergusson, E. Barnes, Thos. Reynell.

India Board, 15th March, 1836."

CHAPTER THREE

THE DECLINE OF CORPORAL PUNISHMENT AFTER 1850

I

The publication of the Report of the Royal Commission did not in itself abolish flogging, but its recommendations were received by the King, Parliament, and the country in general with some relief. Custom in respect to flogging had not endeared itself, but, while hardening the skins of its victims, it had also hardened the sensibilities of those in authority. Many felt that perhaps "things had gone too far", but, as Joanna Baillie wrote, "What custom hath endeared We part with sadly, Though we prize it not". Burke reminds us that "Custom reconciles us to everything", and this was very true in the matter of flogging; true to the officers that ordered the excessive punishments in the early nineteenth century, and true to the men who received the lashes.

John Stuart Mill, in *Liberty*, wrote : "The despotism of custom is everywhere the standing hindrance to human advancement". And this was especially true of the custom of flogging, a punishment that had grown in merely a hundred years to become the most habitual punishment in the Armed Forces under the Crown. While it did not abolish the custom, the Royal Commission of 1835-1836, threw upon it the searching light of publicity and, in so doing, gave vital and balanced support to its *inevitable* abolition.

Henry Marshall, Deputy-Inspector-General of Army Hospitals, one of our best authorities in this work, himself remarked in support of the above : "It must seem strange to persons who do not observe the extreme difficulty with which old-established customs and prejudices, however ill-founded, are subverted, that the practice of awarding excessively large sentences of corporal punishment for trivial offences should so long and so obstinately have withstood the most convincing arguments and most conclusive statistical evidence. It is hard to say how far a man may be carried by the influence of bad example, and by the practice of vile custom, when we see that men, otherwise humane, may become the champions of a system so revolting to a feeling man, *and so liable to abuse*, as flogging".

In support of which observation we quote a Judge-Advocate attached to Wellington's headquarters during the Peninsular campaign : "I have now got a court martial", he writes in his private journal, "in the fourth division, the only one which has hitherto been free, to sit near Escalpaon, and to try three fellows for going out at night and stealing several sheep, keeping sentry as guard over the two shepherds, whilst they skinned the sheep and divided the meal; two other men, of better characters, were with them, and they are therefore to be admitted as witnesses against the three. The court at Coimbra has suffered the two worst fellows to escape almost with twelve hundred lashes; they ought to have been hung, for they are desperate fellows, both Irishmen".

Which is *typical* of the attitude of mind of high-ranking officers, at the time of the Royal Commission, when thinking of the soldier in the ranks below them.

In 1834, the *Sunday Times* published the following paragraph : —

"By a return laid before the House of Commons, it appears that public opinion has at length had some effect in bringing the cat-o'-nine-tails into less frequent use on the naked backs of British soldiers. According to this return, the number of floggings in 1830 was six hundred and fifty-five; in 1831, six hundred and forty-six; and in 1833, three hundred and seventy."

In 1836, the award of a general court martial was limited by the Articles of War to two hundred lashes, a district court martial to one hundred and fifty, and a regimental court-martial to one hundred.

In 1837, the words "reward for good conduct" passed the lips of the Secretary-at-War, and although nothing was done about it for some 'time—that being characteristically British—at least it had been *said*, in furtherance of the Commission's recommendations.

In 1842, on the order for the third reading of the Mutiny Bill, a Captain Bernal proposed a clause to prohibit flogging in the Army during peace, except on the march or for theft, but this motion was lost by a majority of one hundred and eighty-seven to fifty-nine.

In this debate, which was heated, a Mr. Stanley said that he was convinced that if flogging took place in the sight of the public the practice would not be suffered to continue one day longer. Sir Howard Douglas, though objecting to the motion, admitted that "he shuddered when he recollected the scenes which it had been his lot to witness". This debate established that military men were, for the most part, still averse to the abolition of flogging, and it was observed that there were at that moment no less than four Colonels in the British Army who, when they were privates, underwent corporal punishment.

In 1836-1837, of the regiments stationed in depots in England, three hundred and sixty men were flogged, fifteen of them for more than once in that year; but these figures exclude artillery stationed in England, and marines, so that the total of men flogged in 1836-1837 was considerably in excess of the figure of three hundred and seventy in 1833.

The Appendix to the Report of Commissioners on Military Punishments gives interesting figures of the floggings in the British Army during the years 1825-1834 —the years in which public opinion had its strongest effect upon Military Authority, immediately prior to the institution of the Royal Commission in 1835. For

s

example : In 1825, four thousand seven hundred and eight soldiers were tried by courts martial, two thousand two hundred and eighty were sentenced to punishments other than flogging, one thousand seven hundred and thirty-seven were flogged, *and one man in every fifty-nine men in any Army Establishment was flogged for one reason or another in that year.* There is, unfortunately, no record of the *average* number of lashes inflicted per delinquent, though we may safely judge it to be an average in excess of seventy-five !

In 1834, one year before the Commissioners began their Inquiry, ten thousand two hundred and twelve men were tried by courts martial—*an increase in nine years of five thousand five hundred and four men in one single year!* Of the number tried, nearly nine thousand were sentenced to punishments *other* than corporal, and only nine hundred and sixty-three were flogged. Only one man in one hundred and eleven men in each Army Establishment was flogged in that year, showing clearly that with *less* flogging there was *more crime.*

In March, 1842, a discussion in the House of Commons established that of the seventy thousand prisoners in civilian gaols in England and Wales, one thousand two hundred and seven were flogged while in prison, and of these, seven hundred and eighty-nine were juvenile offenders. We mention this to show that flogging was by no means a military prerogative or a punishment reserved exclusively for the soldier.

In 1838, a regulation was introduced into the Army directing that before a soldier was brought to trial by a court martial, he was to be examined by the medical officer. If that officer thought the soldier was in a good state of health and capable of undergoing a flogging he had to grant a certificate to that effect or otherwise, and recommend alternative punishment. This was a great step forward, for, from that time on, all cases could be reviewed *after* the flogging had been inflicted, and the medical officer held responsible if the man suffered too much. Consequently, the medical officers, by profession humanitarians, on behalf of the soldiers *and also on their own behalf*, from 1838 acted as an essential brake and mitigating factor with regard to excessive corporal punishments. However, many mistakes were still made. Moreover, medical officers before this date were often intimidated by their Commanding Officers into allowing excessive punishment, and this was established by Question 40, *Evidence on Military Punishments.* That they were similarly coerced after 1838, we cannot doubt, conditions of service being what they were, and medical officers being often in their early twenties. The "old school" of Commanding Officers, martinets of discipline, were very unlikely in those days to pay much heed to the opinion of a junior officer, medical or otherwise. But the fact that a document had to be certified, recorded, and filed, stating that a delinquent was fit to suffer a flogging was, in itself, a progressive achievement.

In 1840, branding by means of a cold instrument which discharged a set of needle-sharp pins into the skin to a depth of a quarter of an inch, was used in the case of desertion. The mark left was a "D", and into the tiny wounds, by no means excessively painful, gunpowder was rubbed to make an indelible tattoo. This punishment was inflicted before the regiment, with great ceremony, and often as a preliminary to a flogging. The *infamy* of this punishment was the deterring factor; not the pain involved, which was negligible.

II

In May, 1850, a Circular Memorandum from Horse Guards stated that whenever corporal punishment was to be inflicted in a Military Prison (some of which had by this date been established, further to the recommendations of the Royal Commission, 1836), under the provisions of the 27th Clause of the Mutiny Act, the Commitment must contain a Special Order for such corporal punishment, with a Certified Extract of the court's award, and a copy of the order mitigating or commuting the same to imprisonment and corporal punishment combined, without which the latter could not be inflicted.

The 24th Clause to which the above refers states that in any case in which corporal punishment forms the whole or part of a sentence, the Confirming Officer could commute that punishment to imprisonment, etc. And if corporal punishment were not commuted and deleted, or changed to another form of punishment, only twenty-five lashes could be given under such a sentence for execution in a Military Prison.

Less than two months later, a further Circular from Horse Guards made it clear that the lash was only to be inflicted in prison in cases in which the sentence had been mitigated by commuting a portion of it for an additional term of imprisonment; but that when any part of a sentence were remitted or forgiven, without substituting additional imprisonment, the remainder of the corporal punishment was to be inflicted in the usual manner on parade.

Under the Queen's Regulations, 1850, the infliction of corporal punishment a second time under the same sentence was *again* confirmed illegal. The Regulations also directed that attention be paid to the weather prevailing at the time and place of execution, and further that the delinquent was to be subject to a searching medical examination before and after flogging. (See Appendix for Forms of Court Martial and Surgeon's Certificate at this time.)

After the middle of the nineteenth century, England underwent changes in every sphere of life. Industry, commerce, science, art and literature, all and each experienced revolution. The humanities came to the fore and, with national prosperity, thought on almost every subject became more liberal. Under Victoria the Empire prospered and with that prosperity there came a more humane and religious attitude to the value of life, social conditions in general, and especially conditions of service within the Armed Forces under the Crown.

The franchise was considerably enlarged and with a stronger voice the people of England demanded social reforms. The British Army was not involved in any major action in Europe and Parliament was able to consider its construction and conditions of service, its discipline and efficiency with a more dispassionate and liberal attitude than had ever before been practicable. Throughout the world, in the 1860's, authority was beginning to consider the many, the masses, the "under-privileged"; social reforms of every description were being talked of and often put into effect. It was natural, therefore, that the matter of military punishments should again be reviewed, for agitation for total abolition of corporal punishment was still active in the Press and Parliament. As we have shown, much had been gained by 1830, and by 1865 the cat-o'-nine-tails was more frequently quoted to frighten and deter than it was used to wound and punish.

In 1868, the Articles of War decreed that : "No court martial shall for any offence whatever during a time of peace within the Queen's dominions, have power to sentence any soldier to corporal punishment; provided that any court martial may sentence any soldier to corporal punishment while on active service in the field or on board any ship not in commission, for mutiny, insubordination, desertion, drunkenness on duty or on the line of march, disgraceful conduct, or any breach of the Articles of War; and no sentence of corporal punishment shall exceed fifty lashes".

In other words, in time of peace the cat-o'-nine-tails was outlawed and banished from the barrack-square, and the long and bloody history of the drum-head courts martial was at an end. For over a hundred years the lash had reigned as the main military punishment. Its victims ran into uncounted thousands, possibly hundreds

of thousands. But in 1868 the dread command : "Strip,
sir !" and "Drummer, do your duty !" were heard in
England for the last time upon parade.

III

The history of corporal punishment in the British
Armed Forces after 1868 is very brief, conspicuous
mainly for the scarcity of its infliction. Certainly the
number of soldiers flogged before the end of the century,
after that date, was a very small percentage of the number of civilians flogged by order of the civil courts within
civil prisons.

Corporal punishment was legally abolished in the
British Army by an Act of Parliament in 1881. There
have been instances, however, of later flogging.

As recently as 1917, in Mesopotamia, Indian soldiers
were flogged as an alternative to imprisonment. The
cases we know of concerned men who had enlisted but
who had tired of service and had attempted to obtain
discharge from the Army by wounding themselves.
Because a sentence of imprisonment would have meant
sending them out of active service—which was what they
wanted—and would have been a bad example and no
punishment, they were flogged on parade instead, as a
punishment and a deterrent to others with similar
intentions. The soldiers were tied to a triangle and
flogged with thirty strokes of a regulation cat-o'-nine-
tails. The fact that the cat was available to the Provost
Marshal's office and that our informant tells us that the
triangles were "professional" equipment immediately
available, implies that these floggings were more
frequent than he suspected or knew from personal
experience. It is probable that these corporal punishments, though illegal, were condoned by Army
Authority in that theatre of war for special reasons
relating to the conditions prevailing at that time.

In July, 1946, newspapers reported a London court
martial of especial interest to readers of this history. A

CANING IN BURMA, 1943

[*Face page* 264

Major, D.S.O., M.C., was charged with "conduct to the prejudice of good order and military discipline", while on active service in Burma, 1943. Alleged incidents during the Burma campaign were involved.

Within a few days the case was earning big headlines and long columns in the national Press. The right of General Wingate of Burma to order his Chindits to be flogged, shot, or turned loose in the jungle for an offence that would endanger their comrades' lives, and his right to break King's Regulations was challenged, discussed, argued, and debated in print.

The Major was charged on two counts of ordering his Regimental Sergeant-Major to flog two privates, both of the Yorkshire and Lancashire Regiment, for going to sleep while on sentry duty two hundred miles behind the Japanese lines. One of the punished men, interviewed at the court martial, said to a journalist, "*I'm* not complaining".

High Commanding Officers were involved in the defence and on behalf of the defendant, and part of his plea was that the offences of flogging were condoned by General Wingate, and that flogging "was a recommended procedure".

The flogging that was the subject of this case was carried out, it was alleged, with a thin cane after both privates had signed a document saying that they were willing to take such punishment as an alternative to twenty-eight days field punishment, which punishment —because of the "hellish" conditions prevailing in the jungle—would be mild if compared with their everyday life at that time; no punishment at all, in fact.

"The soldiers concerned took their punishment like sportsmen. It was more of a schoolmaster's caning than the old two hundred lashes," said one witness.

Wingate, it was said at the court martial, was in favour of unorthodox punishments, including corporal punishments, being the only kind that could be inflicted on jungle service; thus echoing the sentiments of officers answering questions before the Royal Commission over a hundred years before.

A Brigadier, in evidence, agreed that King's Regulations did not allow flogging and that if Parliament had been flaunted, it was because of the abnormal conditions and that he himself would definitely have authorised the flogging of soldiers in such circumstances. It was he who took over the Burma Command after General Wingate was killed in 1944.

The Brigadier said punishment awarded in the first expedition of long-range penetration columns behind enemy lines in the Burmese jungle, included flogging for severe offences. He was not asked and did not volunteer any information on the frequency, amount, and precise details of such punishments. From our point of view, this is unfortunate, though we feel that the facts stated provide enough evidence for the reader to draw his own conclusions. This witness further said that he saw instructions from Higher Authority as to the punishments which were regarded as proper, and that these included flogging.

General Wingate's view, it was said, was that the punishments should fit the crimes and the conditions under which they were committed, and the conditions under which the punishments had to be executed.

At a lecture in Bangalore, on Military Discipline, Wingate said that for serious offences which might result in the loss of lives of men, the officers under his command were empowered to flog offenders, turn men loose in the jungle with limited rations, or in extreme cases to shoot them.

The two privates, the subjects of this court martial, and the only soldiers from this campaign that were ever *named* as having been subjected to corporal punishment, were each given twelve strokes. It was not given in evidence on what part of their anatomy they were caned, but other sources contacted by the author of this history have assured us that they have seen such caning while on active service in Burma, and that it was administered on the buttocks—and that twelve strokes was a moderate infliction; they had seen three times as many inflicted.

The Major, in evidence before the court martial, said that such caning punishments had been given to other men—he did not say how many, nor was he asked —and that he could speak highly of the discipline of the men under his command; presumably as a result of such chastisement, according to his evidence.

In October, 1946, the Secretary of War announced in the House of Commons that no further action was to be taken about the "allegations of flogging in Burma", and that the Major was held to have been condoned by his superior officers and that therefore his defence was to be allowed. On 24th October the Major was formally acquitted.

* * * *

A circular letter was issued by the Admiralty in December, 1871, directing that corporal punishment could be inflicted only for mutiny or for using or offering violence to a superior officer. Another letter eight years later directed that no Commanding Officer should award a sentence of more than twenty-five lashes.

Although in 1881 a Bill to amend the Naval Discipline Act of 1866 with a view to abolishing corporal punishment was withdrawn, administrative action was taken the same year to ensure that corporal punishment could not be inflicted without Admiralty approval. It can only be presumed that approval would not have been given. It was not until March, 1949, that an Order in Council was made to remove authority to award corporal punishment, which authority endured under the 1866 Act. Boy seamen, though, may still be caned.

Below is an example of corporal punishment to-day in Army and Royal Navy Training Schools and Ships : —

THE CANING OF BOYS IN A TRAINING SHIP, 1950

As told by an ex-Boy-Trainee : —

"I was caught doing something which, if I had been in the Navy proper, would have got me 'cells'. I was taken before the Captain of the training ship and after much questioning he said I would have to take twelve cuts of the cane. Twelve is usually the most given. Often the sentence is six, or nine. I was taken at once to the sick-bay and told to strip except for my socks. This I did, and I got the usual medical inspection. Next I was given the pair of punishment duck trousers. They are always worn by a boy who is to be caned. Then I was marched into the gym where the Master-at-Arms examined me to make sure I wasn't padded, nor wearing pants or football shorts. I was told to stand to attention, and the Surgeon-Lieutenant came in with the Regulating Petty Officer. The R.P.O. always gives the cuts, and he was carrying two long, thin, bamboo canes in his hand.

"I was ordered to lie over the end of the gym horse, and this I did, with my feet dangling. I was held in this position by the two biggest boys on board and the Captain came in and said, 'Carry on'. The R.P.O. lifted the cane in a wide semi-circle to the back of his head, and brought it down with such force that my body seemed to jump up from the middle of its own accord. After the first stroke I was let down from the horse and told to take my trousers down. This I did and the Surgeon examined me. I was ordered back on the horse, held down again, and the Captain again said, 'Carry on'. The R.P.O. again took aim. After each stroke the Master-at-Arms said, 'Cut delivered, sir'.

"After the twelfth I was lifted down and taken to the sick-bay. Here they examined my marks, which were a blue-mauve colour.

"Then they put me in football shorts and made me double to get back the circulation".

* * * *

In November, 1952, publicity was given to alleged caning at the Guards Depot at Caterham, where it was reported that young Guards cadets, including a young earl, "received ten on the backside from their squad Sergeant's cane". The implication of the article was that caning was an accepted and traditional punishment in training schools, and that though illegal, was accepted by cadets who "would die of shame before making a complaint".

The caning of boys is still a legal punishment in the Naval Training Schools and Military and Army Apprentice Schools, and is the sole surviving example of corporal punishment in the Armed Forces at the present time.

It is, obviously, very difficult to estimate exactly to what extent the Queen's Regulations and Articles of War are violated in respect to illegal and semi-official corporal punishment in the Armed Forces at the present time, but there is no doubt that while human nature remains as it is such incidents will and do occur, but there is no doubt in our minds that such incidents are "very few and far between".

Thackeray called corporal punishment "that punishment which it is generally thought none but a cherub can escape", and while that description is less true to life to-day than it was when he wrote *Vanity Fair*, it is still true that men are not appreciably nearer being angels or cherubs than they were a hundred years ago.

* * * *

It is hard to be precise as to the increase in crime in the Army and Navy to-day as compared to one hundred and twenty-five years ago. The Army and Navy are many times the size they were at that time, there have been industrial and social revolutions, and conditions in the Army cannot be compared at all.

There are no figures available for reference to show the punishments awarded expressly between regular soldiers and sailors as against those awarded to conscripted men. Therefore, we are also unable to muse, or to draw deductions between those men who have chosen the Forces and those who have been "pressed" into them.

I make the above points in order to show that the Forces must be taken as a whole when assessing punishment for them to-day. Together for two years, each fraction will learn from the other; and those of the Regulars will always have new civilian faces with them as more conscripted men come and go, bringing their "side of the fence" into barracks, and taking things learnt in barracks outside into civilian life.

Throughout my investigations I have found one thing which cannot be ignored : it is that wherever the whip has been a threatening factor, though not necessarily much used, there we find less crime and more discipline. Putting aside the findings of the Royal Commission (which came to the same conclusion), statements which cannot be doubted, all made by eminent men, will have been found in this volume to prove conclusively that those armies which had little room for the whip, had, also, less discipline and less success in battle—for it is in battle where discipline proves itself. The Royal Commission had proof given to it that the French Army was in no way as well disciplined as the British, and that the Americans, when they suppressed whipping, were faced with a great increase in insubordination.

It has not been the purpose of this work to embark upon a dissertation as to discipline in these days. If the reader has observed the behaviour of troops, he will have been drawn to the conclusion that the general behaviour of the troops under the Crown of Britain is better than most, and that, on the other hand, in those armies where the whip was first abolished, there is found less discipline—possibly more "personality"—but *not necessarily* greater leaders just because "personality" has been allowed to develop in its own way.

This is not a book written for, or against, corporal punishment, but it draws its own conclusions, and those of Her Majesty's Judges who claim that the fear of the rod deters crime must be right. If young lawbreakers were whipped once, they would seldom return a second time. We are told that it is crimes which were *not* punishable with the rod that have shown the greater increase since the war, but we think that there would have been less crimes of violence if the shadow of physical pain had been there. And *after* those who would not be warned had been flogged, these people, as shown in this volume, would take good care not to return for a second dose : and if they did return, certain it is that five years in prison without the cat will have as little effect as, say, three years and eighteen strokes of the cat. Who can say which sentence is likely to have the most effect, any effect, or *what* effect, on different criminal minds? We must judge by experience, and the experience and the findings are behind you in this work. Taking the overall view, it is where the whip has held sway longest, that the general discipline has died hardest.

Opponents of corporal punishment claim that this country would be the "laughing-stock of the world" if the whip were re-introduced; but *which* countries of the world? Those where gangsterism is rife? Those where killers are not put to death? Why do we not go the whole way and do away with hanging? If it is "backward" to beat a batterer, then it is "backward" to kill a killer. If beating won't stop thugs, then hanging won't stop murderers. If you want "an eye for an eye" justice, you must be consistent.

But this Last Word continues too long. We will take an "acid test" . . .

A violent prisoner recently attacked a warder in one of H.M. prisons. He has been flogged : because flogging is still permitted in such cases. Why? "Because," three warders tell me, "we'd find other jobs *if the constant threat and fear* of the cat was removed from the minds of the prisoners." One warder added, "Things have been much quieter in the prison since news of the flogging got round".

Can calmer methods than violence calm, or make fearful, the violent mind? Is the would-be bully a coward? Is the violent mind a sick mind which *is* curable?

The Preface of this book began with the words . . . "there are three subjects over which tempers become strained . . .

I hope that this volume has thrown some light on the third.

APPENDIX

ARMY

.... Regiment.

Headquarters, ... 18...

Application for a .... Court Martial.

Sir,

I have the honour to submit a charge (or charges) against No. .... Sgt., of the Regiment (or depot) under my Command, and request you will obtain the sanction of the Major-General (or other officer) commanding the Division that a .... Court Martial may be assembled for his trial at ....

The Prisoner is now at ....

The Witnesses are at ....

I have the honour to be, Sir,

Your most obedient, humble Servant,

Signature of Commanding Officer ....

The Assistant Adjutant-General, or Brigade-Major.

(Insert here Charge, or Charges. Time. Place. Circumstances.)

SURGEON'S CERTIFICATE

I certify that No. .... Sgt., of the .... Regiment, is in a .... state of health and .... to undergo Corporal Punishment or Imprisonment, solitary or otherwise, and with or without hard labour; and that his present appearance and previous medical history both justify the belief that hard labour employment will neither be likely to originate nor to reproduce disease of any description. The prisoner is (or is not, as the case may be) marked with the letter "D".

Signature of Surgeon or Assistant Surgeon.

....

CHARGE

For disgraceful conduct, in having on or about the
.... day of ...., at ...., in
his capacity of Sergeant, produced to the Paymaster
certain false certificates, as follows ....

RESULT

At a General Court Martial held at, etc., upon, etc.,
.... the accused .... Sgt.
was found Guilty of the Charge(s) brought against him.
The Court does therefore sentence the said ....
Sgt. to be reduced to the Rank and Pay of a Private
Soldier and in addition to receive a Corporal Punishment of fifty lashes on his bare back with a cat-o'-nine-
tails in the usual manner and at a time conveniently to
be chosen.

NAVY

In 1850, the Form of Sentence in the Navy was as
follows : —

"At a Court Martial assembled on board Her
Majesty's ship ...., at ...., on the ....,
the ...... day of ...., 18..., and by adjournment every
day afterwards, to the ...... day of ...., 18....

PRESENT
(Insert list of names.)

The Court, pursuant to an order from Sir ....
Commander-in-Chief of Her Majesty's ships, dated ......
............, 18..., directed to .... Rear Admiral,
having been duly sworn according to Act of Parliament,
proceeded to the trial of ...., of Her Majesty's
ship ...., on the following charges exhibited
against him by ...., Captain of the said
ship, viz.

"For that he, the said ...., being in actual
service and full pay in the Fleet, did, on the ...... day
of ...., 18..., behave in a disrespectful and contemp-
tuous manner to me (Captain ....), his

superior officer, by stating on the quarter-deck of the said ship, that I encouraged insubordination amongst the crew, by not punishing them sufficiently, or words to that effect."

(Court Martial.)

FINDINGS

"Having carefully and deliberately weighed and considered the evidence in support of the charges, as well as what the prisoner had to offer in his defence, as also the evidence adduced in his behalf, and having very maturely considered the whole, the Court is of the opinion that the charge is proved against the said .... And the Court doth therefore adjudge the said .... to receive forty-eight lashes on his bare back with a cat-o'-nine-tails, alongside or on board of such of Her Majesty's ships and vessels, at such time, and in such proportions, as the Commander-in-Chief shall direct."

TO CARRY OUT SENTENCE

Order to the Captain of the Ship to which the Prisoner belongs to carry the Sentence of Corporal Punishment into Execution.

"Whereas, at a Court Martial held on board Her Majesty's ship ...., at ...., on the .... instant, being president thereof, a sentence was passed to the effect following, viz. The Court (here insert sentence). And whereas I have thought fit to approve same, and do hereby require and direct you, when the signal is made to the effect, on board the ...., on .... morning next, the .... instant, at .... o'clock, or the first favourable day afterwards (Sundays excepted), to cause a Lieutenant of Her Majesty's ship under your command, to attend and see the sentence put into execution, by the said .... receiving

T

forty-eight lashes on his bare back with a cat-o'-nine-tails, alongside the ....; and you will here-with receive a copy of the sentence which is to be publicly read alongside that ship by the Provost Marshal. You will order the Surgeon of the ship you command to attend in the boat with the Lieutenant, and one of the Assistant Surgeons in the boat with the prisoner, and you will direct the Lieutenant to stop the punishment till further orders, whenever the Surgeon shall give it that in his opinion the prisoner cannot bear more with safety.

Given under my hand, etc., etc."

Order to the Captain of the Flag Ship to cause the Signal to be made for the Boats of the Squadron to attend to the Execution of the Sentence of Corporal Punishment.

"Whereas ...., of Her Majesty's ship ...., has been sentenced by a court martial to receive forty-eight lashes on his bare back with a cat-o'-nine-tails alongside, or on board such of Her Majesty's ships and vessels at this port, at such time and in such proportion as I shall direct : You are hereby required and directed to cause the proper signal to be made from the ship bearing my flag, at .... o'clock in the morning of .... next, the .... instant, or the first favourable day afterwards (Sunday excepted), for the boats of the squadron, manned and armed, to assemble alongside Her Majesty's ship ...., to attend the said Punishment.

Given under my hand, etc.,

By Command of the C.-in-C.

The Orders to the Provost Marshal, to the respective Captains, etc., various."

LIST OF PUNISHMENTS

Banishment.
Barrel Pillory.
Bastinado.
Beheading.
Bilboes.
Blistering.
Black Hole.
Black List.
Booting.
Branding.
Bread and Water.

Caning
Capstein.
Carrying Capstein Bar.
Cat-o'-Nine Tails.
Chains.
Cobbing.
Cold Burning and Bottling.
Cudgel.
Cutting off Ears.

Death with Torments.
Dismemberment.
Dry Room.
Ducking at Yardarm.
Ducking in Sea.

Execution.

Face to Wall, fully equipped.
Fine.
Flogging.
Flogging round the Fleet.
Fracturing of Limbs.

Gagging.
Gallows.
Gatloupe, Gauntelet, Gantlope.

Gybbets.
Gyves.

Hanging by Thumbs.

Irons.

Keel Hauling.
"Kissing Gunner's Daughter."

Log.
Losing Hand.

Maiming.

Picket, Piquet.
Pillory.
Pioneer-scavenging.

Scaffold.
Shackles.
Shooting to Death.
Shot from a Gun.
Spreadeagle.
Starting.
Stigmatising.
Stocks.
Strappado.
Stripes.

Throwing into Sea.
Tied to a Gun.
Tongue-boring.
Trotting in a circle.

Whirligig.
Wooden Collar.
Wooden Horse.

277

BIBLIOGRAPHY

An Act for Punishing Mutiny and Desertion. London, printed by George E. Eyre and Andrew Spottiswoode, 1842.

Anon., *The Naval and Military Sketch Book, and History of Adventure by Flood and Field,* c. 1845.

Anon., *Naval Sketch Book : or, the Service Afloat and Ashore.* Second Series, London, Whittaker & Co., 1835.

Anon., *Scenes from the Life of a Soldier on Active Service.* London, John Murray, 1850.

Christopher Biden, *Naval Discipline : Subordination contrasted with Insubordination; or, a View of the Necessity for Passing a Law establishing a Naval Discipline on Board Ships in the Merchant Service.* London, J. M. Richardson, 1830.

J. G. Bullocke, *Sailors' Rebellion, a Century of Naval Mutinies.* London, Eyre & Spottiswoode, 1938.

Robert Burgess and Ronald Blackburn, *We Joined the Navy; Traditions, Customs and Nomenclature of the Royal Navy.* London, A. & C. Black, 1943.

Capt. Chamier, R.N., *The Arethusa, a Naval Story.* Second edition, London, Richard Bentley, 1837.

Charles M. Clode, *The Administration of Justice under Military and Martial Law as applicable to The Army, Navy, Marines and Auxiliary Forces.* Second edition, London, John Murray, 1874.

Colburn's United Service Magazine and Naval and Military Journal.

G. L. Newnham Collingwood, *A Selection from the Public and Private Correspondence of Vice-Admiral Lord Collingwood, interspersed with Memoirs of His Life.* Third edition, London, James Ridgway, 1828.

Lt.-Gen. Sir George D'Aguilar, K.C.B. (Ed. by John Endle), *Observations on the Practice and the Forms of District, Regimental and Detachment Courts Martial.* Dublin, J. M. O'Toole, 1861.

Richard Henry Dana, *Two Years Before the Mast,* 1840.

Joseph Donaldson, *Recollections of the Eventful Life of a Soldier.* Edinburgh, Robert Martin, 1837.

Arthur Parry Eardley-Wilmot, *Manning the Navy; a Statement in which the Evils and Losses arising from the Present System are Set Forth and a Remedy Proposed.* London, W. J. Cleaver, 1849.

Frederick Waldermar Engholm, *The Story of H.M.S. Victory, a Ship Unsurpassed in Naval History.* London, Lindsay Drummond, 1944.

Col. C. Field (Ed.), *Old Times Afloat, A Naval Anthology.* London, Andrew Melrose, 1932.

Col. C. Field, *Old Times Under Arms, A Military Garner.* Edinburgh, William Hodge, 1939.

Vice-Admiral H. L. Fleet, *An Admiral's Yarns.* London, Swan Sonnenschein, 1910.

Conrad Gill, *The Naval Mutinies of 1797.* Manchester, University Press, 1913.

Lt.-Col. W. Gordon-Alexander, *Recollections of a Highland Subaltern.* London, Edward Arnold, 1898.

Francis Grose, *Military Antiquities Respecting a History of the English Army.* London, 1786-8.

Lt.-Col. Gurwood, *The General Orders of Field-Marshal the Duke of Wellington, K.G.* London, W. Clowes, 1837.

Robert Hamilton, *The Duties of a Regimental Surgeon Considered,* 1787.

David Hannay, *Naval Courts Martial.* Cambridge, University Press, 1914.

Capt. B. H. Liddell Hart (Ed.), *The Letters of Private Wheeler, 1809-1828*. London, Michael Joseph, 1951.

William Hickman, R.N., *A Treatise on the Law and Practice of Naval Courts-Martial.* London, John Murray, 1851.

Capt. W. Hough, *The Practice of Courts-Martial, also the Legal Exposition and Military Explanation of the Mutiny Act and Articles of War.* Second edition, London, Kingsbury, Parbury & Allen, 1825.

Capt. W. Hough, *Simplification of His Majesty's and E.I. Company's Mutiny Acts and Articles of War, Proposed Military Police and Legislative Enactments.* Calcutta, 1836.

Sir William Kennedy, *Hurrah for the Life of a Sailor!* Edinburgh, Blackwood, 1900.

Alexander Laing (Ed.), *The Life and Adventures of John Nicol, Mariner.* London, Cassell, 1937.

Sir George Larpent, Bart. (Ed.), *The Private Journal of Judge Advocate Larpent attached to the Headquarters of Lord Wellington during the Peninsular War.* Third edition, London, Richard Bentley, 1854.

John McArthur, *Principles and Practice of Naval and Military Courts Martial.* Third edition, London, J. Butterworth, 1806.

G. E. Manwaring and Bonamy Dobrée, *The Floating Republic : An Account of the Mutinies at Spithead and the Nore in 1797.* London, Geoffrey Bles, 1935.

Henry Marshall, *A Historical Sketch of Military Punishments*, c. 1840.

John Clark Marshman, *Memoirs of Major-General Sir Henry Havelock, K.C.B.* New impression, London, Longmans Green, 1909.

Herman Melville, *Billy Budd, Foretopman.* London, John Lehmann, 1946.

Lt.-Col. J. Mitchell, *Thoughts on Tactics and Military Organization*. London, Longman, Orme, Brown, Green and Longmans, 1838.

Lt.-Col. A. F. Mockler-Ferryman, *The Life of A Regimental Officer During the Great War 1793-1815*. Edinburgh, William Blackwood, 1913.

James Moore, *A Narrative of the Campaign of the British Army in Spain, commanded by his Excellency Lieut.-General Sir John Moore, K.B.* London, Joseph Johnson, 1809.

Thomas Morris, *Recollections of Military Service, in 1813, 1814 & 1815 through Germany, Holland & France*. London, James Madden, 1845.

Maj.-Gen. Charles J. Napier, C.B., *Remarks on Military Law and the Punishment of Flogging*. London, T. & W. Boone, 1837.

The Naval Chronicle. London, 1798-1820.

Charles Nordhoff and James Norman Hall, *Mutiny on the Bounty*. London, Chapman & Hall, 1933.

C. W. C. Oman, *Wellington's Army 1809-1814*. London, Edward Arnold, 1913.

Edmund Packe, *An Historical Record of the Royal Regiment of Horse Guards, or Oxford Blues*. London, William Clowes, 1834.

Reuben and Sholto Percy (Ed.), *The Percy Anecdotes*. London, Frederick Warne, c. 1868.

The Queen's Regulations and Orders for the Army. London, H.M.S.O., 1873.

Thomas Reide, *A Treatise on the Duty of Infantry Officers and the Present System of British Military Discipline*. London, J. Walter, 1795.

Report from His Majesty's Commissioners for Inquiring into the System of Military Punishments in the Army; with Appendices. H.M.S.O., 1836.

George W. M. Reynolds, *The Soldier's Wife*. London, John Dicks, c. 1850.

Sir Samuel Romilly, *The Life of Sir Samuel Romilly*. Third edition, London, John Murray, 1842.

George Ryley Scott, *Flogging: Yes or No?* Torchstream Books, London, 1953.

George Ryley Scott, *The History of Corporal Punishment: A Survey of Flagellation in Its Historical, Anthropological and Sociological Aspects*. Ninth impression, London, Torchstream Books, 1952.

John Shipp, *Flogging and Its Substitute*. London, 1831.

John Shipp, *Memoirs of the Extraordinary Military Career of John Shipp, late a Lieutenant in His Majesty's 87th Regiment*. London, 1829.

John Shipp, *The Military Bijou: or the Contents of a Soldier's Knapsack*. London, 1831.

Thomas Simes, *The Military Guide for Young Officers, containing the Arts of War*. Third edition, London, J. Millan, 1781.

Capt. Thomas Frederick Simmons, R.A., *Remarks on the Constitution and Practice of Courts Martial*. Fifth edition, London, John Murray, 1863.

Maj.-Gen. William Starke, *Obsolete Military Punishments* (reprinted from *Notes and Queries*). London, John Edward Francis, 1901.

Statement Respecting the Prevalence of Certain Immoral Practices in His Majesty's Navy. London, Ellerton & Henderson, 1821.

Sir Robert Steele, *The Marine Officer, or Sketches of Service*. London, 1840.

John Teesdale, *Military Torture: a Letter addressed to the People of England . . . on the Use of the Cat-o'-Nine-Tails in the British Army*. London, 1835.

Alexander Fraser Tytler, *An Essay on Military Law, and the Practice of Courts Martial*. Edinburgh, 1800.

Rear Admiral Gerard Wells, *Naval Customs and Traditions.* London, Philip Allan, 1930.

T. H. Wintringham, *Mutiny : Being a Survey of Mutinies from Spartacus to Invergordon.* London, Lindsay Drummond, c. 1935.

Gen. Sir Evelyn Wood, V.C., *Cavalry in the Waterloo Campaign.* London, Sampson Low, 1895.

R. G. Van Yelyr, *The Whip and the Rod : An Account of Corporal Punishment among All Nations and for All Purposes.* London, Gerald G. Swan, 1941.

Lionel Yexley, *The Inner Life of the Navy.* London, Pitman, 1908.

INDEX

Adolphus, Gustavus, 9
Alexander, Bombardier, 52
Army, flogging in (*see* Flogging)
Arthur, Col., 225
Auckland, Gen., 26

Back-boards, 142
Banishment (*see* Transportation)
Barclay, 16
Barrel-pillory, 117
Bartley, Lt.-Col., 220-2, 224
Belfast, proclamation at, 22
Bell, Dr., 49, 50
Bermuda, 226
Best, Rev. Mr., 22
Biden, Christopher, 143
Bilboes, 8, 100, 113
Black-hole, 36, 175, 221
Black-list, 117
Black Watch mutiny, 70
Blasphemy, punishment for, 7
Blistering, 21, 197-8
Booting, 21
Boring the tongue, 7
Bottling (*see* cold burning)
Boulet, 243
Boy seamen and apprentices, caning
  of, 267-8
Branding, 11
Branding with letter D for desertion,
  67, 83, 95-6, 177-8, 213, 261, 273
Brighton, execution at, 16
Bruce, 11
Buckingham, Duke of, 100
Buckingham, Marquis of, 24
Burdett, Sir Francis, 24, 198
Burma, 265-7
Burney, Dr. William, 115, 133
Byng, Sir John, 200

Cape of Good Hope, 62
Capstein, 113
Carlyle, 97
Carrying a capstein bar, 117, 150
Castlereagh, Lord, 24
Cat-o'-nine-tails (*see* Flogging)
Chaining to wheelbarrow, 17
Champian, Major, 226
Charles I, 100
Charter of Richard I, 4

China, 117, 132
Civil jurisdiction, appeal to, 15, 61
Clarence, Duke of, 101
Cobbett, William, 26
Cobbing, 21, 106, 147, 150, 221, 225
Cold burning, 20
Collingwood, Capt., 120, 136
Conscription, 242, 249, 255
Cornwallis, Admiral, 133
Corporal punishment (*see* Flogging)
Courts-martial, forms relating to,
  273-6
Crimes, military, 3, 40, 41, 86-7, 95-7
Cromwell, 107
Cutting off ears, 9, 11

Dalrymple, Lieut.-Col., 11
de Vigny, Count Alfred, 2
Death after flogging, 23, 52, 53, 54,
  74, 106-7, 127, 128, 131, 160, 215
Death penalty, 5, 6, 8, 10, 15, 16, 17,
  70, 80, 102, 119, 121, 123-4,
  153-4, 180-6, 197, 217, 242-3
Denham, Sir J., 97
Desertion, punishment for, 95-7 (*see*
  also Branding)
Doctors' attendance at floggings, 18,
  23, 32, 33, 49, 55, 57, 70, 127,
  130-1, 139, 171-3, 215, 268, 276
Doctors' examination before courts-
  martial, 260-2, 273
Douglas, Sir Howard, 259
Drink and drunkenness, 75, 77, 89,
  103-4, 201, 208, 219, 222, 224,
  226, 228, 237, 249
Drum-head courts-martial, 38, 263
Drum-major's flogging charge, 46-7
Dry-room, 36
Ducking at the yard-arm, 100, 114

Edward I, 99
Elizabeth I, 99
Ellice, Mr., 201
Ely, mutiny at, 26
Essex, Earl of, 6
Ewart, Gen., Sir John Alexander, 60
Exeter, Duke of, 99

Fane, Sir Henry, 71, 236
Fining, 6, 12, 22

Lightning Source UK Ltd.
Milton Keynes UK
UKHW012025050122
396671UK00002B/672